Designing Object Systems

Designing Object Systems
Object-Oriented Modelling with Syntropy

Steve Cook
John Daniels

Prentice Hall

New York   London   Toronto   Sydney   Tokyo   Singapore

First published 1994 by
Prentice Hall International (UK) Ltd
Campus 400, Maylands Avenue
Hemel Hempstead
Hertfordshire, HP2 7EZ

A division of
Simon & Schuster International Group

Printed and bound in Great Britain at
The University Press, Cambridge

Library of Congress Cataloging-in-Publication Data

Cook, Steve.
 Designing object systems : object-oriented modelling with Syntropy
/ Steve Cook, John Daniels.
  p. cm.—(object-oriented series)
 Includes bibliographical references and index.
 ISBN 0-13-203860-9
 1. Object-oriented programming (Computer science) I. Daniels,
John. II. Title. III. Series.
 QA76.64.C64 1994
 005.1′2—dc20   94–30446
                                                              CIP

British Library Cataloguing in Publication Data

A catalogue record for this book is available from
the British Library

ISBN 0-13-203860-9

---

1 2 3 4 5   98 97 96 95 94

Contents

Preface

This is a book about object-oriented analysis and design for software developers. There are many such books, so why write another one? The answer is that we wish to make some specific contributions to the philosophy and practice of object-oriented software development which are significantly different from those that can be found in any of the other available books.

This is not an introductory book[1]. It is for software practitioners with some experience of using object-oriented languages and methods. We assume that the reader understands the basic principles of object-orientation, especially encapsulation and abstraction, classes and instances, polymorphism, and inheritance. We are aiming the book at those software developers who are perhaps a little dissatisfied with the informal interpretations of most published object-oriented analysis and design methods, and who are looking for a more fully defined treatment.

This book does not aim to set out a complete method for software development. In it we describe a range of techniques, notations, principles and procedures, and although we offer some advice on their use, we leave to the reader the matter of arranging these ideas. Indeed, we hope they will be useful to software developers using any kind of object-oriented analysis or design method, by helping them to think more clearly about what their descriptions and notations mean and when they can best be used.

Precision and formality

In this book we are rather stubborn about precision. Most books on object-oriented analysis and design introduce some notations, explained informally by the use of examples. Typically, for example, there is some notation to represent the concept 'is-a-part-of', often called aggregation or containment. The reader is expected to understand what this means: and indeed, we *do* understand what it means, in the

---

[1]For those readers who would like to read an introductory book on object-oriented software development we recommend 'Object-Oriented Software', by Winblad, Edwards and King [Winbl90].

intuitive sense that I understand that my arm is-a-part-of me, the wheel is-a-part-of the car, and so forth. But what does it mean *in software*? After all, the ultimate purpose of our activity is to build software.

This is the kind of question which must necessarily be answered by the builder of a CASE (Computer Aided Software Engineering) tool based on a published notation. A typical answer is to equate aggregation with the concept of an embedded object in the C++ language. We are unhappy with this, on the grounds that the semantics of an abstract modelling technique should not be decided by the detailed semantics of a particular programming language. After all, if the implementation is to be done in some other language, then these semantics are likely to be confusing and difficult to implement.

Alternatively, the modeller might argue that the purpose of the object-oriented analysis is to model the world, not to model the software. We have some sympathy with this view, as you will see. But we should enquire about why the existence of an intuitively understood is-a-part-of relationship in the world is relevant to our real purpose, which is developing software. If it is relevant, then exactly how does it translate into some property of the software; and if not, why is it being modelled at all? This book provides clear and unambiguous answers to these questions.

There are two communities which at first hand seem to have remarkably little in common, and yet are actually trying to solve the same problem. The first community is the one already referred to, namely the methodology authors who invent informal analysis and design notations. The second is the formal methods community, who use the ideas of discrete mathematics: sets, relations, functions and logic, to describe the abstract properties of software systems. Both communities are trying to address the same overall problem of building models of software, in order to understand a problem situation and specify possible solutions at a more abstract level of detail than the program code.

One of our goals in writing this book is to help build some bridges between these two communities. On the one hand, popular analysis and design notations provide easily understandable diagrams, but lack the formal precision necessary for specifying software systems completely and unambiguously. On the other hand, formal notations such as Z [Abria80] or VDM [Jones86] provide the means for specifying software systems accurately and completely, but are quite inaccessible to the vast majority of today's software practitioners whose experience of formal set theory is limited to the little they did at school and have now forgotten. Faced with the need to learn new complex notations and today's job market, any practising software developer can be forgiven for learning C++ rather than Z.

Our approach is to take the most popular existing object-oriented analysis and design notations and give them a more formal interpretation. The first main notation we have chosen is the Object Modelling Technique (OMT) notation, originally introduced by Loomis, Shah and Rumbaugh [Loomi87] and subsequently popularised in the book by James Rumbaugh *et al.* [Rumba91]. The second main notation is the Statechart notation introduced by David Harel [Harel87] and also popularised in the book by Rumbaugh *et al.* We also introduce a number of other notations, some original and some derived from other authors, including Grady Booch [Booch91].

For formal descriptions we have adopted the basic notations of Z to describe sets and their properties. But don't be put off, because we use very little formal mathematical notation. We do not include all of the ideas of Z, by any means. Neither do we attempt to give our notations a proper formal semantics, or discuss proofs of correctness; both of these would be proper for a book about a formal method, and this is not one of those.

A completely different approach would have been to add object-oriented ideas to an existing formal method. This kind of work has led to techniques such as Object-Z [Carri89]. We believe our approach to be much more accessible, because all of the formal material may be omitted while retaining a substantial part of the meaning of the diagrams.

This book can be read by people with no experience of formal methods. Hopefully it will teach even the complete beginner in discrete mathematics something about the power of these methods. Most statements requiring significant mathematical background have been relegated to footnotes and may safely be ignored by all but those particularly intrigued by the mathematics.

Consistency and complexity

There are times when consistency with theory is not the ideal it seems. For example, theoreticians will extol the virtues of programming languages with sound and unbreakable type systems. This ideal has been challenged on many occasions by Bertrand Meyer, inventor of the Eiffel language, who stresses the importance of a *useful* type system over one that is merely *correct* with respect to some theory. We have used this principle ourselves on occasion in this book, notably when considering type-conformance. A theoretically driven definition of type-conformance might result in rules so limiting that conformance would cease to be a useful tool for facilitating reuse. In type-conformance as elsewhere, we don't claim our rules are the paragon of theoretical virtue – we merely claim them to be *useful*. Given this, formal proofs of the soundness of these rules might be impossible and we don't attempt them.

A superficial glance at some of the diagrams in this book might lead a casual reader to the view that our notations are very complex – indeed, excessively complex. Not surprisingly, we do not share that view. Some software systems *are* complex, and require complex design representations. The secret to successful design is to be able to deal with complexity at the right time; at each level of abstraction to have a design that is, to use the phrase attributed to Einstein, *as simple as possible and no simpler*. The simple fact is that the final representation of the design is likely to use a notation far more complex, both in syntax and semantics, than that used in this book: a programming language. The most widespread object-oriented programming language, C++, is more complex than the notations we use in this book, but, we believe, offers much less overall benefit to the software designer.

Analysis, specification and implementation

We have puzzled for years about how to make clear sense of the word 'analysis' in the context of software development. A typical distinction is the following: 'analysis describes *what* the system is to do; design describes *how* it will do it.' The trouble with this distinction is that it is entirely relative. One person's *what* is another person's *how*. It seems that the only way to resolve this dilemma in practice is within the context of a particular project: 'within this project we shall call *this* activity analysis and *this* activity design'.

Because of this dilemma we have tried to avoid the word 'analysis' as much as possible. Instead we use the word 'design' in a wider sense than normal, to refer to all the creative aspects of software system construction: hence the title of this book. We discuss design from three distinct viewpoints: the viewpoint of an observer in the world, the viewpoint of a software specifier, and the viewpoint of a software implementor. These different viewpoints, each with their own modelling interpretation, provide a framework in which each issue can be addressed at the correct time.

Completeness and bureaucracy

Formal methods? Admittedly complex notations? *Three* distinct model interpretations? Surely this is a recipe for overwhelming method bureaucracy?

Although we would robustly defend the need for each and every fine distinction in our approach, we urge you not to turn our design techniques, which, after all, are supposed to be an aid not an impediment, into a pointless grind, where 'standards' and 'procedures' force a relentless and fruitless pursuit of completeness at the expense of inspiration and understanding. This book is bold enough to acknowledge software design as a creative activity, carried out by inventive, imaginative people. Don't stifle creativity.

History, development and use

The ideas presented in this book are the result of the many years spent by the authors in the construction of software systems, since 1985 almost exclusively using object-oriented methods and technology. They form the basis of the Syntropy™ method, pioneered by the authors and used by the consultants of Object Designers Limited and their clients.

The material is intended for designing software to run on conventional platforms, such as workstations, PCs, mainframes or embedded processors. We do not consider other kinds of computational environment, such as special-purpose processors or neural networks. Neither do we consider 'rule-based' software, whose execution is based on the concept of logical inference.

As we make clear in the text, we recognise that full application of the ideas presented here will require the use of powerful tools. No such tools exist at the time of writing, although we are certain of their feasibility. One of our major goals is to mastermind the creation of these tools. Nevertheless, the principles underlying our ideas and most of the notation for expressing them can be utilised today using the simplest of computerised support – or even paper.

More than twenty years after the beginning of the methods revolution, most software produced today is not consciously *designed*. While this state of affairs may be satisfactory for simpler systems, the more complex software being produced now, and the even more complex systems of tomorrow, will require precise and expressive but flexible design techniques. We hope this book will make a valuable contribution to the successful construction of complex software systems.

Using this book

We hope this book builds through its chapters a consistent and convincing story concerning the way to think about software design. We urge you to read it from cover to cover, but we understand that this will take some time and effort, given the level of detail it contains.

Part One of this book, comprising chapter 1, sets out our philosophy. Part Two, comprising chapters 2–5, describes techniques useful for modelling the world. Part Three, comprising chapters 6–9, describes techniques useful for modelling software. Part Four, comprising chapters 10–12, discusses various aspects of system architecture. Part Five, comprising chapter 13, addresses some of the issues that arise when these techniques are used practically to develop software.

The first time through we suggest you read chapters 1, 2, 4, 6, 7, 10, 11 and 13. This route through the material will give you a complete impression of the techniques, without delving into the finer details contained in the other chapters. Some of the listed chapters end with material which should be skipped on a first reading; this material is marked in the text.

For a brief introduction to our approach to software design and development, we suggest you read just chapters 1 and 13.

Acknowledgements

This book has been written over several years. It represents not only the individual work of the authors, but also the fruits of collaboration with a great many other people.

The starting-point for this work was the OODLES object-oriented design working group, under the auspices of the British Computer Society's OOPS (Object-Oriented Programming and Systems) Specialist Group. OODLES met regularly during 1987, and was the forum in which we discovered our common interests and began to articulate our ideas. We thank the members of OODLES, particularly Bruce Anderson and Chris Wallace, for setting us off on the right road. Bruce's ideas about how people can work together effectively have influenced us greatly, and Chris's design examples (notably his Petrol Station) have found their way into our training courses, this book, and many other places.

In a wider context, OOPS has provided a focus since 1985 for the development of the object-oriented methods community in the United Kingdom, by organising many meetings and conferences in which ideas about object-oriented systems have been presented and discussed. We thank all of the organisers and participants in these events for providing a fertile environment for us to develop our ideas. Special thanks are due to Ralph Hodgson for his enthusiasm and encouragement.

Since 1990 the full-time consultants of Object Designers Ltd., including Gary Birch, Dave Cleal, Iain Cooke, David Harvey, Geoff Mohamed and Charles Weir, have taken pains to understand, interpret, constructively criticise, enhance and ultimately use our ideas. We thank them for their patience and their contribution to this book.

We also thank the students on our many training courses and workshops in object-oriented analysis and design over several years, who have tried out our ideas and let us know whenever they found them wanting.

We thank the following people who gave us useful feedback on drafts of this book: John Cameron, Franco Civello, Ian Maung, Richard Mitchell, Meilir Page-Jones, Paul Taylor, and the anonymous referees.

We owe our heartfelt thanks to our wives and children for their unfailing support throughout the months we spent in front of our computers on this project.

References

[Abria80] J-R. Abrial, S. Schuman and B. Meyer. A specification language. *On the Construction of Programs*, R. McNaughten and R. McKeag (eds.), Cambridge University Press, 1980.

[Booch91] G. Booch. *Object Oriented Design With Applications*, Benjamin/Cummings, Redwood City, California, 1991.

[Carri89] D. Carrington, D. Duke, R. Duke, P. King, G. Rose and G. Smith. Object-Z: An object-oriented extension to Z. *FORTE89 – International Conference on Formal Description Techniques,* North-Holland, 1989.

[Harel87] D. Harel. Statecharts: a visual formalism for complex systems. *Science of Computer Programming* 8:231–274, 1987.

[Jones86] C. Jones. *Systematic Software Development Using VDM*, Prentice-Hall International, Hemel Hempstead, Hertfordshire, 1986.

[Loomi87] M.E.S. Loomis, A.V. Shah and J.E. Rumbaugh. An object modeling technique for conceptual design. *ECOOP'87 European Conference on Object-Oriented Programming,* Lecture Notes in Computer Science no. 276, Springer-Verlag, Berlin, 1987.

[Rumba91] J. Rumbaugh, M. Blaha, W. Premerlani, F. Eddy and W. Lorensen. *Object-Oriented Modeling and Design*, Prentice-Hall, Englewood Cliffs, New Jersey, 1991.

[Winbl90] A.L. Winblad, S.D. Edwards and D.R. King. *Object-Oriented Software*, Addison-Wesley, Reading, Massachusetts, 1990.

Part One

Systems, models and views

CHAPTER 1

Systems, models and views

1.1 The ecology of software

Object technology holds out the promise of a breakthrough in software productivity. But this breakthrough will not be achieved by continuing to develop software systems in the same old ways using object-oriented programming languages instead of procedural ones. Instead, the breakthrough will be a consequence of building software systems by assembling them from pre-fabricated parts, rather than repeatedly starting system development from scratch.

Many technical and organisational changes are needed to bring about this revolution. These changes might be summarised as a change in the *ecology* of software. *The Oxford English Dictionary* defines ecology as 'a branch of biology dealing with relationships of organisms to one another and to their surroundings'. In software, we deal with the relationships of software components – objects – to each other and to their surroundings. These relationships are the subject of this book.

Our own vision of object technology is heavily influenced by many years of experience with the Smalltalk programming environment [Goldb83]. Developing software in Smalltalk brings several insights whose importance extends well beyond the boundaries of the Smalltalk system itself to shed new light on the overall software development process. These are as follows:

- Software development takes place within an extensive, evolving environment of multi-purpose computational components.
- Structures and relationships are vastly more important than algorithms and functions.
- Every element has its proper place within the whole.
- New software is created as an extension of what already exists.
- The system is built from a small number of powerful and orthogonal concepts.
- The software development activity consists at least as much of learning as of creating.

Influential as it is, Smalltalk is far from being an adequate solution to the overall problem of software development. Although Smalltalk is an excellent way of building some kinds of software, the true potential of object technology will not be achieved through any particular programming language. It will be achieved through an evolutionary process during which new insights into software development will be translated into products and standards.

1.2 Modelling

This is a book about building models. The entire field of object methods is based on the notion that 'objects' identified in the problem (analysis) have a meaningful place in the solution (design). This book explores this notion in considerable detail, and shows that although it contains many elements of truth, it should not be taken too literally.

As a first approximation, we can say that object-oriented methods focus on structural, problem-directed approaches rather than functional, solution-directed approaches. To understand this difference think about maps. If you want to find out how to get from your house to the office you have two choices: ask someone for directions or buy a map. We express directions functionally: 'Go west for four miles, turn right, proceed a further three miles and take the second left after the Post Office.' Provided they are good directions and you follow them precisely they will solve your immediate problem. But they are not a general, reusable solution and if you miss a landmark you are probably lost. A map is a model based on real-world entities. It is rich in contextual information; you don't have to rely on spotting isolated landmarks, they are all captured on the map. Experience tells us that trying to follow directions is much easier if you have the map first! The richness of a map allows us to relate more closely to the real-world situation being modelled. The map represents a structure (roads, etc.) through which we navigate functionally.

Models can be very versatile. We can often use a well-designed object model to answer questions about the situation being modelled which we had no plans to ask when the model was built. Maps are an extreme example of this. Not only did the cartographer not know (or care!) about the routes you want to follow when he drew the map, he also allowed you to answer questions ('how high is that hill over there?') which were completely outside your interest ('what's the quickest route to the office?') when you bought the map.

Another argument in favour of models is that they change less frequently than the functions applied to them. Using our map analogy, the routes we follow are more likely to change than the terrain over which those routes pass. We don't always go from A to B. When A is our home and B is the office, the A's and B's change regularly for most people. Maps do become out of date but the lifetime of a map is usually longer than our need to follow any particular route. (Interestingly, even an out-of-date map is very useful.)

There have always been areas of software design where modelling is paramount. One is database design. Databases are a clear example of structure pre-empting function. One particular field of database design research, semantic data modelling, has contributed greatly to the development of today's object-oriented analysis and design methods. Semantic database models were first devised as tools that allowed high-level descriptions of data to be captured and visualised prior to their translation into the less expressive database models, such as network, hierarchical and relational, used for implementation. Although the relational model is very flexible, and does a good job at separating the logical from the physical, its strongly record-oriented nature limits its expressive power. Recently, semantic data models have been used as the basis for actual databases, rather than as an intermediate description.

While the connection between object-oriented models and semantic data models is strong, object-oriented models go much further, using the data/function merging features of objects to describe the functions that navigate through the model as well as its structure. Indeed, it is a primary tenet of object technology that the underlying representation of objects is hidden behind a procedural interface. This is true for maps, too, in this technological age: the *real* map is a collection of 1s and 0s on a magnetic tape; the map we buy is but one possible visualisation of those data.

A word of caution here. You may be aware of the millions of dollars wasted on attempts to build huge software 'maps' (actually, corporate data models) of all aspects of a large company's operations. Part of the problem here is the sheer scale of the undertaking; the map is out of date before it's finished. But there's another problem. These huge models often lack purpose. We've said that models are versatile but you can only take that so far: road maps don't generally include geological survey data. It's all a question of the richness of the information. If you try to solve too many problems with a single model it becomes unmanageably large and cumbersome. Instead of a single centralised model, the solution is to build many small intersecting models, each under the control of people who understand a particular area of the business well. Object technology can simplify the construction of such models, using techniques such as those described in this book.

Simulation is another area of software design where modelling is crucial. In fact, object technology has its roots in the Simula language, which was designed for programming discrete-event simulations. In simulation, the software models a system for the purpose of understanding the system itself. The model does not correspond in real time to any portion of the world; instead it is used to ask 'what if' questions about the simulated system. Closely related to simulations are systems which maintain an artificial interactive reality. These systems allow users to create and interact with information structures which correspond to concepts in their minds. Examples are word-processors, graphical editors, mathematical processing systems, and music composition systems.

Controlling a process is another important application of software models. In a process such as a chemical plant or an aircraft, software responds to stimuli generated within the process and produces appropriate responses to control the future development of the process.

Many software systems combine aspects of all of these. For example, software for supporting trading activities on financial markets is one of the most demanding applications of object technology so far, where data structure, simulation and process control are all vital aspects of the overall complexity to be modelled.

1.3 Software and the world

We have said that the entire field of object methods is based on the notion that 'objects' identified in the problem (analysis) have a meaningful place in the solution (design). An important question is the extent to which the activities of analysis and design can be merged. The simplistic approach is to say that object-oriented development is a process requiring no transformations, beginning with the construction of an object model and progressing seamlessly into object-oriented code. This approach is based on two questionable principles: (1) the set of concepts found in object-oriented programming is appropriate for building abstract models of reality, (2) there is essentially no difference between an analysis model and an implementation model.

While superficially appealing, this approach is seriously flawed. It should be clear to anyone that models of the world are completely different from models of software. The world does not consist of objects sending each other messages, and we would have to be seriously mesmerised by object jargon to believe that it does. Nevertheless, it may be worth considering the notion that it would be useful to *model* the world as objects sending messages, as a precursor to building software. If we had such a model, it would immediately constitute an executable simulation, and the transition to a useful software system would be easy. Indeed, this is the promise often held out for objects.

Unfortunately, there are some fundamental problems with this view. The first is *predictability*. Much as we might sometimes like it to be otherwise, the world is unpredictable. If it were predictable we could determine all future behaviour by reasoning about currently known facts. On the other hand, software is predictable because its behaviour is determined by its code. Therefore, software cannot model the world in general.

But the world is *partially* predictable. We can predict that the sun will rise, and having risen will not rise again until after it has set. Perhaps we can still use objects sending messages to model the predictable part of the world. The problem with this is *causality*. Which object will send the sun the message asking it to rise? Is it to be the earth, the laws of physics, the sun itself? There is no logical basis on which to make this choice by considering just the situation itself.

What about the effects of the sunrise? We predict that in summer lots of birds will start to sing around sunrise. Here we need to describe many things happening at once, that is, *concurrency*. Does the sun send a message to all of the birds individually? If so, in what order? Is there a problem of deadlock? These are silly questions, because they are questions about software execution, not the sunrise. It seems that if we insist on choosing 'objects sending messages' to model even the predictable part of the world, we must ask nonsensical questions.

So we see that applying the object-oriented programming concept of messages to abstract specification leads to inflexibility and over-commitment. Object-oriented programming languages (OOPLs) also have serious limitations in the important modelling concepts of association and aggregation. We conclude that the set of concepts found in OOPLs is inappropriate for building abstract models of reality.

In any case, software systems must also deal with interfaces, data storage and a host of other low-level issues. Even if the process of translating an analysis object model into equivalent classes in an OOPL were trivial (which it isn't), only a small part of the whole job would be completed.

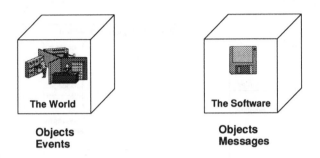

The World — Objects Events

The Software — Objects Messages

Fig 1.1 *The world and the software*

Because of these problems we use different sets of building blocks for modelling the world and modelling the software, as illustrated in figure 1.1. To model the world we use two basic concepts: objects and events. Objects model things and events model occurrences. The things modelled by objects can be concrete or abstract, transient or permanent, real or imaginary. The occurrences modelled by events are names for the changes of state of the things being modelled.

All a thing needs in order to be modelled by an object is a name: bricks, Bessel functions, ducks, dreams and unicorns can all be objects. In fact, we normally model object *types*, rather than individual object instances. For example, let's go back to the sunrise. What are the facts? Given a location on the earth, there is one sun, which alternately rises and sets. There is some number of birds. Given a bird, we cannot say when it will start to sing, but we can definitely say that it won't stop singing until after it has started. We have identified:

- some object types: Location, Sun, Bird;
- some events: rise(Location, Sun); set(Location, Sun); startSinging(Bird); stopSinging(Bird);
- some simple relationships between these object types and events.

To model *software* we also use two basic concepts: objects and messages. Software objects refer to encapsulations of data with their associated operations, and messages refer to invocations of these operations.

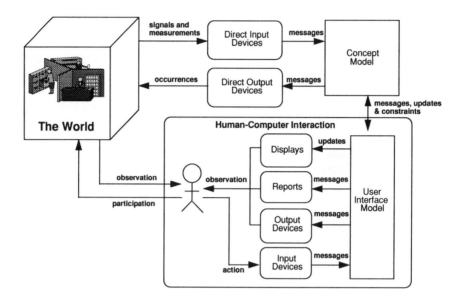

Figure 1.2 *Linking the world and software*

Now let's examine the relationship between the world and a software system, illustrated in figure 1.2. Somewhere in the software is a *concept model*, a model in software partially mimicking the behaviour of certain things in the world. This software model must be updated whenever relevant changes occur in the world. The speed and frequency of update is a design parameter. In any system there are two possible paths for these updates. The occurrences may be detected and measured by sensors or transducers, called direct input devices in the diagram, and notification passed from these to the concept model. Alternatively, the occurrences may be detected by human operators and fed to the concept model via a human–computer interface. It may also be the job of the software to *cause* occurrences in the world. These are either applied immediately by direct output devices, such as valves or relays, or are passed to the human operator for action.

The diagram is only partially accurate for several reasons. Firstly, software is, of course, itself part of the world – increasingly so, for in today's world some very common phenomena, such as money, have no recorded existence other than in software. Hence it is not possible to design software on the basis that its existence will leave the world unchanged; the introduction of a software system into the world changes the world irrevocably and often unpredictably. Sometimes it is useful to pretend that the introduction of a software system will not change the world. On other occasions such a pretence is unhelpful and best avoided.

Secondly, the diagram distinguishes between those humans whose purpose is to act explicitly as operators for the software system, thereby appearing inside the human–computer interaction box, and those who are simply part of the world and whose actions are detected by direct measurement. Making this distinction clearly requires us to know something about the intentions of the people concerned. Nevertheless in many cases the distinction is perfectly clear. For example, a system controlling the sprinklers in a building will have sensors to detect a fire, a concept model representing the physical layout of the building, valves to turn the sprinklers on in the right areas, and a user interface to help fire-fighters find out where the fire is and other relevant parameters. In this system the occupants of the building are in the world, whereas the fire-fighters are part of the human–computer interaction system.

Lastly, it is often possible to re-interpret the diagram simply by a shift of perspective. Consider a word-processing system. What is the concept model? Does it include:

- the meaning of the words being written?
- the letters, words and paragraphs, considered as objects in their own right?
- the visual appearance of the letters, words and paragraphs, taking into account fonts, styles, etc.?
- the interaction properties of the letters, words and paragraphs?
- the way the word processor manages windows on the display?

The first interpretation may seem unlikely, until we consider the possibility of syntax-directed editing of formal texts such as computer programs or specifications. But all of the rest seem quite plausible. Where shall we draw the line?

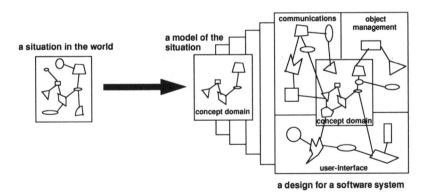

Figure 1.3 *Domains*

The answer to this question lies in a discussion of *domains*. Domains are separately considered sub-systems. Some domains are *concept domains*, whose primary role is to mimic the world, whereas other domains are *interaction domains*, whose primary role is to provide the mechanisms for keeping the concept domains and the world in step. Figure 1.3 illustrates how a model of a situation in the world – a concept domain – is embedded in a number of typical interaction domains acting as intermediaries between the concept domain and its environment. The diagram shows interaction domains for object management, communications, and user-interface. We discuss domains further in chapter 11. For now, the discussion will assume we are focusing on one domain, and the general assumption will be that it is a concept domain. Nevertheless, all of the modelling techniques we propose can be applied to any domain, although some may be more appropriate than others in particular circumstances.

In this book we present three kinds of object-oriented model. The first kind, which we call the *essential model*, considers the model to be a description of some real or imaginary *situation*, which may or may not contain software. We use the word *situation* rather than *system* because 'system' has so many possible meanings including the software we may be trying to build, and rather than *world* to emphasise that we are considering purposeful systems situated in a context rather than trying to describe all of some supposedly objective reality. The purpose of building the essential model is to understand and establish the facts about this situation. The building blocks which we use to build essential models are objects (actually object types) and events (actually event types). An essential model is built by drawing annotated diagrams, and interpreted as descriptions of sets, functions and sequences with meanings in the situation being described.

In the second kind of model, called the *specification model*, we are concerned with specifying software. To create a specification model it is necessary to establish which parts of the overall situation will be implemented in software. In some cases this might be a large part of the situation, whereas in others it might not be a part at all. The activity of specifying exactly what is to be implemented in software is quite different from the activity of establishing the facts about the overall situation; however both of these activities would conventionally fall under the heading of 'analysis'. Like essential models, specification models deal with objects and events and are built by drawing annotated diagrams. They are interpreted as a description of the abstract stimulus–response behaviour of the software. The specification model describes software at a high level of abstraction, and in particular says nothing about internal sequencing or concurrency. An important part of building a specification model is the allocation among object types of responsibility for aspects of software behaviour.

The third kind of model, the *implementation model*, is concerned with establishing patterns of control flow within the software. In this model we take into account the fact that computer programs have a limited number of well-defined flows of control, which execute at a finite speed. The building blocks for implementation models are objects and messages. Object interactions are described as messages sent from one object to another, and the implementation model describes message sequencing and concurrency control. Annotated diagrams are used again, although in the implementation model our repertoire of diagrams is richer than for the other kinds of model.

Figure 1.4 summarises the three kinds of model. It illustrates how essential models are built to understand the world, whereas specification and implementation models are built in order to describe the behaviour of software. It also shows a systematic correspondence between the essential model and the concept domain part of the software models: this is the same correspondence as is illustrated in figure 1.3.

Note that the specification model stands between the essential and implementation models, in the sense that it uses the same concepts as the essential model but has the same intention – the description of software behaviour – as the implementation model.

For object-oriented methods to offer significant advantages there must be consistency and systematic correspondence between these three models of a system. We do not, however, expect the three models to be identical; indeed, because the formal interpretations of the three models are different, this is not possible. But we certainly expect a systematic correspondence between the essential model and the concept domain part of the specification and implementation models. Exactly what kinds of correspondence we may expect will emerge as we look at the models in detail.

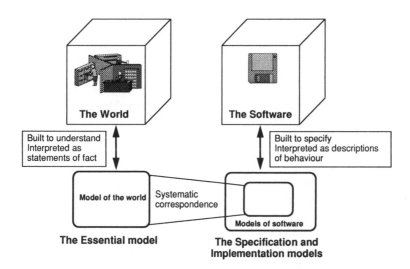

Figure 1.4 *Relationships between models*

1.4 Essential models

The purpose of an essential model[1] is to understand a situation, real or imaginary. The building-blocks of an essential model are objects and events, and its interpretation is a set of facts. Chapters 2–5 describe in detail the notations for building essential models, and what kinds of facts can be expressed using them.

Building an essential model may be a matter of establishing the facts about a pre-existing situation, or it may involve designing the facts about a situation yet to be constructed. For example, we might be designing a new video game, in which alien monsters compete for advantage in a world full of weird and wonderful dangers. This imaginary, designed world contains facts just as much as does a payroll system, and it is equally appropriate to build essential models of it.

The facts about a situation which are described by an essential model are as follows:

- the possible states that the situation can be in;
- the set of events which cause changes between one state and another; and
- the possible sequences of events which can occur.

The states of a situation are described in terms of objects, which have properties, and their relationships. Any particular state consists of a set of objects, each with specific properties, participating in particular relationships.

An important activity when building an essential model is to decide what to include. In any situation there may be an infinity of phenomena which can be perceived and which might be included in an essential model. The way to decide is to refer to the purpose for which the model is to be built, and hence select what is relevant.

Events in an essential model are simultaneously observable everywhere. They may carry information, in the form of object identities and other values. All events are instantaneous, regardless of how long they might actually take in the world: either an event has happened or it hasn't; events are never in the middle of happening. If we need to model overlapping activities, then we model them using distinct events to mark where they start and where they finish. If we need to model events occurring at particular times, then we model the passage of time with events.

The essential model does not describe cause and effect relationships. We do not wish to consider what causes what in the world, which we think is an infinitely complex, mysterious and non-deterministic place. However, we do notice that some sequences of events do occur in the world, whereas others don't. For example, a switch is either off or on, and the events *on* and *off* invariably alternate. Two *on* events simply never happen without an intervening *off* event. In the essential model, what we leave out is just as important as what we include.

An essential model acts as an external observer of a modelled situation. Events 'leak out' from the situation being observed and are detected by the essential model,

---

[1]The terminology 'essential model' has been used elsewhere, notably in the work of McMenamin and Palmer [McMen84]. Our usage is different, although the intention is somewhat similar.

which tracks the changes of state of the observed situation. The essential model states which sequences of events can happen, and which cannot. There are no 'run-time errors' in a correct essential model: if an event occurs which is not allowed by the model, then the model does not describe the situation properly.

An essential model, once built, could in principle be executed, and would act as a kind of simulation of the modelled situation[2]. At any point it would expect one of a certain set of events, and would need to be told which of these events had occurred; it would then shift to a new state, with another set of possible events.

Essential modelling techniques are applicable to a wide range of situations, regardless of whether software is to be written. All that is necessary for these techniques to be useful is that the modelled situation can be usefully described in terms of discrete states and events. For example, the techniques could be used to describe the rules of a game or the operation of a business enterprise.

Most often, however, we want to build a software system. To do this it is necessary to define the boundary between the software and its environment. Many software development methods assume that the environment and the boundary for a software system are given as known facts at the beginning of development. In our experience, although this is sometimes the case, often it is not. We can identify three general categories of system on the basis of what is known about the software boundary and environment at the outset, as follows:

1. The environment is given and the software boundary is implicit in the definition of what the overall system is to do.

   This category of systems, which we sometimes call 'hard' systems, consists of those where the performance of the system depends completely upon the software. An extreme example is a video game. Here there is no ambiguity about the role of the software; the software is the entire system. Another example would be a guided missile, where the purpose of the software is to get the missile to the target by controlling the engine, navigation and other functions.

2. The environment is given, but the software boundary is a matter of choice.

   This category of systems, consisting of systems which we call 'semi-hard', are those where the introduction of software does not change the behaviour of the overall system, but the role of the software within the overall system can be chosen depending upon non-technical factors such as cost, ergonomics or political issues. For example, we might automate some aspect of the overall operation of a business – say payroll processing – without appreciable impact on the operation of the business as a whole.

---

[2]We believe that a tool which executes essential models in this way would be very useful for validating the model for people with experience of the subject domain who don't understand the diagrammatic and mathematical formalisms.

3. The introduction of the software will change the environment in unpredictable ways.

> This third category of systems, whose members we call 'soft', are those where introducing software will have consequences which cannot be predicted in advance of its introduction.   An electronic mail system is an example. Introducing an electronic mail system into an organisation can have far-reaching consequences on the organisation, such as the way meetings and diaries are organised, the amount of time individuals spend processing their mail, or even the physical location in which individuals carry out their work.   Sooner or later the software will need to be changed to reflect and incorporate the changes it has precipitated in the organisation.

These distinctions are relative.   One person's hard system is another person's soft system – introducing video games into an organisation of undisciplined staff might wreak havoc on its productivity.   Much of the history of information technology consists of the introduction of computer systems into organisations on a piecemeal basis, on the assumption that the software does not affect the basic structure of the organisation.   However, it often does, and more recently there have been many initiatives to try and redress the balance, by applying techniques for corporate information modelling and business process re-engineering [Hamme93].

It is important not to under-estimate the changes which introducing software can make to a situation.   Traditional methods of systems development, which analyse and automate existing data-flows and data stores, have resulted in software systems which perpetuate organisational practices established when the business was run using paper. Many organisations are having to rebuild their information systems around models which represent the essence of the business, rather than models which simply implement outmoded business practices.   Some have tried to build complete, centralised models of everything that happens in the business.   This is often a mistake, for reasons pointed out earlier.   This book is not about information systems methodology or business process re-engineering; nevertheless we believe the modelling distinctions made here are necessary (although not sufficient) for thinking clearly about those subjects.

1.5 Specification models

The purpose of a specification model is to state what the software will do.   The specification model describes the states that the software can be in, and the way that it responds to stimuli (events) by changing state and by generating responses (also events).

Like the essential model, the specification model is built in terms of events and states, and the formalisms we use are extremely similar for both models. The main practical differences are as follows:

- the specification model can generate events itself;
- a specification model can leave the response to an event undefined.

Although the diagrams we draw for the specification model are very similar to those for the essential model, the theoretical interpretation is significantly different. One important difference is the concept of sub-type, often informally called an 'is-a' relationship. Chapter 6 provides a detailed discussion of the notations used for specification modelling and their interpretation.

A specification model describes software at a level of abstraction which ignores implementation issues such as control flow, concurrency, user-interface details, persistence and so on. Any practical implementation will have many intermediate states of execution between the states described by the specification model, because of the limitations of speed and space imposed by computer hardware. However, the specification should describe the implementation accurately, in the sense that it would be possible in principle to produce a formal proof that the implementation implements the specification correctly. We do not provide any apparatus for doing such proofs in this book; indeed, in the current state of the art, such proofs are rarely a practical proposition for software systems of any significant size or complexity.

To create a specification model we must draw a boundary between the software and the rest of the situation, which we will call the *environment*. To design a specification model requires considerable thought about how the software and its environment will interact. In general, it may require the design of a complete user-interface, together with the design of the tasks which the operator of that interface will need to undertake. Often this design will involve prototyping the user-interface, and other disciplines such as ergonomics and graphic art will be brought into play.

A proper discussion of user-interface design is well outside the scope of this book, but we can make some general comments about the considerations which come into play when designing interactions.

Firstly, in determining the boundary and responsibilities of the software we must identify all of the stimuli and responses. Sometimes these are simply given, and sometimes we identify them by first building an essential model. If we have an essential model defining a set of events, we must decide for each event whether it is detected by the software, generated by the software or irrelevant to the operation of the software. This question provides a systematic way of thinking about the software boundary based upon the essential model.

The second important principle to use when designing the software boundary is to consider untimely occurrences. For example, an essential model might declare that the event of withdrawing money from an account cannot happen when the account is overdrawn by more than a certain amount. However, in an implementation, somebody might well attempt to withdraw the money. Attempting to withdraw the money is different from succeeding in withdrawing it, and the specification model could make this distinction precise by specifying a detected event representing an attempt to withdraw the money, and a generated event representing the actual withdrawal.

The third principle we use is to think of the specification model as a 'transparent box', that is, to assume that the state of the model can be observed by its users at any time, without the need for explicit events to carry information from the software to the situation. The decision about which information should be transferred from the software to its environment explicitly by means of events, or implicitly by observing the state, is not an absolute one; it depends upon assumptions made in the design of the user-interface such as the expectations of the users of the software. For example, in an air traffic control system, will operators be notified by an audible alarm when an aircraft enters their zone (a generated event) or will they simply notice it on the screen (an act of observation)? In any case, making the software state visible in an implementation can be a complicated exercise, requiring mechanisms such as dependencies, triggers and display updates. All of this can be ignored in the specification model for a concept domain, although it may be crucial in a specification model for an interaction domain.

As well as providing an abstract specification of the overall behaviour of the software, a specification model establishes which object types have responsibility for which aspects of this behaviour. The vision of building software from pre-fabricated parts applies just as much to specifications as it does to implementations. Hence specification model object types should provide robust abstractions which may be reused in different models (although for performance reasons allocation of responsibilities may change when moving from a specification model to a particular implementation).

1.6 Implementation models

Implementation models describe the objects in the executing software and how they communicate. The primary building blocks for the implementation model are objects, which have types, states and properties, and communicate by sending messages. The implementation model is semantically close to the execution model of popular object-oriented programming languages, such as Smalltalk, C++ and Eiffel. Particular languages have particular quirks which may filter up through the design to be represented explicitly in the implementation model. Indeed, the pragmatics of the implementation language sometimes impact the entire development process in quite profound ways, and affect the essential and specification models, too.

However, it is in the implementation model that the effects of the language are most likely to be seen, for example:

- where class libraries already exist;
- where there are particular subtleties about the semantics of inheritance; or

- where choices between object and value types are predetermined by efficiency considerations.

In this book we approach the implementation model from a language-independent viewpoint. One of the most important strengths of object technology is its ability to integrate heterogeneous systems. In the future, any focus on a particular programming language will become less and less relevant as systems start to be constructed from parts written in many different programming languages, communicating via a language-independent substrate such as the Object Management Group's Common Object Request Broker Architecture [CORBA92].

Traditional approaches to software development make a strong distinction between data and processing. This distinction lies at the heart of the design of programming languages such as COBOL, C and Pascal, and also at the heart of traditional data-processing architectures which separate the shared database from the programs which access it. With the advent of object technology this traditional distinction is beginning to break down, to be replaced by the distinction between the *insides* and the *outsides* of objects. Objects encapsulate data together with the operations that act upon those data. Objects are only accessed via operations, which provide services to the object's clients. A single object can be thought of as a stimulus–response mechanism, where a stimulus is a message causing the invocation of one of the object's operations. From the point of view of the message sender, the response is a value returned from the operation. From a more global perspective, the response includes a set of messages sent by the object to others, each of which causes its own response.

The distinction between the insides and outsides of objects is captured by the *egg model* (figure 1.5). If an object is an egg, then the yolk of the egg represents the object's data. Completely surrounding the yolk is the white, representing the object's operations. On the very outside is the shell, representing the interface that the object offers the world. The arrows denote references[3] from one object to another, which always end at the shell, indicating that the shell is the only visible part of the egg. The white and yolk are inaccessible to an observer outside the egg unless the egg is broken open – which would be called a 'violation of encapsulation' in object-oriented terms.

In an implementation model, external stimuli are converted into messages which are sent from point to point between objects, eventually being converted back into responses in the external world. In slightly more detail we expect an event to be detected by a hardware device first, then handled by some interaction domain objects which will send appropriate messages to concept domain objects. On the output side, a messages is sent from a concept domain object to an interaction domain object, which co-operates with other interaction domain objects, eventually manipulating hardware devices which cause occurrences to be manifested in the external world.

---

[3]These arrows represent inter-object references, not message-sending: arrows representing message-sending would go from the white of one egg (its methods) to the shell of another.

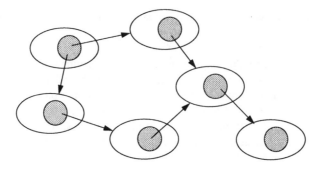

Figure 1.5 *Objects as eggs*

Object technology is often described as encouraging reuse. At the level of program code this ability is a direct consequence of pursuing the distinction between insides and outsides. The inside of a client object contains assumptions about the outside of the supplier objects it uses. Any supplier which offers an outside conforming to these expectations is a valid partner in this relationship. Building software systems by assembling pre-fabricated components is made possible by software technology which allows many different actual suppliers (actual outsides) to conform to a single expected outside: a property often called *polymorphism*. This matching between suppliers and clients may occur either at system assembly time (typically when modules are compiled together), or at run-time, that is, when several different suppliers with the same interface co-exist in an executing system.

Bertrand Meyer has emphasised this idea using the phrase *design by contract* [Meyer92]. Each relationship of usage between two objects has a supplier and client. The supplier offers the client a contract, as illustrated in figure 1.6. In Meyer's language, Eiffel, such a contract is specified in terms of pre-conditions, which the client must satisfy before calling an operation, and post-conditions, which the server promises to satisfy afterwards. We follow these ideas in the implementation model, using annotated diagrams to express the interfaces instead of a programming language. The idea of design by contract also applies in a modified form to the specification model, as we will see in chapter 6.

One of the crucial issues addressed in the implementation model is concurrency. In the essential and specification models speed of execution is not an issue: all responses are simply defined to be sufficiently quick. However, in a software system it is often the case that a rapid response is required to a stimulus, even though the software is in the process of calculating the response to an earlier, but less urgent, stimulus. User-interface feedback is an obvious example of this requirement. Simply serialising all inputs to the software is not often an adequate solution, and in general there is a need for several concurrent processes, whether on the same or different physical processors.

As soon as there are concurrent processes, there is a need to manage concurrent access to objects. As we will see in chapter 9, concurrent processes cannot be allowed to access objects in an arbitrary way, because the semantics of shared objects cannot be guaranteed without a coherent scheme for making competing processes co-operate with each other. Also, unfortunately, the basic principle of design by contract is violated as soon as concurrency is introduced. The implementation model extensions described in chapter 9 contains process synchronisation constructs which allow the principle of design by contract to be re-introduced, although in a modified form.

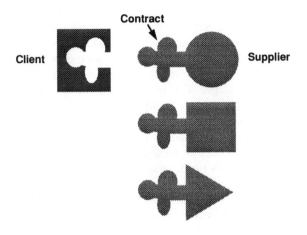

Figure 1.6 *Design by contract*

1.7 Views and notations

Each of the three models is expressed in a series of views, where each view shows a different aspect of the model. Some of these views are textual, some are graphical. Some have a formal interpretation, some are informal.

The two most important views, applicable to every model are:

- type view – a view showing the types of object in the model, their properties and relationships;
- state view – a view showing how the state of objects changes over time as a result of events.

Both these views are based on existing notations: OMT's object modelling notation [Rumba91] for type views and Harel Statecharts [Harel87] for state views. However, we give these diagrams precise meanings expressed in terms of sets and functions, so that they may be interpreted unambiguously, and to ease the construction of tools.

As described in later chapters, the type view consists of rectangles representing types, containing expressions describing properties and invariants, with annotated lines between them describing relationships. Many object-oriented design methods have notations consisting of bubbles and lines, and what mainly differentiates the methods is the shape of the bubbles. Many methods simply say that bubbles describe classes, and attributes describe instance variables (data members, in C++ terminology). Indeed, this is a tempting interpretation, because CASE manufacturers can easily generate code templates, one class per bubble, and claim that they have a code generator; it also greatly simplifies the task of producing diagrams from code – a feature which can be readily marketed as 'reverse engineering'. We take the position that this simplistic interpretation is inappropriate, certainly for essential and specification models. The main reason for our reluctance to equate bubbles and classes is that the semantics of constructs such as inheritance or pointers are language-dependent, and by equating bubbles and classes we would make the semantics of our notations dependent on a particular programming language. This may arguably be appropriate for implementation design, but is certainly inappropriate for the more abstract structures represented by essential and specification models.

We much prefer to define our notations in terms of abstract sets and functions, so that they can be used to reason about models in a language-independent way. Hence we choose to call our rectangles types, rather than classes, and the things inside them properties, rather than attributes. How they are implemented in a particular OO or non-OO programming language is an important aspect of the overall design; it is often dependent on project-specific issues, and in general the mapping from diagrams to code may be different for each new project. Frequently, another important consideration is the mapping from objects to database constructs, such as relational tables. How to do these mappings in detail is outside the scope of this book.

In addition we define how formal, mathematical, specification can be used to enhance these views. We do not believe formal specification should be applied everywhere in every case but we think it a useful technique that every designer should have available. We have tried to make the formal specification an adjunct to graphical notations that already have a formal meaning. Our mathematical notation is based on the formal specification language Z [Words92].

The third kind of view shown in figure 1.7 is directly applicable only to implementation models. It shows how software objects interact by message-passing. For this view we use the concept of scenario-based *mechanisms*, as promoted by Booch [Booch91], drawn using the object diagrams found in [Rumba91]. Being based on examples, this view cannot realistically be made complete or formal. Statecharts in the implementation model are given different semantics to allow the specification of message interaction. Thus they provide the formalism missing from mechanisms.

The most important view is the type view, closely followed by mechanisms. If time and effort are limited, these are the ones that we recommend producing. Statecharts are more difficult to understand and to get right, and tend to be less familiar, especially to programmers. However, statecharts are necessary for completeness.

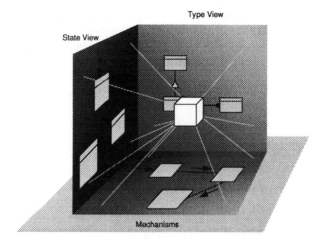

Figure 1.7 *Views*

1.8 Encapsulated software components

We started to discuss reuse in the introduction to the implementation model, and introduced the idea of design by contract, which enables reuse of executable software components. But the need for reuse goes well beyond executable software. We would like to be able to reuse elements from our essential and specification models, too.

We cannot address this desire in any of our models without being able to construct partial models, and to define formally systematic ways of putting them together to produce composite models. Our basic vision for this is set out in chapter 12, where we discuss how to define encapsulated software components which may be stored in a repository for reuse.

Such a vision cannot be realised without support from computer-based design tools, which do not exist at the time of writing in 1994, although they form a clear part of our plan for the future of our ideas.

1.9 Method

This book introduces a number of ideas and techniques which we have found helpful in software projects. But we do not by any means recommend that all the techniques be used for all projects. Indeed, without CASE tools in advance of anything available today, this would be an exceptionally time-consuming and bureaucratic task for all except the simplest projects. Which techniques are most appropriate depends upon the starting-point for the project, and which part of the project is being considered.

Software developments generally fall into one of two categories, depending upon whether *functional* requirements for the project are known in advance.

For some software projects the starting-point is a set of functional requirements, that is, a concrete specification in some form of what the software is to do. Usually this boils down to a description of desired stimulus–response behaviour. Typically, software for use in embedded systems falls into this category. In such projects, the boundary of the software has already been defined, often through some intrinsic characteristic of the wider system into which this particular component is to fit: conformance to a published standard, for example.

For such projects, a specification model is a natural starting-point. An essential model can be built if required to provide a description of the assumptions made by the software about its environment. The essential and specification models will typically be very similar. In such projects it is important to remember that functional requirements tend to be much more volatile than the essential subject-matter which they are dealing with – after all, this is a basic principle of object-oriented software. Hence considerable emphasis should be placed on designing a robust model which will survive changes in the functional requirements over time.

Other software projects start from more abstract non-functional requirements. Often this is because functional requirements are difficult to establish without building prototypes and/or models in order to obtain informed input from end users. In these projects an essential model is likely to be the appropriate place to start. The process of constructing an essential model gives insight into the problem, delimits the relevant subject-matter and provides a systematic way of making decisions about the software boundary.

Above all, we don't believe that any prescriptive method is suitable for all software projects. Every software development organisation needs to develop its own methods and processes which are suitable for the kinds of software it builds, the staff it employs, the equipment it uses and many other factors. Sometimes the most appropriate techniques are entirely outside the scope of this book (e.g. the use of blackboard architectures, constraint-satisfaction techniques, neural networks, attributed grammars, etc.). We do believe that there are some generally applicable disciplines for managing software development, which we return to in chapter 13.

1.10 Summary

- Object technology promises a revolution in software productivity through changes in the ecology of software.
- This book is about building models.
- Modelling the world and modelling software are fundamentally different.
- Within a software system is a *concept model* which mimics the behaviour of the software's environment.
- A software system is sub-divided into *domains*.

- The *concept domain* describes the concept model, and *interaction domains* keep the concept domain and the world in step.
- We introduce three kinds of model:
  essential models, describing situations in the world;
  specification models, specifying software in the abstract;
  implementation models, describing the details of software implementation.
- There is a systematic correspondence between the three kinds of model.
- Essential models describe states of the world in terms of *object configurations*, *events* which cause state changes, and the possible sequences of those events.
- Specification models describe the stimulus–response behaviour of software in terms of object configurations, *detected stimuli* and *generated responses*. Specification models assume infinitely fast processing and infinite execution resources.
- Implementation models describe the details of software execution in terms of collections of objects communicating by sending *messages*. Implementation models assume finite processing speed and limited execution resources.
- *Polymorphism* is the ability for many different kinds of object to act as *servers* for a given *client*.
- The relationship between clients and servers is called a *contract*.
- *Design by contract* promotes software reuse.
- Each model is expressed using several different *views*.
- *Type views* and *state views* are applicable to every model.
- The meaning of type views and state views is given in terms of abstract sets and functions.
- Additional views are used in the implementation model, particularly *mechanisms*.
- Reuse requires a discipline of *encapsulated software components*.
- The techniques in this book are not intended to be a prescriptive method for software development.

1.11 Bibliographic notes

Recommended books on user-interface design include [Schnei87] and [Laure90].

1.12 References

[Booch91] G. Booch. *Object Oriented Design With Applications*, Benjamin/Cummings, Redwood City, California, 1991.

[CORBA92] *Common Object Request Broker Architecture and Specification*, Object Management Group, Framingham, Massachusetts, 1992.

[Goldb83] A. Goldberg and D. Robson. *Smalltalk-80: the Language and its Implementation*, Addison-Wesley, Reading, Massachusetts, 1983.

[Hamme93] M. Hammer and J. Champy. *Re-engineering the Corporation: a manifesto for business revolution*, Nicholas Brealey, London, 1993.

[Harel87] D. Harel. Statecharts: a visual formalism for complex systems. *Science of Computer Programming* 8:231–274, 1987.

[Laure90] B. Laurel (ed.). *The Art of Human–Computer Interface Design*, Addison-Wesley, Reading, Massachusetts, 1990.

[McMen84] S. McMenamin and J. Palmer. *Essential Systems Analysis*, Yourdon Press, New York, 1984.

[Meyer88] B. Meyer. *Object-oriented Software Construction*, Prentice-Hall, Hemel Hempstead, Hertfordshire, 1988.

[Meyer92] B. Meyer. Applying 'Design by Contract', *IEEE Computer*, 25(10): 40–51, 1992.

[Rumba91] J. Rumbaugh, M. Blaha, W. Premerlani, F. Eddy and W. Lorensen. *Object-Oriented Modeling and Design*, Prentice-Hall, Englewood Cliffs, New Jersey, 1991.

[Shnei87] B. Shneiderman. *Designing the User Interface: strategies for effective human–computer interaction*, Addison-Wesley, Reading, Massachusetts, 1987.

[Words92] J. Wordsworth. *Software Development with Z*, Addison-Wesley, Wokingham, Berkshire, 1992.

Part Two

Modelling the world

CHAPTER 2

Describing structure: the basics

2.1 Objects, values and events

The world is a very complicated place. As software developers, we need to produce models of it and make them come to life. Fortunately, we only need to construct small and partial models of the world; models just rich enough to meet our purpose. To reflect this limited ambition, we prefer to talk about modelling *situations* in the world. A situation is a set of things and occurrences which describes some kind of activity in the world: situations have a purpose. Two very similar sets of things and occurrences may be part of totally different situations, with very different purposes, so it is important to understand the purpose for which a model is being constructed. We would contrast this goal of modelling situations (having a purpose) with that of building generic models, such as the attempts to construct corporate-wide data models, where the ultimate purpose is poorly understood.

Our stated goal is to use the concepts of object technology to describe situations in the world. Which concepts are relevant and how should we apply them? For the purposes of modelling, we consider the world to consist of *objects*, *values* and *events*.

Objects have identity: one object can always be distinguished from another. In this sense, object identity is rather like a key, a concept familiar to anyone who uses a database, but even objects with no obvious key have identity. Imagine building a model of a bottling plant, where bottles move along a production line being filled, capped and labelled. Sensors on the line detect the presence of a bottle and monitor its progress. We might wish to model each bottle as an object that comes into existence (in our model) when first detected by a sensor. We can then tie-up subsequent sensor detections with a particular bottle (because of a fixed-order constraint) even though the bottles appear identical. Objects also have observable properties, such as the weight and size of the bottle. An observable property does not equate to a data attribute; we are not attempting to model the world in data. It is just something that can be observed in some way. A bottle has a volume. It is unnecessary and not useful to say whether that property is 'stored' or 'computed'. On the other hand, we may wish to state a mathematical relationship which always holds between the bottle's size and its volume.

Such relationships are called *logical invariants* and we will discuss them further later in this chapter. The properties of objects may be other objects: a useful property of a bottle might be the company which made it. Properties that are other objects or collections of objects are called *associations*. The properties of objects may change over time, and this mutability is an important difference between objects and values.

Values don't change. The best examples of values are the numbers. There is no mathematical operation that allows the integer 3 to be mutated into the integer 4. It is certainly possible to take a bottle object and change its value property describing the amount of fluid in it. But the number has not been mutated: one number has been replaced by another. By contrast, the state of the bottle object *has* changed. Since values are immutable, they have no identity separate from their value; we can have no concept of replicating a value to obtain another copy of it.

Except for things like numbers, the distinction between objects and values is largely one of convenience. The designer must choose which things will be objects and which values. A disadvantage of values is that there can be no notion of sharing them, and hence no notion of navigating *from* them to find all objects holding a particular value. Values simplify the designer's job because pre-defined value types, such as strings, can frequently be used to represent problem-domain concepts. For example, we might decide to use a number to represent the speed property of a car object, rather than design a new kind of value type for speed; defining a new value type for speed would bring with it a consequential need to define an algebra for manipulating speeds. On the other hand, the algebra for numbers might not exactly fit our understanding of speeds – what does it mean to multiply two speeds together? The choice of value types is a trade-off between convenience and accuracy.

Events bring new objects into existence (within our model), cause objects in our model to leave it, and change the properties of existing objects. Events have no duration, they have either not yet happened or have already happened. We will discuss events in detail in chapter 4.

2.2 Types

In this chapter we wish to consider how to describe the structure of a model of a situation; in chapter 4 we will consider how the model is affected by events. We could depict our model using just the concepts already introduced.

Figure 2.1 depicts three objects, two bottles and one manufacturer, and their associations. Describing the model like this is perfectly correct but rather limiting. It doesn't say anything about situations where there are three bottles, or one bottle or two manufacturers. We need a more generic description of the model, which we can only obtain by generalising. We need a concept which will allow us to describe all bottles in the situation at once, a concept that supports the description of the properties they all share. We call this concept *object type*. An object type represents a particular kind of object; it is analogous to the concept of entity type in data modelling.

In line with emerging industrial practice, we use the phrase *object type* for this concept in preference to the phrase *object class*. The idea of class is closely linked, through its use in object-oriented programming languages, with the description of implementation details of software objects. This idea is clearly inappropriate when considering objects in the world. Here we wish to consider the capabilities of objects, to discuss objects in terms of the facilities and knowledge they possess; we are not in any way concerned with the details of possible software implementations for objects. We use the phrase *object type* to represent this idea of object capabilities.

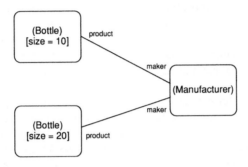

Figure 2.1 *Object diagram*

Using the concept of object type, we can draw a more generic description of the model.

Figure 2.2 *Type view*

Figure 2.2 is drawn using the OMT notation [Rumba91]. Each rectangle represents an object type and lines between rectangles represent associations between objects. The name of the object type appears at the top of the rectangle, separated from the rest of the contents by a horizontal line. We require object type names to begin with an upper-case letter. The remainder of the rectangle is used to hold value-typed properties, such as **size**, and invariants. We call diagrams of this kind *type views*.

Values also have types: 3 is a value, **Integer** is the type of that value; 1st January 1999 is a value, **Date** is the type of that value. In figure 2.2, we have used the value type **Number** as the type of the property **size**. We use the value type **Number** to represent any kind of number, whole or fractional.

One major difference between the notation presented here and that found in [Rumba91] is the lack of separation of the lower part of the rectangle into attributes and operations. We do not believe such separation is appropriate in an object modelling technique because we do not want to consider the data representation of objects. It should be a matter of no concern whether or not a particular property is modelled as stored data. The value-typed properties we show in the lower part of the rectangle are just 'observable'; we wish to make no decision about how they are observed. Also, we think the concept of operations is inappropriate in essential models because it is too restrictive to begin allocating responsibilities to particular kinds of objects at this stage; such allocation is a matter of software design. In particular, we have no concept of 'update' operations which change the values of properties or the membership of associations. When we build state views, as described in chapter 4, we assert changes in the values of properties as a consequence of events – clearly, then, the properties are changing but not as a result of operations being invoked: they just change.

So the type view above tells us that in the model of the situation there will be objects which we will treat as bottles and others which we we will treat as manufacturers. Although it is convenient to talk about 'bottle objects' and 'manufacturer objects' (indeed we will do so in this book) it isn't strictly correct. We have no way of knowing, from this model alone, exactly what the objects *are*, we just know that they will exhibit the properties of bottles and manufacturers. We say the objects *conform* to the relevant object types.

How do we know that bottles and manufacturers are important object types in our situation? This is a significant issue in object modelling, and the question can only be answered by considering each case. The identification of object types comes from an analysis of the vocabulary of the situation, as expressed in specifications, process manuals and by problem-domain experts. From this vocabulary it is possible to draw up a list of potential, or candidate, object types which must be considered and refined. In fact, within a given situation, expressed for a given purpose, problems in doing this seldom arise; it is usually quite clear to an experienced designer which kinds of object play an interesting and important part in the situation. We give some guidelines on identifying objects in appendix C.

2.3 Properties

We distinguish between value-typed properties of objects, which from now on we will just call properties, and object-typed properties, called associations. A property is a named value that an object knows about. These are listed in the type boxes on type views. Each object has its own set of properties, as defined by the types to which it conforms. Properties are pieces of information about an object which can be observed by a second object that knows the identity of the first. As we said earlier, they are not intended to represent stored data; an object model *is not* a model of data representation. In essential models we are not concerned with physical data representations and we make no distinction between basic properties and derived properties. However, when two properties are functionally related we specify their relationship with a logical invariant. In our state views we show how events affect property values.

We define a property by stating its name and type, which must be a value type. The usual syntax is:

propertyName : propertyType

2.3.1 Value types

The most common value types used in this book are **Number, Integer, String, Date, Time** and **Symbol**. A description of these types appears in appendix B.

Literal **Numbers** and **Integers** are shown using digits in the usual way. Literal **Strings** are shown enclosed by single quotes. Literal **Symbols** are sequences of characters preceded by a '%' sign.

2.3.2 Parameterised properties

Properties may be parameterised. For example, the volume property of a bottle might be dependent on temperature. We would write this as:

volume(temp : Number) : Number

or just **volume(Number) : Number** if the meaning was unambiguous[1].

2.3.3 Multi-valued properties

Properties may be multi-valued: they may yield a collection of values of the same type.

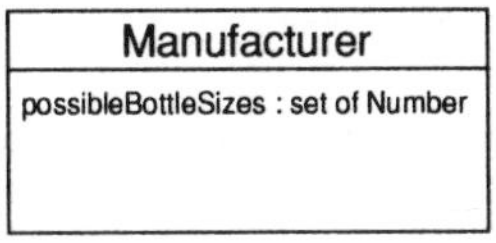

Manufacturer
possibleBottleSizes : set of Number

Figure 2.3 *A multi-valued property*

---

[1]All properties can be considered to be functions that return a value-typed result. Some of the functions will take parameters, others will not.

In figure 2.3, the **possibleBottleSizes** property of **Manufacturer** yields an unordered set of numbers when observed. The options are:

set of X	An unordered collection of values of type **X**, with no duplicates allowed
bag of X	An unordered collection of values of type **X**, with duplicates allowed
seq of X	An ordered collection of values of type **X**, with duplicates allowed

In general, a multi-valued type may appear wherever a single-valued type is valid[2].

2.4 Associations

In figure 2.2 above we show an association between objects conforming to the type **Bottle** and objects conforming to the type **Manufacturer**. How should we interpret that association? Informally, we say it means that if you identify a bottle object you can also identify, by virtue of the association, a manufacturer object, the manufacturer who made it. If you identify a manufacturer object you can also identify the set of bottles made by that manufacturer. We know that this will be a set, rather than a single object because of the black blob on the end of the line. When we use an association in this way, to identify the objects at the other end, we say we are 'following', or *navigating*, the association. Remember, we are not describing software or even a database design here, we are just trying to formalise our understanding of a situation. So you shouldn't read into a term such as *navigating* anything connected with access paths or implementation visibilities.

Every association can, normally, be navigated in both directions. In fact, we have a pair of related associations, each with different characteristics[3]. To make this clear,

---

[2]In the appropriate places, such as in event specifications, we also allow multi-valued object types, defined using the same syntax.

[3]Formally, we say that an association describes two functions, in this case one mapping each object of type **Bottle** to one object of type **Manufacturer** and another mapping each object of type **Manufacturer** to zero or more objects of type **Bottle**. The functions described are:

> **maker : Bottle → Manufacturer**
> **product : Manufacturer → set of Bottle**

The function **maker** is a function mapping members of **Bottle** to members of **Manufacturer** and **product** is a function mapping members of **Manufacturer** to sets of members of **Bottle**. These two functions are logically related.
Given **m : Manufacturer**

> **product(m) = {b : Bottle | maker(b) = m}**

The mathematical notation used throughout this chapter is described in appendix A.

when we are considering a particular navigation direction we refer to the *source* and the *destination* types. The source type is the type being navigated from, the destination is the type being navigated to. The pair of associations are related in that they yield consistent results: for any given bottle, the set of products of the bottle's manufacturer must include the bottle.

2.4.1 Roles

The ends of the association line can be annotated, as shown above, with a string that identifies the role played by the object(s) at that end of the association with respect to the object(s) at the other end. So, in figure 2.2, the bottles are the products of the manufacturer and the manufacturer is the maker of the bottles. When there is only a single association between two object types it is not mandatory to use role labels. If a role label is omitted the role is given a default name equal to the name of the type at that end of the association, with the first, upper-case, letter replaced by lower-case.

When there are two or more associations between two object types, role names become essential to distinguish the associations.

In figure 2.4, an extra association between **Bottle** and **Manufacturer** has been added to represent the bottles held as stock by the manufacturer. Each association must have a unique role name. For the manufacturer the role names are **product** and **stock**; for the bottle they are **maker** and **stockist**. Since these two associations are distinct, a bottle's maker and stockist may be two different objects.

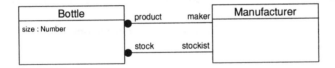

Figure 2.4 *Role names*

2.4.2 Multiplicities

Placing different symbols at the end of the association line modifies our expectations of what we will obtain when we navigate the association. An unadorned line means that navigating the association, in that direction, will always yield a single object conforming to the type at that end, as with the bottle maker above. A black blob indicates that navigation will yield a collection of objects; a black blob by itself indicates a *set*. We call associations with a black blob *multiple* associations.

We use the word *set* in its mathematical sense here: the set may have zero or more members but cannot have duplicates. So, in figure 2.4, the *same* **Bottle** object cannot appear twice in the manufacturer's **product** collection.

As we will see later in this chapter, constraints may be added to associations to limit the size of the collection represented by the black blob. One particular constraint, the constraint that limits the size of the collection to zero or one, occurs very frequently and so a special notation is provided for it.

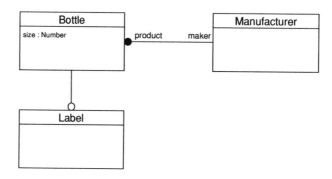

Figure 2.5 *Association multiplicities*

The white blob that appears in figure 2.5 indicates an optional, single association. If we identify a bottle we might be able to identify a single label associated with it, or maybe not. As things stand, the model gives us no indication of why or when a label will be associated. However, it does clearly indicate that once a label becomes known in the situation it is always associated with a bottle; the situation does not allow unaffixed labels.

There is no reason why associations should not have adornments at both ends. For example, consider figure 2.6.

Figure 2.6 *A many-to-many association*

Each company has many employees and each person may have many employers (many jobs at once). When trying to understand these kinds of association it pays to remember that the line really represents *two* quite distinct (but related) associations, one in each direction.

2.4.3 Qualifiers

Sometimes we want to be more specific about a multiple association by showing how the source distinguishes between the destination objects. We do this by adding a qualifier to the association, at the source end.

Figure 2.7 *Qualified association*

Let's make the crazy assumption that the manufacturer makes exactly one bottle per day. In figure 2.7, we have replaced the manufacturer's product association by a qualifier box. The name of the qualifier becomes the default role name at the other end of the association, but another role name can still be specified if desired. The qualifier must have a type: the value type **Date** is used in this example. We interpret the qualifier, informally, as meaning that given a manufacturer and a date we can identify a particular bottle (the bottle made on that date)[4]. Since the association has no adornment at the bottle end, we must assume that each possible combination of a manufacturer and a date will yield exactly one bottle. This cannot be true because the type **Date** represents all possible dates; its domain is infinite. In fact, in any reasonable model, only certain dates will yield bottles. Unless we can use a different qualifier type, which limits the range of dates, we must change our model to make it correct, as shown in figure 2.8.

More likely is that the manufacturer makes a variable number of bottles each day. We can show this by making the destination end of the qualifier a multiple, as in figure 2.9.

A qualifier may have more than one parameter. The type of each parameter must be shown inside the parentheses.

---

[4]If we think of an association as a function that takes an object of the source type as a parameter and returns an object, or a set of objects, of the destination type, then a qualifier describes a similar function that takes two parameters: an object of the source type and another of the qualifier type. In this example the qualifier describes a function of the form:

    product : (Manufacturer × Date) → Bottle

Since **product** is also the default role name in this case, the association also describes a secondary function:

    product : Manufacturer → set of Bottle

Since any adornments placed at the end of a qualified association affect the primary function (the first one shown in this footnote), we always assume that this secondary function yields a set. The choice of primary or secondary function is made according to the number of parameters supplied.

Figure 2.8 *Optional qualified association*

Figure 2.9 *Qualifier yielding a set*

2.4.4 Aggregation

Aggregation is often referred to as a 'whole-part' or 'is-part-of' relationship, where the whole, the aggregate, is made up of its parts. While this seems satisfactory at a superficial level, it is much more difficult to say exactly how such a relationship differs from associations such as those we have already been considering. Is a bottle in a whole-part relationship with its label? Is a company in a whole-part relationship with its employees? Unless we can come up with some concrete semantics for whole-part relationships which go beyond those defined for associations, the concept has no place in our modelling discipline.

The OMT notation we have adopted has notation to represent aggregation: a small diamond is placed at the end of an association line. The challenge is to define a precise meaning for this notation. We can think of the following three possible 'meanings' for aggregation, which could be combined in various ways:

- **An implied sharing of properties.** Let us say that a car is an aggregate of its parts. Give the car a property that represents its colour. We might say each part shares that property, so that the doors will be the same colour as the car. So this implies that properties of the aggregate propagate to its parts. But the opposite is true, too. If each part has a property that is its weight, the car also has a weight property that is a direct function of the properties of its parts. Somewhat reluctantly, we discard this notion of aggregation as too imprecise, particularly since the same effect can be obtained using invariants.
- **Encapsulation.** The idea here is that the aggregate encapsulates its parts in some way. There might be two reasons for wanting to do this: the first is to enable the construction of more robust and modular software, the second to control

complexity in the model. We disregard the first of these because, in the essential model, we are not considering software at all. The second is a powerful argument, since the abstraction provided by encapsulation is a vital part of object theory. The idea that one object is composed of others, and that the components are not known to clients of the whole, is a powerful structuring principle in object technology. We reject the idea that the diamond notation be used to represent this powerful concept because, visually, it does not imply encapsulation. We have developed our own notational conventions to deal with levels of encapsulation which are discussed in chapter 12.

- **Life-time dependency.** We might say that the parts in an aggregate cannot move from one aggregate to another. That is, each part must, at the time it becomes known in the situation, become connected with an aggregate and must remain connected until it or the aggregate is destroyed. Alternatively, we might say that when the aggregate is created it takes on a fixed structure of parts that cannot be changed during the life-time of the aggregate, but when the aggregate is destroyed the parts may become components of another. Both of these imply that aggregation is a constraint on the relative life-times of the aggregate and its parts: either the life-times of the parts are contained within the life-time of the whole or the life-time of the whole is contained within the life-times of its parts.

We choose aggregation to mean life-time dependency; in particular, that the life-times of the 'parts' are contained within the life-time of the 'whole'. The 'parts' are permanently attached to the 'whole', and cannot be removed from it without being destroyed. Conversely, destroying the 'whole' destroys the 'parts'.

Aggregation is shown as a diamond placed on the association line adjacent to the type whose instances have the containing life-time (the 'whole' or 'aggregate').

Figure 2.10 gives a classic example of an 'is-part-of' relationship: A division is part of a company. Using our semantics for the diamond we can offer a more precise meaning. We define this diagram to mean that each division must be associated with a single company (because there is no blob on the line at that end) and it must remain associated with that company throughout its life-time. Divisions can be created and destroyed during the life-time of a company but a division cannot be moved from one company to another. If the company is destroyed, so are the divisions. The effect of the diamond is to 'freeze' that end of the association.

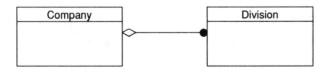

Figure 2.10 *Aggregation*

By moving the diamond to the other end of the line, we change the meaning completely. In figure 2.11 we have made the life-time of the company contained within the life-time of any associated division. The company is now a static structure. It must be associated with the required divisions on creation and they cannot subsequently be changed. Although the company can be associated with any number of divisions, that number is fixed on creation of the company. Although each division must be associated with a single company, there is no reason why a division shouldn't be attached to a different company when its current one is destroyed. By putting a diamond at both ends we make the life-times of the associated objects equal. In this example it would mean that a company and its divisions must be created and destroyed as a unit.

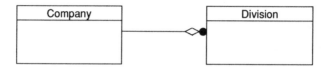

Figure 2.11 *Static company structure*

2.4.5 Association properties

Associations may be given their own properties, as shown in figure 2.12. Each association between a person and a company has a **salary** property. If a person has two employers, he or she has two distinct salaries, as you can see from the object diagram in figure 2.13. In this diagram, the association properties have been shown explicitly as ovals on the links between objects.

Association properties are most useful on associations that are multiple at both ends (often called 'many-to-many' associations), because it is difficult to position the property at one end or the other in these associations.

The name of an association property is introduced into the name space of the types at both ends of the association, and its name must not clash with the names of other properties defined for the types, nor with any role names.

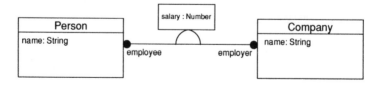

Figure 2.12 *Association property*

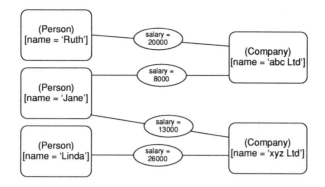

Figure 2.13 *Example of association properties*

In principle, more than one property may be attached to the association, and shown in the box. However, when there are several properties it is more usual to create a new object type and attach this to the association, as shown in figure 2.14.

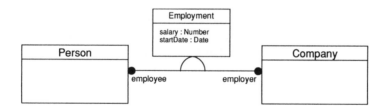

Figure 2.14 *An association type*

The new object type can then be used in the normal way and have other associations. Attaching an object type to an association introduces a new role name to the association, which can be shown explicitly near the arc if necessary. Otherwise, the usual default role name rule applies. In figure 2.14, attaching the **Employment** type to the association introduces the (default) role name **employment**. This name must not clash with any other role names already defined for the types at either end.

We need to consider the difference between the model shown in figure 2.14 and that shown in figure 2.15, which is a more traditional way of dealing with many-to-many associations.

When you navigate from person to company in figure 2.14, you identify a set of companies so it is not possible for a person to have two or more jobs with the same company. No such constraint applies in figure 2.15 because the set of employments associated with a person might all be legitimately associated with the same company. We would need to add specific constraints to give figure 2.15 the same meaning as figure 2.14.

Figure 2.15 *Splitting a many-to-many association*

2.4.6 Ternary associations

Occasionally, we desire to model associations between three or more types. A rather informal notation for this appears in [Rumba91] which is useful for sketching ideas. However, all ternary and other higher-order associations can be modelled more precisely using binary associations together with new types that represent the association explicitly, attached properties and/or qualifiers.

2.4.7 Use of '?'

Drawing a simple line between two type boxes means something quite specific: a one-to-one association. Sometimes we want to be rather less precise than this, to say 'there is an association between these types but I haven't yet decided on their multiplicity'. We can say that by placing a **?** at the ends of the association about which we have yet to decide.

Figure 2.16 *Undefined associations*

In figure 2.16, we have decided that each bottle is associated with exactly one manufacturer, but we have not yet decided how many bottles are associated with each manufacturer. We cannot navigate the association towards **Bottle** meaningfully until we have decided.

We also use **?** for another purpose: when to provide details about one end of an association would be to over-specify the model. This happens when we wish to divide our model into parts but limit the knowledge that one part has of another. By using a **?** we can indicate that an association exists but avoid exposing details of it. You will see **?** being used for this later in this book (e.g. in chapter 11).

2.5 Type extension

One type may be defined as a sub-type of another. This is often called an 'is-kind-of' relationship. A sub-type 'inherits' all the properties, constraints and associations of its super-type[5]. The word 'inherits' is used with caution here because we are not defining type extension to be linked to the class inheritance found in object-oriented programming. It is true that, in implementation, the second can be used to implement the first, but that is not relevant here. We define sub-typing to imply object conformance: an object conforming to the sub-type also always conforms to the super-type. The exact rules governing conformance vary between the essential, specification and implementation models but, broadly, the sub-type can extend the capabilities of the super-type but not restrict them.

Type extension, or sub-type, relationships are shown by a line between the super-type and its extensions. Somewhere along the line between the super-type and the first line junction (or the sub-type, if only one) there must be an equilateral triangle with one apex on the line and the opposite side perpendicular to the line. The triangle must point towards the super-type.

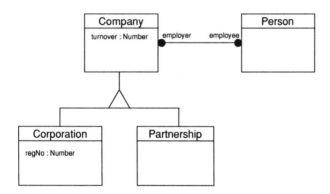

Figure 2.17 *Type extension*

Figure 2.17 shows that a corporation is a kind of company, as is a partnership. An object conforming to **Corporation** also conforms to **Company**. Each corporation object has a registration number property plus all the properties and associations of a company, such as a set of employees. The value of type extension is that it allows us to describe clearly the differences between related types. It also introduces the idea of object equivalence, often called *polymorphism*. The model shown in figure 2.17 makes it clear that a person expects to work for an object displaying the characteristics of a

---

[5]But we may wish to constrain the set of inherited features to encapsulate the elements of our design better. This is discussed further in chapter 7.

company; the person does not distinguish between corporations or partnerships, they are happy to work for either.

2.5.1 Abstract types

Figure 2.17 does not imply that all objects which conform to **Company** must also conform to one of its sub-types. We could have an object that is a **Company** but not specifically either a **Corporation** or a **Partnership**. We can introduce a constraint that all objects conforming to the super-type must also conform to one of its sub-types by defining the super-type as *abstract*. We can constrain **Company** to be an abstract type by adding a special kind of type invariant to its representation in the type view, as in figure 2.18. The general use of type invariants will be discussed shortly.

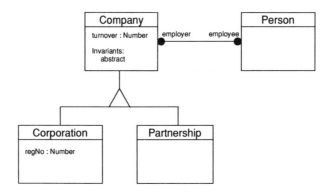

Figure 2.18 *An abstract type*

The difference between figures 2.16 and 2.18 can be explained by Venn diagrams (see figure 2.19). In figure 2.16, objects conforming to **Corporation** and **Partnership** make up disjoint subsets of the set of objects conforming to **Company** (figure 2.19(a)). In figure 2.18, the disjoint sets completely partition the superset (figure 2.19(b)).

As an aid to understanding type extension with Venn diagrams, we suggest you think of the extension triangle as meaning 'subset', and the set of sub-types as meaning 'partitions'. If the super-type is abstract, the 'subset' is just the same as the super-type set, and hence the edge of the subset circle lies on top of the enclosing circle, as in figure 2.19(b). According to this interpretation, figure 2.19(a) should really be drawn as is figure 2.20.

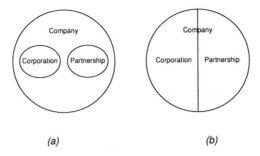

Figure 2.19 *Effect of abstract type on Venn diagram*

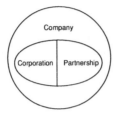

Figure 2.20 *Applying the partitioning rules*

2.5.2 Using sub-types to eliminate optional associations

The introduction of a sub-type will often eliminate optional associations, as in figure 2.21.

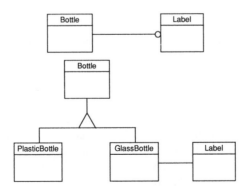

Figure 2.21 *Eliminating optional associations*

The top part of the diagram shows that each bottle may optionally have a label. This optionality can be explained using bottle sub-types: plastic bottles never have a label; glass bottles always have one.

2.6 Constraints and invariants

2.6.1 Logical type invariants

You will have noticed our attempts to make the meaning of the modelling notation as precise as possible. One reason for this is to allow a common understanding among a group of designers, but another, perhaps more important, is to allow us to use the formal precision of mathematics, in the form of set theory and logic, in conjunction with the model.

An important use for mathematical expressions is the specification of logical type invariants. A logical type invariant is a logical expression that will always be true for every object conforming to the type. Some examples are given in figure 2.22.

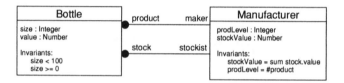

Figure 2.22 *Type invariants*

The invariants are shown in the type rectangle, under their own heading. In figure 2.22, the **size** of bottles must be non-negative but less than 100, the **stockValue** of a manufacturer is defined to be the same as the sum of the values of its products, and the **prodLevel** is defined to be the size of the set of products. These last two require some explanation:

> **sum stock.value**

is an expression that includes a navigation through the model. For any given **Manufacturer,** the simple expression **stock** represents the set of **Bottles** obtained by navigating from that **Manufacturer** along the association with the **stock** role name. The addition of **.value** indicates that we want to collect the **value** properties of the **stock** bottles. Finally, we sum this collection of numbers.

In the other invariant, **#product** means the size of the set of **Bottles** obtained by navigating the association called **product**. The # operator allows us to obtain the size of any collection. The two invariants for **Manufacturer** *do not* imply in some way that **prodLevel** and **stockValue** are 'derived' rather than stored. Since properties are not data representations, merely an indication that an object 'knows about' a value, the notion of 'derived' has no meaning. We are merely indicating the fixed relationships that exist between properties.

2.6.2 Sub-ranges

Simple restrictions on the range of integers can be specified in the property definition, rather than as an invariant, by using sub-ranges. Sub-ranges take the form:

m..n

where **m** and **n** are positive integers, or expressions yielding positive integers (interpreted in the name space of the type). In the case where m = n, the single integer or symbol can be used alone, e.g. 6. So, in figure 2.22, the size property could have been defined as:

size : 0..99

and the invariants removed.

2.6.3 Property invariants

We can constrain individual properties such that their values remain fixed during the lifetime of their owning object. We indicate this constraint using the special type invariant **const**.

Another constraint that we can apply to individual properties is to require them to yield a unique value for every object in the model conforming to the type. We indicate this constraint using the special type invariant **unique**. In figure 2.23, the property **size** is constrained to be both constant and unique[6].

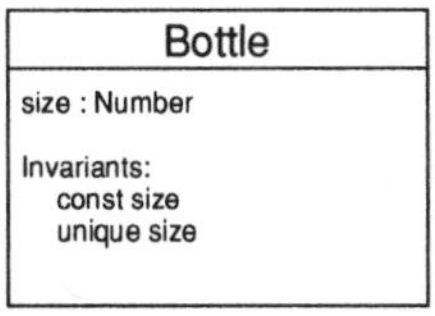

```
┌─────────────────────────┐
│          Bottle         │
├─────────────────────────┤
│ size : Number           │
├─────────────────────────┤
│ Invariants:             │
│    const size           │
│    unique size          │
│                         │
└─────────────────────────┘
```

Figure 2.23 *Property invariants*

---

[6]Mathematically, the unique constraint can be expressed as:
$$\forall \ \mathbf{b} : \mathbf{Bottle} - \{\mathbf{self}\} \bullet \mathbf{b.size} \neq \mathbf{self.size}$$

2.6.4 'nil'

The special value **nil** is logically a member of all object and value types, and it represents an undefined or unset property. Properties that can take the value nil are called *optional* properties, and must be specified as such using a type invariant.

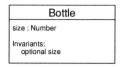

Figure 2.24 *The optional invariant*

In figure 2.24, the **size** property of **Bottle** is defined to be optional; that is, it may take the value **nil**. Without the **optional** invariant, the property could not validly take a **nil** value.

2.6.5 Constraints on associations

A constraint indicates some limitation which applies to the model. Type invariants are a form of constraint. Constraints that appear outside type rectangles are enclosed within square brackets. We can write informal constraints by writing a comment (enclosed by double-quotes) inside the brackets; alternatively, we can write a precise constraint using navigation expressions and mathematical symbols.

A common kind of constraint is one that limits the size of the set of objects yielded by an association. A completely unconstrained association is shown by placing a black blob at the end of the line, as we have already seen. Two constraints have been used already: an unadorned line constrains the size of the set to be one; a white blob constrains the size of the set to be zero or one. Any other constraints must be shown as annotations placed next to the black blob. Constraints on multiplicity are specified using sub-ranges, as defined on page 47, enclosed, like all constraints, inside square brackets.

In figure 2.25, each person can have between zero and six employers. Also, each company has a property representing the maximum number of staff it may employ; this property is used to specify a limit to the size of the employee set. As a special case, when only a lower limit is required, the lower limit may be followed by a + sign, for example [1+].

Another kind of constraint that we can apply to an association specifies the order of objects yielded by the association. By default, navigating an association yields a set, which is unordered and cannot have duplicates: in figure 2.25, the same person cannot

Figure 2.25 *Constraints on multiplicities*

be employed twice (at the same time) by a company. We can use constraints to specify a sequence, a bag or a sort order. These are described in the following table.

name	syntax	ordered?	duplicates?
bag	[bag]	NO	YES
sequence	[seq]	YES	YES
sort	['sort spec.']	YES	YES

The sort spec. may be informal or formal. If formal, it must declare two variables of the type being sorted (commonly called **a** and **b**) and include a logical expression that relates them. In the sequence represented by the association, **a** will come before **b** if the expression is true.

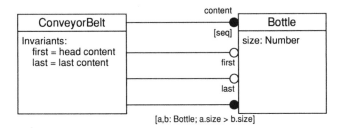

Figure 2.26 *Sequence and sorted constraints*

Figure 2.26 shows examples of the sort and sequence constraints. In the sorted association, the bottles will be arranged in descending order of size. The contents of the conveyer belt are defined as a sequence, allowing two other associations to be defined as the first and last elements of the sequence. These associations must be optional because the sequence might be empty[7].

---

[7]We define the result of applying the first or last operator to an empty sequence to be **nil**.

2.6.6 Constraints between associations

Constraints may exist between two or more associations. These are shown as dashed or faint arrows drawn between the association lines, with a description of the constraint alongside, enclosed by square brackets.

In figure 2.27, the constraint indicates that the number of bottles a manufacturer has in stock must always be less than half those produced. It is exactly equivalent to writing the same expression as an invariant for **Manufacturer**. However, we sometimes prefer to show the constraint directly between the associations because it reduces the coupling between the type and its associations[8].

All constraints between associations are directional. In figure 2.27, we are describing a constraint on the results of navigating from **Manufacturer** (the *source*) to **Bottle**; the direction is established in this example by the use of the **Manufacturer's** role names[9]. It is a logical consequence of constraints between associations that the constrained associations always yield the same source object when navigated in the opposite direction. In this example, it is a constraint that, for any **Bottle**, the **maker** and **stockist** of that bottle will be the same **Manufacturer** object.

Figure 2.27 *Constraint between associations*

2.6.7 Subset constraints

A subset constraint is a special kind of constraint between associations that occurs so often that we give it its own syntax. A subset constraint specifies that the set of objects yielded by one navigation is a subset of the objects yielded by another. For example, in figure 2.28 we specify that the manufacturer's stock is a subset of all its production[10]. The arrow has a single arrowhead to show which is the subset: the arrow points to the superset.

This constraint is also directional: from **Manufacturer** to **Bottle**. We can deduce the direction by examining the multiplicities; a subset constraint can only apply between

---

[8]If we use an invariant we have made knowledge of the associations explicit in the main description of the type.

[9]Clearly, then, the expression could not use role names taken from both the source and the destination. For example, this expression could not reference **maker** or **stockist**.

[10]**Manufacturer::stock ⊆ Manufacturer::product**

Note also that ∀ **b** : **Bottle** • **b.maker** = **b.stockist**

two multiple associations (i.e. black blobs). If there were block blobs at both ends of the associations, we would need to indicate the direction explicitly by naming the source type in the constraint, as follows:

[Manufacturer::subset of]

A slightly different form of the subset constraint occurs when we wish to indicate that the object yielded by a single or optional association is a member of a multiple association. In this case we replace **subset of** by **member of**.

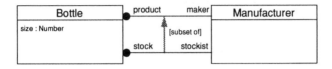

Figure 2.28 *Subset constraint*

2.7 State types

Let us revisit an earlier example and change the situation slightly. Figure 2.29 represents the employer/employee relationship between people and companies that we have seen before, changed so that a person may have only zero or one employer.

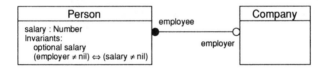

Figure 2.29 *The Person–Company relationship*

Since a person's salary is now a single-valued property, we have placed it within the **Person** type. This is a bad choice because it must be **nil** when the person has no employer. A better choice would be to attach it as an association property, as before, but we might decide to build a more descriptive model by creating two sub-types of **Person**.

In figure 2.30, we have moved the **salary** property into the **EmployedPerson** sub-type, and we have also been able to remove the optional association and replace it by one with a tighter constraint. In general, this seems a great improvement, but it has one very significant drawback: we have condemned unemployed people to a life-time of leisure.

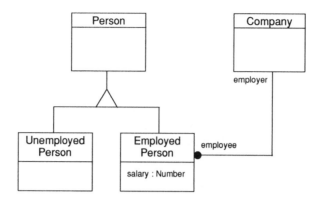

Figure 2.30 *Sub-types of Person*

The semantics of our models are such that objects cannot change the set of types to which they conform during their life-times, so an object created to conform to the **UnemployedPerson** type can never become an **EmployedPerson**. You might argue that this is an unnecessary and artificial restriction but it can be justified by considering the requirements for dynamic models. As you will see in chapter 4, we wish to construct a precise model that describes all possible changes in state in the situation, using a set of state machines, one for each object type. If we were to allow objects to change their type, this would imply terminating the state machine defined for one type and initiating the state machine for another. But an object changing its type is just another example of a change in state in the situation, and so, to maintain our precision, we must represent that change as a transition on a state machine. On which type's state machine would the transition appear? The lack of any reasonable answer to this question has led us and others to find alternative ways of dealing with this problem.

We introduce the concept of *state types*, which behave as normal types in nearly every respect but are not described by state machines. Instead, they represent states in the machine of their super-type. State types are distinguished in type views by having a diagonal line across their top-left corner.

Figure 2.31 shows the use of state types. State types must always be a sub-type of a normal type because they represent one possible state for objects conforming to the normal type. Objects cannot be explicitly created to conform to a single state type; conformance with state types will change as the object changes state. Not all the possible states need be shown in the type view, but each state type in the type view will correspond to exactly one state on a statechart in the state view.

State types cannot have normal types as sub-types but they can have other state types; this represents a nested state structure: if the object is in the state represented by a state type it must also be in one of the states represented by its sub-types[11]. A group of state types connected to their super-type by a single extension triangle, as in figure 2.31, represents exclusive states. A type may have several such groups connected to it, each connected via a separate triangle. The object must be in one state from each group.

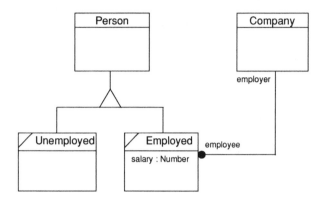

Figure 2.31 *State types*

The use of state types provides a direct link between the type view and state view of a model. Their use implies a high degree of understanding of, and confidence in, the model. Typically, all types are initially treated as normal types; those which prove to be best treated as states are converted later to state types.

The names of state types are added to the name-spaces of their parent types, and can be used in navigation expressions. State type names need not be globally unique.

2.8 Summary

- We model situations in the world using the concepts of *objects*, *values* and *events*.
- Models of situations in the world are called *essential models*.
- An *object type* represents a particular kind of object, and is drawn as a rectangle.
- Diagrams called *type views* are constructed from object types and their relationships.
- Type views describe the structure of the model.
- Object *properties* are shown inside the object type rectangle and represent named values.

---

[11]But it might be in one of the states not shown. To understand the state structure completely it is necessary to refer to the state view.

- *Associations* between object types represent possible links between objects of those types.
- Considerable detail can be specified for associations, through multiplicities, qualifiers, aggregations and association properties.
- One object type can be defined as a specialisation of another, inheriting its parent's associations and properties.
- The semantic content of the model can be increased by adding a variety of constraints, to types, properties and associations.
- *State types* allow detailed definition of the properties and associations gained and lost by an object as it moves from one dynamic state to another. They also provide a link with state views.

2.9 Bibliographic notes

An excellent discussion of the differences between objects and values appears in [Kent91].

Our ideas for mathematical specifications, and the notations used to describe them, derive from the formal specification language Z. An excellent introduction to Z can be found in [Words92].

The idea of using OMT-style type boxes to represent object states seems to have been first mentioned in [Rumba92]. However, that article acknowledges Desmond D'Souza for the original suggestion. D'Souza himself expands on the theme in [D'Souz92].

The formalism in [Marti92], which is derived from the (apparently unpublished) Ptech technology, considers types and states to be equivalent. We find it more useful to distinguish between them because it provides a more straightforward mapping onto available object-oriented implementation technologies, in which objects cannot normally change their type dynamically.

2.10 References

[D'Souz92] D. D'Souza. Education & training: Teacher! teacher!. *Journal of Object-Oriented Programming* 5(2):12–17, 1992.

[Kent91] W. Kent. A rigorous model of object reference, identity, and existence. *Journal of Object-Oriented Programming* 4(3):28–36, 1991.

[Marti92] J. Martin and J. Odell. *Object-Oriented Analysis and Design*, Prentice-Hall, Englewood Cliffs, New Jersey, 1992.

[Rumba91] J. Rumbaugh, M. Blaha, W. Premerlani, F. Eddy and W. Lorensen. *Object-Oriented Modeling and Design*, Prentice-Hall, Englewood Cliffs, New Jersey, 1991.

[Rumba92] J. Rumbaugh. Modeling & design: Derived information. *Journal of Object-Oriented Programming* 5(1):57–61, 1992.

[Words92] J. Wordsworth. *Software Development with Z*, Addison-Wesley, Wokingham, Berkshire, 1992.

CHAPTER 3

Describing structure: adding more detail

3.1 In search of expressive power

In the preceding chapter we presented the basic elements of structural views. Although basic, these elements are not imprecise; they have a precise interpretation underpinned by mathematical logic and set theory. When notations have a precise meaning it becomes important that they are capable of expressing everything that needs to be expressed. In this chapter we present a few additional pieces of notation that improve the expressive power of type view diagrams, and discuss in more detail the meaning of some ideas already introduced.

3.2 Navigation

In chapter 2 we used some simple expressions to navigate around type views. These navigations can become quite complex, and we need to be clear on their exact formulation.

3.2.1 Name-space

Figure 3.1 uses most of the notation described so far. We will use it to explore the way in which navigation expressions are written.

Each type view represents a separate name space; that is, within a type view the only names that may be referenced are those on the diagram. All navigation expressions are written from the point of view of some particular object, conforming to one of the types in the type view. We need to define the set of names in scope for any particular type. These are as follows:

- property names of the type and its super-types;
- the role names (including implied role names) of associations;

- qualifier names of the type and its super-types;
- the names of properties attached to associations connected to the type or one of its super-types;
- the names of exposed states.

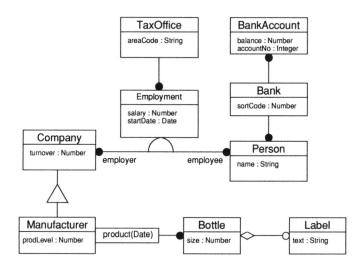

Figure 3.1 *Type view for employment examples*

So, for the **Manufacturer** type in figure 3.1, the following names are in scope:

- **prodLevel** – property defined locally;
- **turnover** – property defined by super-type;
- **product** – name of qualified association to **Bottle**;
- **employee** – name of inherited association to **Person**;
- **employment** – implied role name of association type on **employee** association.

Notice that the properties of **Employment** are not in scope; they must be accessed via the **employment** name.

3.2.2 Expressions

To write a navigation expression we must start with an object of a known type and we must have a way of referring to that object. Let us use the symbol **m** to refer to an object conforming to the type **Manufacturer**.

We would write this declaration as:

m : Manufacturer

meaning that m is a variable that can refer to an object taken from the set of objects conforming to the type Manufacturer. We are using the type name to represent the set of objects in the model that conform to it[1]. Given this declaration, the expression:

m.prodLevel

represents the production level (a **Number**) of the object represented by **m**. Let us be a little more ambitious. The expression:

m.employee

represents the set of Persons employed by **m**.

Frequently, we want to define the starting scope of a navigation by saying 'Given some arbitrary object conforming to type X, the result of navigating from that object...' Rather than declaring a symbol to represent an arbitrary object, as we did with **m** above, we can just start the expression with a type name followed by two colons:

Manufacturer::employee

This means 'the set of employees of some object conforming to **Manufacturer**.' We frequently write navigation expressions within the context of a type; for example, when defining type invariants. In this case we omit the type name at the beginning of the expression because it is implied by the context.

Having navigated to **Person** objects, we can access names in scope for type **Person**. So:

Manufacturer::employee.bank

represents the set of banks used by employees of a manufacturer. As we move along the navigation expression the name scope changes to be that of the type of objects being considered at that point. Since **Manufacturer::employee** represents a set, any subsequent navigation must be applied to each member of the set and the result formed by constructing a set from the objects located[2].

---

[1]We discuss how this set is defined in chapter 4.

[2]If we use mathematical set notation we can express this more clearly:

    Manufacturer::employee.bank ≡ {p : Manufacturer::employee • p.bank}

We apply slightly different rules when accessing value properties:

Manufacturer::employee.name

represents the *bag* of names (i.e. a bag of **Strings**) of employees of a manufacturer. When we collect together a *value* from each member of a set of objects we obtain a bag not a set[3]. Since values have no identity separate from their value, duplicates would be removed if we put them in a set, and this is not usually what we want. You will appreciate the benefit of collecting values in a bag by considering:

sum (Company::employment.salary)

This expression represents the sum of the salaries paid to the employees of a company. If we collected the salaries in a set we would obtain the wrong answer (or, at least, an unexpected answer) if two employees were paid the same amount.

   If each subsequent navigation from members of a set yields, in turn, another set, the result is the union of the sets. Consider:

Manufacturer::employee.bank.bankAccount

This expression represents the set of all the bank accounts of all the banks used by the employees of a manufacturer[4].

   To navigate via a qualifier we must supply a parameter:

Manufacturer::product(1-Jan-94)

This represents the set of bottles made on that date. Optional associations are slightly more complicated:

Bottle::label

may or may not yield a **Label** object. If no label is associated it will yield the value **nil**[5].

---

[3]Using mathematical notation, and taking into account that a bag is a set of tuples relating a member to the number of times it occurs:

> **Manufacturer::employee.name ≡ {p : Manufacturer::employee •**
> **(p.name, #{q : Manufacturer::employee | q.name = p.name}) }**

[4]Using mathematical notation:

> **Manufacturer::employee.bank.bankAccount ≡**
> **∪ {b : Manufacturer::employee.bank • b.bankAccount}**

[5]We sometimes prefer to treat an empty optional association as yielding the empty set, written { }.

This raises a slight problem when we have expressions such as:

Manufacturer::product(1-Jan-94).label

because the first part of the expression yields a set of bottles and we must gather up the results of navigating to the label of each bottle. Some of these results will be **Label** objects, the others **nil**. The solution is simply to say that the **nil** values are ignored.

The following are some other navigation expressions:

Company::employment.taxOffice	The set of tax offices of the company's employees. This set might well be smaller than the set of employees.
Employment::employee	The single person associated with the employment. Navigating from a type attached to an association will always yield a single object.
TaxOffice::employment.employee.name	A bag containing the names of all the people whose employments are associated with the tax office.
Label::bottle.manufacturer	The manufacturer of the bottle to which the label is affixed.

The following are some invalid expressions:

Person::company.prodLevel	The properties of sub-types are not in scope in the super-type.
Company::salary	You cannot navigate directly to a property of a type attached to an association. See the correct example above. The expression shown here would be correct if salary were a simple association property (i.e. not part of an object type).
Manufacturer::bottle	The role name of this association is **product**, the qualifier name.

Given a person **p**, and a company **c**, which is one of **p**'s employers, how would we refer to the start date of the person at that company? We can qualify an associated property or type:

p.employment(c).startDate

This means: 'for person **p** select the employment attached to the association with **c** and yield its start date'[6].

Finally, consider the simpler model shown in figure 3.2.

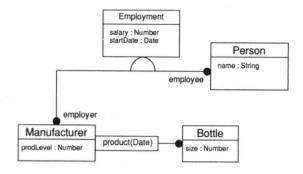

Figure 3.2 *Type view of simpler employment example*

How would you write an expression which meant 'given an employment object, the set of bottles made by the employer on the start date of the employment'? You might try:

Employment::employer.product(startDate)

but **startDate** is not in scope for manufacturers, which is the applicable scope when the qualifier is used.

We can't use:

Employment::employer.product(employment.startDate)

because **employment.startDate** yields a bag of dates (the bag of all start dates of all employees) rather than a single one. Instead, we use the special identifier **self**, which represents the object from which the navigation began, in this case some anonymous object conforming to **Employment**. The expression becomes:

Employment::employer.product(self.startDate)

How would you write an expression which meant 'given a person object, the set of bottles made by all the person's employers on the start dates of their employment'? The problem is, once again, in specifying the qualifier. We need a way of referring to

---

[6]Given **p** : **Person**, **c** : **Company** and the constraint **c** ∈ **p.employer**, we have:

{p.employment(c).startDate} ≡ {e : p.employment | e.employer = c • e.startDate}

each particular manufacturer object as we obtain the correct qualifier for it. This is beyond the scope of our navigation language. If we really wanted to describe this set of bottles we can easily do so with a set expression:

∪ {e: Person::employment • e.employer.product(e.startDate)}

It would really be more reasonable to decompose the expression and show intermediate functions on the type view. We could add a constrained association between **Employment** and **Bottle**, using an invariant as described in the next section, as shown in figure 3.3. Now the navigation expression becomes just:

Person::employment.startingBottle

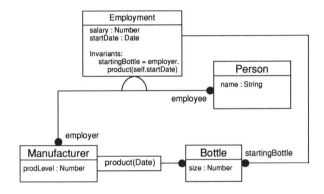

Figure 3.3 *Adding a constrained association to simplify navigation*

3.2.3 Encapsulation – a warning

In this section we have seen how to construct long and complex navigation expressions that wander around the object structure. That we *can* construct such expressions doesn't mean we *should* construct them. As we said when discussing aggregation, the notion of encapsulation is central to object-oriented theory, and should be acknowledged, even in essential models. Long navigation expressions produce undesirable coupling between the starting type of the expression and all the other types visited in it. Details of the associations and properties of one object type become known, and embedded in, other object types only remotely connected to the first. One of our goals in designing object systems, as with all modular approaches, is to minimise coupling between parts of the system.

In general, then, we wish to avoid long navigation expressions; where possible, we wish to limit the knowledge of one type to the details of those types with which it is intimately related. Long expressions can be decomposed by adding derived properties and associations.

We discuss issues of encapsulation in more detail in chapter 12.

3.3 Derived associations

One association can be defined in terms of another, or a collection of others. Associations of this kind are called derived associations and are indicated on the diagram by placing a short diagonal line across the association line.

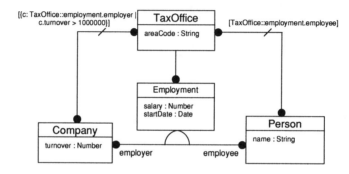

Figure 3.4 *Derived associations*

In figure 3.4, the association between **TaxOffice** and **Person** is derived. Derived associations must be accompanied by an annotation, enclosed by **[ ]**, which describes the equivalent navigation path. This is best done formally, using a navigation expression, as in the diagram. Although the expression defines a navigation path in one particular direction (i.e. from **TaxOffice** to **Person**), the association can be navigated, consistently, in either direction[7]. The other example in this diagram shows that derivation expressions can be more complicated than a simple navigation. Here we have a set construction expression that selects all companies associated with a tax office that have a turnover greater than 1 000 000. The starting set for the selection is defined by a normal navigation expression (**TaxOffice::employment.employer**), and a logical predicate selects the required members.

Both derived associations and subset constraints between associations, described earlier, provide ways of specifying one set of objects to be a subset of another. A derived association also provides a rule by which membership of the subset may be determined; a subset constraint gives no indication of why objects are in the subset,

---

[7]For any navigation expression *e* from type **A** to type **B**, the inverse for a given object **b** : **B** can be expressed as:

{a: A | b ∈ a.e}

although the rule might appear in an associated type invariant. We recommend using derived associations whenever a membership rule exists.

3.3.1 Derived associations to state types

We frequently wish to construct derived associations where the derivation is a function of the state of a set of objects. Consider the model shown in figure 3.5.

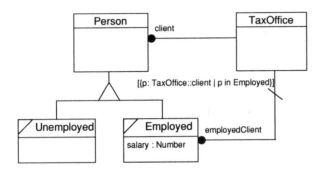

Figure 3.5 *Derived association to a state type*

A tax office is associated with a set of people who are its clients. There is a subset of these clients who are, at any moment, employed. The derived association represents this subset. The expression **p in Employed** evaluates to true if the object **p** is in the **Employed** state. Since this derived association has been drawn with the state type as its destination, there is an argument that the derivation expression contains redundant information, and could have been written as:

[{p: TaxOffice::client}]

The argument is that objects yielded by navigating the association towards the **Employed** state type can only be in the **Employed** state. Although this is true, we prefer to write the derivation expression in full so that it remains consistent with the general rule for such expressions: that they define the required navigation completely.

3.4 Recursive associations

It is quite common for both ends of an association to be attached to the same object type. A simple tree structure is a classic example. To illustrate the interpretations of these recursive associations we present a number of examples based around a single object type, the type **Person**. When you read these examples please bear in mind that several would be better expressed using sub-types.

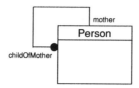

Figure 3.6 *Recursive association*

Every person has a mother; every mother has zero or more children[8]. This structure forms a tree, as shown in figure 3.7.

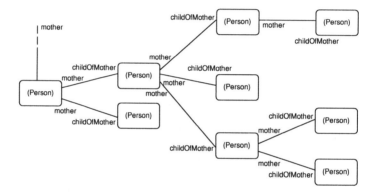

Figure 3.7 *Example of a recursive association*

Notice how we can't draw a complete diagram: every **Person** object has a mother, and nobody has a child who is also their mother, so the set of objects is infinite. Figure 3.8 shows another example. Every person might or might not have a doctor; a person may have patients (if he or she is a doctor – this is very suggestive of a missing object type). Again, there is a consistency constraint: my doctor must have me as a patient.

---

[8]Note that the role name is called **childOfMother** rather than **child**. This is because the association must be consistent when navigated in either direction. Consider what would happen if the role was **child** and we modelled a person who is a father with a single child. Navigating from that person to find his child and then back again *using the same association* to find the mother would have to yield the father if our concept of an association as a pair of related functions were to hold.

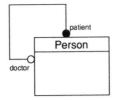

Figure 3.8 *Optional recursive association*

A possible object structure is shown in figure 3.9. Not every person has a doctor: person **d1** in the diagram has no doctor.

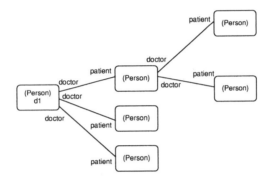

Figure 3.9 *Example of doctor–patient association*

Some recursive associations are inherently symmetric. Consider the **spouse** association, as shown in figure 3.10: if Jack is Jill's spouse, Jill is Jack's spouse. Unlike the doctor–patient association considered above, there is really only one concept here, not the two implied by a double-ended association, hence the same role name at both ends[9].

This association breaks the rule that all the associations emanating from a type must have distinct role names. Since this association really describes only one concept we treat it as a special case. A recursive association with the same role name at each end defines a symmetric association and the multiplicity constraints must be identical at each end.

---

[9]In these symmetrical associations there is really only one function being described, in this case the function **spouse**. Even so, the same constraint logic applies. Given **a: Person**:

  spouse(a) = nil $\Rightarrow$ **{p: Person | a = spouse(p)} = { }**
  spouse(a) $\neq$ nil $\Rightarrow$ **{p: Person | a = spouse(p)} = {spouse(a)}**

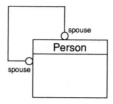

Figure 3.10 *Symmetric recursive association*

With a little rearrangement we could turn this example into a one-to-one association, as in figure 3.11.

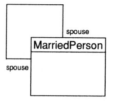

Figure 3.11 *One-to-one symmetric recursive association*

Many-to-many associations of this kind occur frequently. In figure 3.12 we assume that friendship is mutual: if Jack is a friend of Jill, then Jill is a friend of Jack.

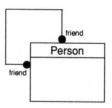

Figure 3.12 *Many-to-many symmetric recursive association*

3.5 Sub-types

3.5.1 Non-disjoint sub-types

In chapter 2 we showed how types can be defined as extensions, or sub-types, of another. In the examples shown so far, the set of objects conforming to one sub-type is disjoint from the set conforming to another. We can also define sub-types with non-disjoint membership by connecting the sub-types to the super-type with separate extension triangles, as in figure 3.13.

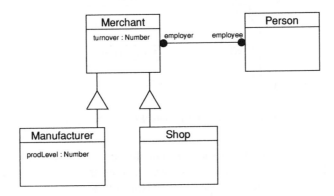

Figure 3.13 *Non-disjoint sub-types*

The sets of conforming objects described by the sub-types are no longer disjoint: an object can conform to both **Manufacturer** and **Shop**. The corresponding Venn diagram appears as figure 3.14. This interpretation is in accordance with the guidelines given in chapter 2: each extension triangle equates to a subset.

Figure 3.14 *Non-disjoint sub-types on Venn diagram*

For a more complicated example, consider figure 3.15.

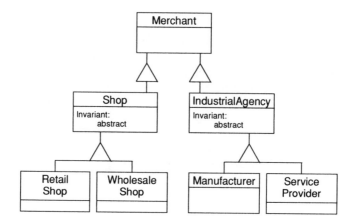

Figure 3.15 *Combining different kinds of sub-typing*

Here, **Shops** and **IndustrialAgencies** are not disjoint, but **RetailShops** are disjoint from **WholesaleShops** and **Manufacturers** are disjoint from **ServiceProviders**. An object could conform to both **RetailShop** and **Manufacturer**. The corresponding Venn diagram is shown in figure 3.16.

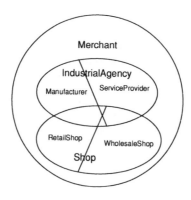

Figure 3.16 *Venn diagram for shop–agency example*

3.5.2 Multiple super-types

Sometimes, a type is-a-kind-of more than one other type. For example, we might want to model a situation that includes both companies and merchants, as separate concepts. We might decide that a manufacturer is both of these kinds of thing, as in figure 3.17.

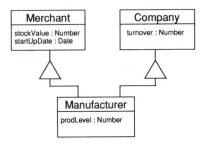

Figure 3.17 *Multiple super-types*

A type with multiple super-types 'inherits' the union of the properties, constraints and associations of its super-types. So a manufacturer has both a stock value and a turnover property. There must not be any name clashes between the super-types. The simple way to eliminate name clashes is to change one of the names!

It is perfectly permissible for two or more super-types themselves to extend a common super-type, as in figure 3.18, but they clearly cannot be disjoint extensions. This is how we define objects that conform to two non-disjoint sub-types.

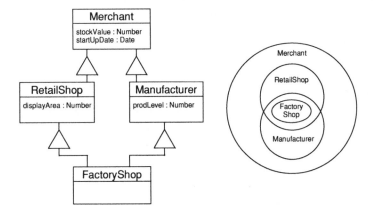

Figure 3.18 *Multiple super-types with common ancestor*

Manufacturer and **RetailShop** are both specialisations of **Merchant** but it is possible to define objects that conform to both, such as **FactoryShop**. This would not be valid if **RetailShop** and **Manufacturer** were shown as disjoint sub-types, using a single triangle. The corresponding Venn diagram is also shown in figure 3.18.

It is clear that a factory shop has a single **prodLevel** property and a single **displayArea** property, but how many **stockValue** and **startUpDate** properties does it have? Should it have two of each because it gains one from being a retail shop and another from being a manufacturer, or just one of each because, ultimately, it is just one merchant? A case can be made for each view: the single stock value might be the total of both the retail shop aspect and the manufacturing aspect; we might want to model a separate start-up date for each aspect. Somewhat arbitrarily, we define this diagram to mean that the factory shop inherits the features of merchant only once. If you want a factory shop to have two start-up dates then you should redesign your model to use association rather than specialisation.

3.5.3 Overriding

Overriding occurs when a sub-type redefines a feature of its super-type. The definition given by the sub-type replaces and hides, from the sub-type and thus from all its sub-types, the definition given by the super-type. Overriding requires care because we need to ensure that sub-types remain conformant with their super-types. The principle is that an object which conforms to the sub-type must also conform to the super-type. We need to define what conformance means, so that we can ensure it is maintained. Unfortunately, a precise definition of conformance is difficult – we discuss this issue in detail later in this book, in chapter 8. In the essential model we are concerned only with *structural conformance*, which only considers navigable structure and properties: if navigation of a model yields a set of objects of a particular type, then observing the properties of the objects in the set should not produce any surprises, even if some (or all) of the objects also conform to a sub-type. The kind of surprise we have in mind would be a constraint violation or a property of the wrong type.

Overriding of associations
Association overriding, or redefinition, occurs when the sub-type has an association with the same type and role name as the super-type. You might want to redefine an association for three reasons:

1. to change the multiplicity constraint;
2. to change both the associated types to be sub-types;
3. to change an aggregation constraint.

We could have drawn an earlier example using redefinition, as in figure 3.19.

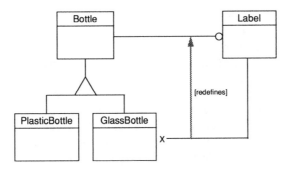

Figure 3.19 *Redefinition*

In this example we are overriding an association to change the multiplicity constraint. A **Bottle** object may or may not have a **Label**; a **GlassBottle** object always has exactly one. The constraint is being changed from **[0..1]** to **[1]**. This is a valid change in the constraint because **[1]** is a sub-range of **[0..1]**. The rule applying here is that the range specified by the sub-type must be a sub-range of the range specified by the super-type. This rule ensures that an observer of the super-type will not be surprised by objects of a sub-type having association sets which would be disallowed for the super-type. **PlasticBottles** are unaffected by this redefinition; they inherit the association from **Bottle** and may still have zero or one **Label**[10].

The following table shows some examples of changes to multiplicities:

Super-type range	Sub-type range	OK?
none given	[0..7]	✓
[1..20]	[10..20]	✓
[1..20]	[0..20]	✗
[1] (plain line)	[0..1] (optional)	✗

The sub-type inherits the association role name and may not change it because to do so would destroy conformance with the super-type. In fact, we could have deduced that the association between **GlassBottle** and **Label** in figure 3.19 was a redefinition, even if the arrow was missing, because, if it were not, **GlassBottle** would have two associations with the role name of **label**, one of them inherited, which is not permitted. Even so, we require all association overrides to be annotated with a constraint arrow. If, in figure 3.19, the association between **Bottle** and **Label** had a role name at the label end, that role name would apply to the redefining association even if it were not re-specified. Any association properties or types also automatically apply to the redefining association.

---

[10]In this respect, this model differs from the similar one that appears in chapter 2.

The designer can choose whether the redefinition redefines both ends of the association or just one. In this example the association is being redefined for the **Label** end only; this is indicated on the diagram by placing a cross at the **GlassBottle** end of the line. A cross at the end of an association indicates that the association is not navigable towards that end. The redefinition in figure 3.19 does not introduce a new name into the name space of the **Label** type: we cannot navigate from **Label** to **GlassBottle**. Navigating from **Label** to **Bottle** will yield a set of objects conforming to **Bottle**; some may also conform to **GlassBottle** but that is irrelevant. The association is being redefined only from the point of view of the sub-type; it has no effect on the super-type, other sub-types or the destination type. This is the most frequent situation for redefinitions.

Removing the cross, as in figure 3.20, changes the meaning completely. Now the association is being redefined at both ends, and **glassBottle** is introduced into the name space of **Label**. We now know that labels are *never* associated with plastic bottles. The role name **bottle** remains in the name space of **Label** and navigations using that name are unaffected; they yield a **Bottle**, not a **GlassBottle**.

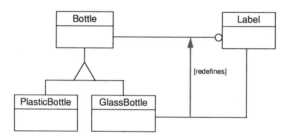

Figure 3.20 *Redefinition with full navigation*

Redefining the sub-type end of the association has an impact on the other sub-types. Since labels are never associated with plastic bottles, the multiplicity of the **Bottle** to **Label** association is effectively being redefined to be zero for **PlasticBottle**. This is fine because **[0]** is a sub-range of **[0..1]**. But imagine that the multiplicity of the **Bottle** to **Label** association had been defined to be **[1+]**. Now, introducing a redefinition like that in figure 3.20 would produce an invalid model because not all bottles (i.e. **PlasticBottles**) can be associated with at least one label.

Another reason for overriding an association is to redefine the associated types. The new source and destination types must be sub-types of the original source and destination types. An example is shown in figure 3.21.

Here we want to show that, while all bottles have an association with a label, glass bottles have an association with paper labels and plastic bottles have an association with plastic labels. In this construction it is normal to redefine the association with respect to both ends; it may be navigated in either direction. The role names at both ends are inherited; for example, the name space of **GlassBottle** includes the role name

label and the role name **paperLabel**. The multiplicity constraints may be changed in a conformant manner, as described earlier.

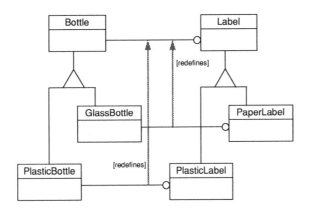

Figure 3.21 *Redefining both ends of an association*

As with the preceding examples, the purpose of this kind of construction is frequently to explain and add information rather than to define new model features. Unless the sub-types have their own associations with other types, these redefined associations can never be navigated. A navigation through **Bottle** using the role name **label** can assume only that the object yielded (if any) conforms to **Label**; it cannot assume conformance with any of the sub-types. Conversely, an explicit navigation through **GlassBottle** using the role name **paperLabel** will always yield an object conforming to **PaperLabel** (if it yields anything at all).

Overriding of properties
The definitions of properties in the super-type are always inherited and their types may not, in general, be changed, but constraints on them may be added or modified according to some simple rules. The types of any property parameters must not be changed.

Type invariants may be overridden in order to be tightened, but not loosened. That is, if the super-type constraint fails, the sub-type constraint must fail, but not necessarily vice-versa. The sub-type constraint must imply the super-type constraint.

For example, given that x is a numeric property of the super-type:

Super-type constraint	Sub-type constraint	OK?
$x > 3$	$x > 4$	✓
$x > 3$	$x > 2$	✗

These rules are, once again, designed to avoid surprises to observers who think they are looking at objects of the super-type. An observer who thinks x will always be greater than 3 will not be surprised to find it is always greater than 4.

The type of an inherited property may be changed in the sub-type where the change is equivalent to an allowed constraint modification; that is, where the type given in the sub-type is itself a sub-type of the type given in the super-type. For example, a property defined to be of type **Integer** might be redefined by a sub-type to be of type **[0..10]**, a sub-range (and hence a sub-type) of **Integer**.

The only sub-typing for value types that we assume to be pre-defined applies to integers and sets of symbols. For integers, a numeric range n_1 conforms to another numeric range n_2 if the starting value of n_1 is greater than or equal to the starting value of n_2 and the ending value of n_1 is less than or equal to the ending value of n_2:

> **[1..10]** conforms to **Integer**
> **[1..10]** conforms to **[0..10]**

For sets of symbols, the sub-type set must be a sub-set of the super-type set:

> **{a b}** conforms to **{a b c}**

For a collection, both the type of the objects in the collection and the possible size of the collection must obey the above rules.

3.6 The meaning of invariants

Figure 3.22 shows two invariants of a company. The first says that the **payCost** property is the same as the sum of the salaries of the employees. The second says that **spouseCost** is the same as the sum of the salaries paid by the company to all the employees whose spouses work for the same company. Notice how **self** is used in the set expression to ensure that the spouse works for the same company and to select the correct employment. Remember that **self** is bound to the object from which the navigation expression begins, in this case an arbitrary object conforming to **Company**.

To understand fully the meaning of logical invariants, such as those in figure 3.22, we must consider the meaning of comparing two expressions for equality. In general, two expressions are equal if they yield results of the same type and the two results match. For example, where expressions yield numbers, the expressions are equal if the numbers are equal. Equality of objects means equality of their identities, that is, that they are the same object. Equality of collections means they have the same members; in the case of sequences they must also be in the same order.

Invariants are assumed to be universally quantified over the type containing them. So the first invariant for **Company** in figure 3.22 is equivalent to:

> ∀ **c : Company • c.payCost = sum c.employment.salary**

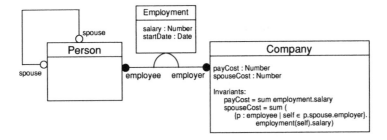

Figure 3.22 *More complex invariants*

Invariants constraining parameterised properties, such as:

> **veryBig(Number): Boolean**
> **Invariants:**
> > **veryBig(x) = (x > 500)**

are assumed to be universally quantified over the parameter type. Here, we are saying that the invariant holds for all valid values of **x**, that is:

> $\forall$ **c : Company** • $\forall$ **x : Number** • **(x > 500)** $\Leftrightarrow$ **c.veryBig(x)**

3.7 Value types

At the beginning of chapter 2 we made a strong distinction between object types and value types. Object types are described using boxes on a type view, value types are the types given to object properties. In fact, we can, if we so choose, represent value types on the type view using type boxes. There are two reasons why we might want to do this.

Firstly, it is sometimes clearer to use graphical notation than textual notation, particularly when there is a variety of constraints to be considered. Secondly, we can use the expressive power of type definitions to describe the characteristics of value types.

In figure 3.23 we represent a value type, **Point**, using a type box[11]. We know it is a value type, and its members are therefore immutable and lack identity, because it has a **value** invariant. The lack of identity is further reinforced by the crosses at the **Graph** ends of the associations; as before the cross indicates that the association cannot be navigated in that direction. It is never possible to navigate *from* a value. The diagram also shows that value types can still be used to type properties inside the type box, as

---

[11]This diagram shows a good example of the difference between derived associations and subset constraints. The negated plots can be derived by a rule; there is no rule to determine which curve contains which plots.

with **originOffset**, even though they also appear as type boxes. A more detailed specification of a **Point** type appears in appendix B.

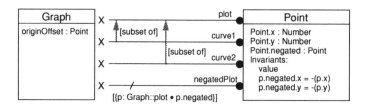

Figure 3.23 *A value type*

3.8 Summary

- *Navigation expressions* allow us to express the results of navigating associations.
- Every type has a *name space* that defines the names which may be used in navigation expressions.
- Expressions that navigate to many objects yield a set, with no duplicates.
- Expressions that navigate to many values yield a bag, with duplicates allowed.
- Care must be taken that navigation expressions do not compromise encapsulation.
- An association that can be defined in terms of others is *derived*. Such associations are marked with a diagonal bar across them and an explanation of the derivation alongside.
- Associations where both ends go to the same type are *recursive*.
- A recursive association that has different role names at each end defines two separate navigation paths.
- A recursive association that has the same role names and multiplicities at each end is *symmetric* and defines only one navigation path.
- Sub-types describe non-disjoint sets of objects when connected to their super-type by separate extension triangles.
- A type can extend two or more other types.
- A sub-type may *override* properties and associations inherited from a super-type provided structural conformance is preserved.
- Logical type invariants are assumed to be universally quantified over the type.
- Value types can be defined in the same way as object types, using type view notations.

3.9 Bibliographic notes

It is worth noting that quite a lot has been published on adding more detail to the OMT method (which uses similar notations to those presented here); we referenced one such source, concerning state types, in the preceding chapter. In particular, the article [Rumba93] describes a number of ideas related to those in this chapter, but which are quite different to our approach.

3.10 References

[Rumba93] J. Rumbaugh. Modeling & design: On the horns of the modeling dilemma. *Journal of Object-Oriented Programming* 6(7):8–17, 1993.

CHAPTER 4

Describing behaviour:
the basics

4.1 Modelling behaviour

Type views give the anatomy of a model; they must be complemented by other views which describe dynamic behaviour. Unlike some authors, we do not believe it appropriate to describe behaviour in the world using point-to-point messages between objects. Our main objection is that such a description over-specifies: it unnecessarily commits to design decisions. This is most noticeable when several objects must each react to an occurrence in the world. A message-based description must decide, often arbitrarily, on the exact order in which the objects will be sent a message notifying them of the occurrence. By contrast, we describe behaviour directly in terms of *events*, and require no artificial sequencing. We say that an event has no duration and is simultaneously detectable everywhere. This mirrors our view of the world.

In this chapter we consider ways to describe dynamic behaviour of essential models, our name for models of situations in the world. We want the essential model to describe all the ways in which the situation can change, by defining all the possible sequences of events. If a sequence of events can be observed in a particular situation, the essential model must indicate that the sequence is valid. Conversely, a correct essential model allows no sequence of events that cannot happen in the situation.

4.2 Events

4.2.1 What events are

Type diagrams tell us about the possible states of a situation, in terms of object configurations, property values and associations. State types, introduced towards the end of the last chapter, describe other possible states and we will develop this theme later in this chapter. To complete the picture we need to consider events, which cause a situation to change from one state to another.

Events are a fundamental part of the structure of experience, and so it is difficult to define them in terms of anything else. Events are the way that information comes into existence. Without events, nothing would happen. Pieces of information are associated with events, but we may not be interested in all possible information. Every event is associated with a date and time, the date and time at the moment the event occurred, but such information may not be relevant in our model.

From a modelling point of view, events have no duration: either they have not yet happened or they have already happened; they can never *be* happening. We can know that an event has occurred only by detecting its effect on our model. This is true in our everyday lives as well as in models. One of the authors was recently sitting at home reading a book when he heard a loud bang outside. His wife asked him to go and see what it was. Without a thought he rose and went outside to look. Only then did the literal absurdity of the situation strike him: how can you look for a bang that has already happened? You can't, you have to look for consequences of the bang, such as fallen masonry or dented cars. (In case you are worried, no consequences other than a change to our memories could be detected.)

When modelling a situation, we are only interested in some of the events, in the same way that we are only interested in some of the infinity of objects which we might perceive when observing the situation. Specifically, we are only interested in those events which cause our model to change its state.

Events are not objects. However, if an event causes our model to change state, the model carries within it a memory of that event having happened. Sometimes we might choose to model that memory as an object, created as a result of the event, and named as though it was the event itself. For example, a marriage event might be represented as a marriage object. You should distinguish between the event itself, and the object representing the memory of that event. Here we are talking about the events themselves; we construct object models to retain the memories of those events in the way which best suits our ultimate purpose.

The purpose of the essential model is to describe what the possible states of the system are, what the possible sequences of events are and how the state changes when the events occur. We consider events to be simultaneously available to all objects in the system. Any object can change its state in response to any event; sometimes several objects may change their state in response to a single event. Conversely, objects change state *only* as a consequence of events.

4.2.2 Describing events

Every event carries some information. We model the information carried by an event in two ways:

- the name of the event;
- the parameters to the event.

Consider the event described by the following English sentence:

'The 09:45 train to Cambridge leaves Kings Cross on 17th June 1993.'

Assume that we are interested in this event because we are building an object model which models, amongst other things, stations and trains. Clearly, this event is one of a family of similar events, representing departures of trains from stations. We might describe this event as follows:

depart('0945 to Cambridge', 'Kings Cross', '17th June 1993')

where **depart** is the event name. This is an instance of the *event type*:

depart(Train, Station, Date)

Here we are assuming that the properties of the **Train** type include its scheduled departure time and its destination. Event types are a generic description of a family of possible events, where each instance of the event carries parameters which are objects and values conforming to the parameter types.

Alternatively, we might be interested in the actual time at which the train starts to move out of the station, in which case we might extend the event type with an additional parameter:

depart(Train, Station, Date, Time)

Another possibility is that we are not interested in the train itself at all, simply in the station, date and time:

depart(Station, Date, Time)

The way in which we describe an event depends upon the information we need from that event to maintain our model.

We prefer to use verbs in the present tense for the names of events, because this helps to avoid confusion with other names. For example, we prefer *depart* to *departed*. Each event type must have a different name.

Event parameters

The parameters to an event can be object types and value types. If a parameter is an object type, it means that the event carries with it the identity of a particular object. We don't say exactly how this happens; designing mechanisms for mapping the identities of objects in the world to and from the identities of the corresponding software objects is an important part of the design of a software implementation, especially a user interface, which we normally ignore when building essential models[1]. State types cannot be used as the types of event parameters. If a parameter is a value type, it means the event carries that value with it. Again we don't specify how the value is determined.

Often the detection of an event will cause the creation, in the model, of a new instance of some object type. A frequent error is to suggest that the event should carry the identity of the new instance as a parameter. This is not possible because the new instance (and hence its identity) does not exist until after the event is detected. The correct parameter for the event would be the identity of an existing object which will participate in an association with the new object.

Objects commonly use an event's parameters to determine whether they are interested in it. For example, for an event:

turnOn(s: Switch)

it is likely that only the switch **s** is interested in that event. However, if we had a row of radio buttons constrained so that only one could be on at any one time, an event which turned one of them on might also cause another to turn off. We use statecharts, described shortly, to specify these behaviours accurately.

An event parameter can be multi-valued; for example, its type might be:

set of Number

meaning that the parameter is an unordered collection, with indeterminate size, of numbers.

4.2.3 Initial object configurations

Consider the type view of an essential model shown in figure 4.1. When an instance of this model first comes into existence, what objects are in it? Should we assume a starting condition where no objects exist?

We require that there must be an initial configuration of objects deemed to exist at the moment of model creation. Further, there must be a type in the model that will only ever have one instance, and that instance must be part of the initial object configuration. This object is called the *initial object*, and its type the *initial type*. All the objects that make up an instance of a model must be reachable by navigation from the initial object. In fact, we define an instance of a model to be an initial object and the objects reachable from it.

---

[1]This matter is discussed further in chapter 11.

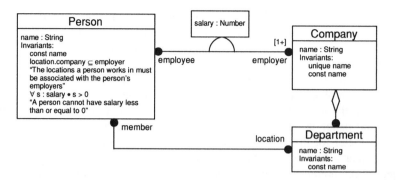

Figure 4.1 *Type view for the company–employee example*

Assuming that we intend to create more than one **Company** object, there is no type in figure 4.1 that can act as the initial type; we must introduce one. We decide that this type will be **RegistrationOffice,** and the single instance of this type represents the office with which all companies must be registered. If we discovered a need for more than one registration office, perhaps responsible for different geographical areas, we would need to introduce a different initial type, perhaps one whose single instance represents the country's government. The new type view is shown in figure 4.2.

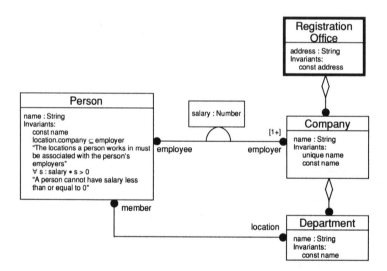

Figure 4.2 *Type view with initial type*

We have distinguished the initial type by giving it a thicker border. In a complete model there will always be exactly one type so distinguished, but it is perfectly permissible not to have decided about this yet, and so not to have selected an initial type yet. The selection of the initial type may sometimes be difficult and can have important consequences on the model. For example, in this model we can deduce the need for the **[1+]** constraint on the association from **Person** to **Company**. If a **Person** object had no employer it could not be reached by navigation from the initial object; to support people without an employer we would need to introduce an association between **Person** and **RegistrationOffice,** representing knowledge by the registration office of all people eligible for employment.

By introducing the concept of an initial object we have greatly simplified the interpretation of treating type names as the set of objects conforming to the type, an idea introduced in chapter 3. For example, with reference to figure 4.2, the word **Person** represents not only an object type but also the set of objects conforming to the type that are reachable by navigation from a particular **RegistrationOffice.**

Associations connecting the initial type will always feature a diamond at the initial type end because we have no concept of objects moving from one instance of the model to another.

The simplest initial object configuration is now a single instance of the initial type, **RegistrationOffice,** as in figure 4.3.

> (RegistrationOffice)
> [address = 'Buck House, London']

Figure 4.3 *A simple initial object configuration*

How was the address of the registration office established? We say that the initial object configuration is the consequence of instantiating the initial type. With essential models, being models of the world, it is not meaningful to discuss how that instantiation took place; in a model of software we would say that the instantiation is the result of running a program.

A consequence of defining an initial object configuration is that it enables us to require that all events have at least one object type parameter. Here, we might envisage an event:

createCompany (RegistrationOffice, String)

that creates a new company[2]. Although we restrict the initial type to have only one instance, we still provide it as a parameter because it gives us a way of identifying existing objects in the model. It allows us, in this case, to write a logical expression showing that the new company becomes a member of the registration office's **company**

---

[2]The **String** parameter is required to provide the company's name.

association, as we will show later in this chapter. It also makes it easy to change the model in the future.

It is never *necessary* to have an initial object configuration larger than a single object, but it is often desirable. It isn't necessary because we can always define events that cause the creation of other objects, as with the creation of companies in this example. If the situation requires us to have events for the dynamic creation of particular types of objects anyway, it seems pointless to place some instances of these types in the initial configuration; they can always be created using the defined event. But when we really do have a static arrangement of objects that includes the initial object, denoted on type views by aggregation constraints at both ends of associations, it is sensible to define the static configuration as the initial object configuration.

4.2.4 Discovering events

If we already have a type view, an excellent way of discovering some of the events is by systematically considering the object types and their associations. For each type, consider how an instance of the type is created, and how it is destroyed. For each association, consider:

- how an instance of it is created;
- how an instance of it is destroyed;
- in the case of an ordered association, how its order is established or changed.

The answer in each case is an event, except when objects and associations exist as part of the initial object configuration.

Referring back to figure 4.2, we can deduce that the following event types are needed to create and destroy objects and establish and remove instances of the associations:

createCompany(RegistrationOffice, name: String)
createDepartment(Company, name: String)
destroyCompany(Company)
destroyDepartment(Department)
addEmployee(Company, name: String, salary: Number)
employ(Company, Person, salary: Number)
leave(Person, Company)
allocate(Person, Department)
deallocate(Person, Department)

Note that **Person** objects are created only as part of their becoming employees.

The event parameters are always the minimum set that specifies everything necessary. We do not have an event type:

allocate(Person, Department, Company)

because the company information is redundant: the department is associated with only one company.

The technique of examining object and association life-times, although an essential part of the discovery process, will not necessarily find all of the events for a model. Other events are needed for those state changes within objects which do not affect any of the associations on the type diagram. These events are discovered by carrying out a detailed analysis of individual object types. For example, all non-constant properties must be able to be changed by at least one event – otherwise, why are they not constant? In this example, we will need an event to change salaries.

4.2.5 Event validity

Imagine we have an instance of the model shown in figure 4.2 whose current state is represented by the object diagram in figure 4.4. We have given the objects symbolic 'names', such as **R** and **C1**, so that they can be referenced in events. What events could happen next?

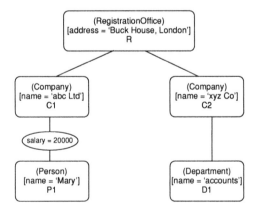

Figure 4.4 *Instance of the company–employee model*

If an event could happen we say it is *valid*. Event validity is a complicated subject, and is studied at some length in this book, both here and in chapters 5 and 6.

Events might be invalid for one of three reasons:

1. erroneous parameters;
2. invalid parameters;
3. model in wrong state.

We will deal with each of these in turn.

Erroneous parameters
An event parameter is *erroneous* if it is of the wrong type or, in the case of object type parameters, if it is an object identity unknown in the model. Referring to the list of event types given above and figure 4.4, the event:

    createDepartment(C1, 20)

is invalid because the second parameter is erroneous: it should be a string. Likewise, the event:

    createDepartment(C3, 'personnel')

is invalid because the first parameter refers to an unknown company. In practice, we always assume that parameters will not be erroneous in this way. We just say that events with erroneous parameters can never occur.

Invalid parameters
An event is invalid if its parameters, taken together, would, whenever the event occurred, have the effect of violating a model constraint. For example, the event:

    addEmployee(C1, 'Peter', -20)

cannot occur because the third parameter, the salary, violates the constraint that salaries must be greater than 0. A rather more subtle example is:

    allocate(P1, D1)

In this case, the event is invalid and could not occur because person **P1** does not work for the company with which **D1** is associated. The event would, therefore, violate the type invariant concerning these associations defined in **Person**.

Model in wrong state
As we saw in chapter 2, some objects have defined states which they enter and leave during their life-times. There may be constraints that certain events can occur only when objects to which they relate are in certain states. This means that the validity of

an event cannot be determined merely by examining the type view and the event parameters.

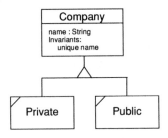

Figure 4.5 *State types*

Consider the enhancement to our example model shown in figure 4.5. A **Company** can be either **Private** or **Public** in its ownership. There might be two extra events:

> **goPublic(Company)**
> **goPrivate(Company)**

A company that is already public cannot go public again, so a **goPublic** event is invalid and cannot occur if the company specified in its parameter is already in the **Public** state. Similarly, a **goPrivate** event cannot occur if the company is already in the **Private** state.

It is clear, therefore, that to determine whether a particular event can occur we need to know the current state of the objects to which the event relates.

4.2.6 Pre-conditions

For each event type we can write down, in natural language, the conditions which must exist for it to occur. This is a useful exercise in its own right, and may also be used as a precursor to more formal specification of pre-conditions.

As we have already seen, pre-conditions fall into two categories: constraints on the event parameters, and constraints on the model. These categories correspond to the 'invalid parameters' and 'model in wrong state' cases above.

Using the events introduced above as examples, the pre-conditions might be expressed as:

addEmployee(Company, name: String, salary: Number)   The **salary** must be greater than 0.

| allocate(p: Person, d: Department) | The person **p** must work for the company owning the department **d**. |
| goPublic(c: Company) | The company **c** must not already be public. |

Irrespective of their category, all pre-conditions have the same effect of defining which events may occur. An event not meeting the pre-conditions just cannot happen.

4.2.7 Consequences

The consequence of an event is usually to change the state of the model in some way. We can write down, in natural language, the consequences of an event. If these consequences are conditional we should make this clear. Once again, this is a useful exercise in its own right, and may also be used as a precursor to more formal specification of consequences.

For the events we are considering here, we might express the consequences as:

addEmployee(c: Company, n: String, s: Number)	A new **Person** object is created, with **n** as their name, employed by company **c**, and earning **s**.
allocate(p: Person, d: Department)	The person **p** is associated with the department **d**.
goPublic(c: Company)	The company **c** moves into the **public** state.

4.2.8 The event table

It is often convenient to document all of the event types in a system using an event table. For the essential model, this has five columns, as shown below:

Name	Object parameters	Value parameters	Pre-conditions	Consequences
The name of the event type	Types of the object parameters, with optional formal name	Types of the value parameters, with optional formal name	Description of conditions that must exist for the event to occur	Description of changes to the model that result from the event

An additional column containing an informal comment is often useful in addition to those shown above.

4.2.9 Event scenarios

As we have seen, not all events can occur at all times. Events can occur in only specific orders. We can produce examples of these sequences, which we call *event scenarios*. An event scenario is a sequence of specific event instances; it shows just one of the many possible sequences of events that could occur.

In essence, an event scenario is just a list of event instances, where each event instance is specified by its type and the values of its parameters. In many cases the event parameters will be identities of objects, which we must represent symbolically. Imagine we have just created an instance of the company–employee model, and have an initial object configuration as in figure 4.3, with the **RegistrationOffice** object known symbolically as **R**.

Consider the event sequence:

    createCompany(R, 'abc Ltd')
    createCompany(R, 'xyz Co')

This sequence creates two new companies. We can draw an object diagram to show the state of the model at this point. The new objects are given symbolic names that can be used in the rest of the scenario. The state of the model after the two events above is as shown in figure 4.6.

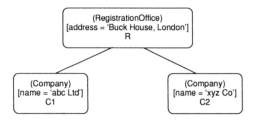

Figure 4.6 *Model after first two events*

Now we can continue the scenario to show an employment:

    addEmployee(C1, 'Mary', 2000)

This gives a new model as in figure 4.7.

By combining the list of events with object diagrams we can describe quite complex scenarios. But these are still only examples. Ideally, we want a precise way of describing all possible scenarios. We will consider this issue next.

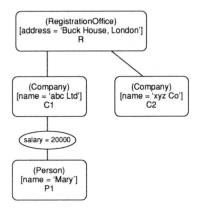

Figure 4.7 *Model after third event*

4.3 Describing behaviour with objects

Other authors [for example Marti91] have defined notations for generic event scenarios, or *event schemata*. The schemata give a model-wide description of behaviour, often with considerable detail. These schema notations exist alongside object-based descriptions of structure, and the relationships between the two are often tenuous. The value of such schemata is in their ability to represent patterns of behaviour observed in the world that act on several different objects over time.

We do not wish to have generic representations of behaviour that are unassociated with specific objects. To use objects to represent structure but not to localise behaviour is, we think, to miss the point about object-oriented techniques. We can achieve the benefits of event schemata by introducing additional objects to the model, objects whose states represent stages in a pattern of behaviour. It is most certainly correct to use objects as abstractions of process as well as abstractions of state.

The remainder of this chapter is devoted to a description of techniques to allow the precise definition of event validity and consequences. The techniques focus on the effect of events on one specific type object, not on the model as a whole. A picture of the whole can be built up from the parts, but, more importantly, the objects to be modelled can be chosen so that their life histories correspond directly to our understanding of processes in the world.

4.4 States

Events can only occur in particular sequences. The sequences are constrained according to the realities of the situation under consideration. For example, a light switch has two events associated with it, **turnOn** and **turnOff**. If at any moment we wish to know which of these two events will occur next, we must know whether the switch is currently on or off, the two stable *states* of a simple switch. If the switch starts in the off state, the only possible sequence of events is **[turnOn, turnOff, turnOn, turnOff, ...]**. Other sequences, such as **[turnOn, turnOn]**, cannot happen. We could draw a simple diagram to describe this situation, as in figure 4.8.

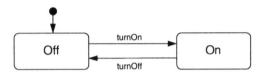

Figure 4.8 *Simple state machine*

In principle, every different set of property values taken by an object represents a different state. Usually this means an object has an infinite number of states, because the domain of at least one property, such as a number, will be infinite. In practice, we choose to model explicitly only those states which distinguish the possible orderings of events, or which relate to dynamically acquired properties and associations. For example, imagine a bottling plant where bottles are filled and capped. The bottles might be described by the object type shown in figure 4.9.

Bottle
capacity : Number content : Number

Figure 4.9 *The Bottle type*

Objects of this type have an infinite number of sets of property values, but we can describe the life-history of a bottle using just three, as in figure 4.10.

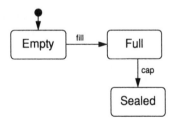

Figure 4.10 *State changes for a bottle*

The **Empty** state in figure 4.10 represents a whole set of property values where **content < capacity**. This diagram gives a precise definition of the possible event sequences. There is just one: **[fill, cap]**.

4.5 Statecharts

The diagrams presented above are examples of *finite state machines*, a technique with a long and mostly respectable history in computer science. A finite state machine depicts the interesting states of a system and the possible transitions between them, in the form of a directed graph. Finite state machines are useful ways of representing the behaviour of objects because they have a memory (their current state) in the same way that objects do. We say 'mostly respectable' because they have one well-known drawback: their complexity increases exponentially with the complexity of the system being described. For finite state machines to be useful we must find ways of controlling their complexity.

It would be possible to draw a single state machine to describe the entire world situation being modelled, but the inevitable size of such a machine might well make it unusable. Instead, we allow each object type to be described by a separate state machine and define the state model of the situation to be the combination of the separate machines, which might well overlap in their coverage, according to some specific rules. It is this separation into separate machines for each object type that is our major and most powerful weapon in the battle against the inherent complexity of finite state machines. It is also strategic in our aim of breaking down a complex model into a number of self-contained, potentially reusable, parts.

The other weapon against complexity is the use of a more powerful visual formalism than that commonly used for state machines: the Harel *statechart* notation [Harel87]. This formalism supports nested states and orthogonal machines, as described below.

Statecharts, as described in the rest of this chapter and the next, meet many different needs. Their primary role is to hold a state machine, drawn in a form similar to figure 4.11, that describes the way an object of a particular type moves between a finite set of distinguished states. Some objects have more interesting state changes than others; some may exhibit no event ordering limitations at all, and hence do not require a state machine. However, statecharts also allow the description of much other important information, with the result that it is impossible to provide a complete description of an object type without drawing a statechart for it.

Statecharts capture the following information:

- a list of the events of interest to an object type;
- a finite state machine;
- details of object creation;
- constraints on the validity of events;
- descriptions of event consequences.

As we mentioned above, an object may not be interested in all defined events, so its statechart will describe only the events in which it is interested. Since an event is interesting in a situation only if it affects the state of the situation in some way, it follows that every event defined must appear on at least one statechart, and may appear on several or all.

4.5.1 Statechart elements

Each state in a statechart, including the whole statechart itself, is shown as a rounded-rectangle (state box). A state box may be divided into up to three sections.

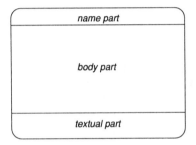

Figure 4.12 *Statechart elements*

Unused sections are omitted. The name of the state is shown inside the name part, which is separated by a horizontal line from the remaining contents. The entire statechart is actually a state, with its name the same as the related type name. State names must be unique within the statechart. The textual part is separated from the body part by a solid line, not necessarily horizontal.

4.5.2 The event list

Figure 4.13 shows a statechart for a bottle in the situation discussed earlier. The textual part of the statechart contains a list of the events in which the bottle is interested; we call this list the *event list*. Event lists can appear only in the textual part of the outermost state. The list of events in the event list is not necessarily the same as the list of events with the **Bottle** type as a parameter.

Each entry in the event list gives the full signature of an event type, including formal parameter names for each parameter (**b** in figure 4.13). When an event is shown against a transition on the state machine, only those formal parameter names needed to describe the transition are shown; the formal parameter names have been omitted from all the transitions in figure 4.13.

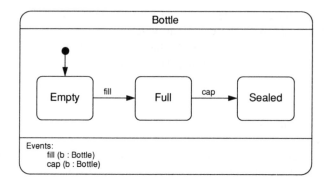

Figure 4.13 *Bottle statechart*

4.5.3 Transitions

How should we interpret this statechart? It shows three states, **Empty, Full** and **Sealed**. Our convention is to begin state names with upper-case letters. The arrow with a black circular tail shows the **Empty** state to be the initial state for objects of this type. When a new bottle object is created it enters this state. Bottles are interested in two events: **fill** and **cap**. Both events carry the identity of a bottle as a parameter. The transition between **Empty** and **Full** shows that the fill event takes a bottle from the **Empty** to the **Full** state; a cap event takes a bottle from the **Full** to the **Sealed** state. A transition is *triggered* when the event labelling it occurs.

Remember that the essential model, of which this statechart is a view, describes facts about the situation being modelled. There is no transition labelled with 'cap' leaving the **Empty** state; therefore it is a 'fact' that, for any newly created bottle **b**, the event sequence **[cap(b)]** cannot occur. What would it mean if we *did* observe such a sequence? It would mean, simply, that the situation being observed was not a bottling plant, according to this model. Event sequences in the world can never be erroneous; either they occur or they don't and, if they do, our model must allow for them. So, not drawing a transition for an event from a state is making just as important a statement as drawing one: it is saying that the event never happens in that state. The following is our basic rule of event validity in statecharts:

> *Events can occur only if they can trigger a transition.*

We call any event sequence that can occur in a situation a *valid* event sequence.

4.5.4 Nested states

Let us enhance the statechart by adding two extra events, as shown in figure 4.14: the **break** event occurs when a bottle breaks while being filled or waiting to be filled; the **reset** event occurs when a bottle is emptied and returned to the beginning of the production line. The diagram shows how the bottle's state is changed by these events. Notice that a **reset** event can occur when a bottle is empty. We call transitions that start and end with the same state *self-transitions*.

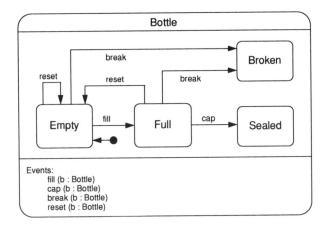

Figure 4.14 *Statechart with extra events*

We can use one of the two major advances provided by the statechart notation, the concept of *nested states*, to reduce the number of transitions in figure 4.14. The revised statechart is shown in figure 4.15.

A new state has been introduced, called **InProgress**, which nests the **Empty** and **Full** states. A transition leaving this state, like the one labelled **break**, applies to all the nested states. The **reset** transition is similar, except that it ends at one of the nested states. We now need two initial state arrows, one showing the initial state at the outer level, another showing the initial state within the nesting. If we had a transition whose destination was the **InProgress** state, the initial state arrow would tell us which of the nested states was to be entered. What we really have here are two state machines: one with the states **InProgress**, **Broken** and **Sealed**, another with the states **Empty** and **Full**. Any state may contain a nested machine.

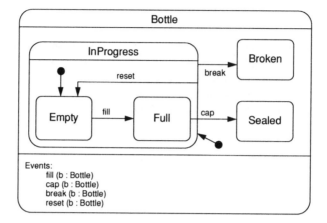

Figure 4.15 *Nested states*

In figure 4.16, an additional transition for the **break** event has been added from **Full** to a new **Leaking** state. This illustrates a possible conflict: the state **Full** now has two transitions leaving it for the **break** event, one direct and the other by virtue of the nesting. We allow this, and say that, when there is a choice, the innermost transition is triggered; in this case, the direct transition[3].

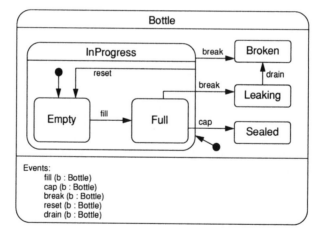

Figure 4.16 *Alternative paths*

---

[3]It would not, of course, be valid to have more than one transition for an event at the same level of nesting, unless they were guarded (see page 98).

4.5.5 Correspondence between the state and type views

The states in a statechart must correspond directly to any state types in the type view. State nesting is depicted in a type view by showing the nested states as sub-types of the enclosing state type. The type view corresponding to figure 4.16 is shown in figure 4.17.

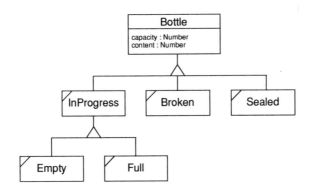

Figure 4.17 *Type view correspondence*

It is not necessary to show all states as state types in the type view; usually, only those needed to show state-dependent properties and associations are included. We can even omit enclosing states, such as **InProgress** in figure 4.17, provided the resulting state type structure does not conflict with the statechart. The rule is that all state types connected to their super-type via the same extension triangle must be mutually exclusive.

4.5.6 Pre-conditions

Earlier in the chapter we introduced the idea that events are subject to pre-conditions. That is, there may be circumstances in which an event cannot validly occur. We have already seen how statecharts show one kind of pre-condition, the kind that requires objects to be in particular states. Pre-conditions of this sort are given directly by the state machine: if no transition exists for an event, the event cannot occur.

In our earlier example of companies and employees we noted another kind of pre-condition, one that limited the values of event parameters. We use logical expressions in the event lists of statecharts to show these pre-conditions. For example, the event list of the **Company** statechart might contain a pre-condition for the **addEmployee** event described on page 87, requiring that the salary be greater than 0.

The event list entry would take the form:

addEmployee(c: Company, name: String, salary: Number) [salary > 0]

The pre-conditions are shown after the event signature, enclosed in square brackets. Similarly, the event list of the **Person** statechart might contain the following entry:

allocate(p: Person, d: Department) [d.company ∈ employer]
'The person p must work for the company owning the department d'

These logical predicates express the conditions under which the event may occur, subject to any other restrictions in the body of the statechart. Pre-condition expressions can use any names in scope for the type; thus they can, in fact, be expressions that do not mention any event parameters, but this is unusual.

4.5.7 Guards

Now let us consider a simple version of our bottle example, where we deal only with the filling of the bottles. Perhaps the filling of a bottle can be considered, at a more detailed level, as a series of squirts of liquid into the bottle. The **fill** event is replaced by a sequence of **squirt** events, where each **squirt** event has an associated numeric parameter, being the volume of liquid squirted. It is possible to define, generically, the number of **squirt** events which occur before the bottle enters the **Full** state, as shown in figure 4.18.

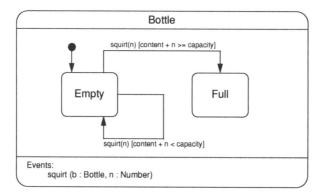

Figure 4.18 *Guards*

The transitions in this statechart have *guards*. A guard is a logical predicate that must be true when the event occurs if the transition is to be taken. By using guards we can have more than one transition for the same event leaving a single state. Here we use guards to show that **squirt** events which occur when the bottle has unused capacity do not cause a transition to the **Full** state, while the **squirt** event which fills the bottle will do so. Guard expressions can use any names in scope for the type plus state names.

A statechart whose guards allow more than one transition to be triggered by a single event is badly specified.

In figure 4.18 the logical *or* of the two guards is *true*. That is, one of the two guards is guaranteed to be true. This doesn't have to be the case. Imagine the guard on the transition from **Empty** to **Full** reads:

squirt(n) [content + n > capacity]

Now neither guard is true when **content + n = capacity**. In line with our rule that every listed event of every valid sequence must cause a transition in the statechart, we can deduce that, in the situation being modelled, no **squirt** event will ever exactly fill the bottle. The guards are now acting as pre-conditions. Not only are they specifying the correct state change but also the conditions under which a **squirt** can occur.

Guards, then, can be used for two purposes. When the logical **or** of the guards for an event leaving a state is **true**, the guards are selecting a path through the machine. When the logical **or** is other than **true** (for example, when there is only one guarded transition for the event), the guards are acting as pre-conditions as well.

All pre-conditions could be shown as guards on transitions. But this complicates the body of the statechart, and has important consequences when we later consider the relationships between the essential, specification and implementation models. Therefore, we recommend that, whenever possible, pre-conditions be specified in the event list. However, there are some pre-conditions, particularly those dependent on particular states, that cannot be shown in the event list.

From this point on in the book, we will use the term *pre-condition* to denote those logical predicates in the event list that limit the conditions under which an event is valid. We will continue to refer to guards acting as pre-conditions simply as *guards*.

4.5.8 Statechart as state

It is not a coincidence that the graphical representation of the outside of a statechart is the same as that of a state within it. In fact, the whole statechart represents a state of the object, a state enclosing all others. We might think of this super-state as the state of existence; when an object is created it is in the state represented by the statechart as a whole.

We can sometimes use the statechart as a state to simplify our diagrams. Figure 4.19 shows a statechart for **Bottle** that uses the statechart as an enclosing state to reduce the number of transitions.

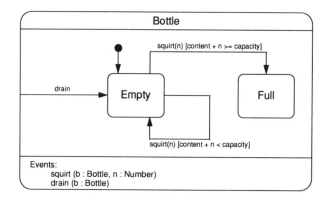

Figure 4.19 *Statechart as state*

A **drain** event has been introduced, which always results in the bottle become empty. We could have drawn this with two transitions, one from **Full** to **Empty** and a self-transition on **Empty**. Instead, we have drawn a single transition starting at the edge of the statechart. Using the statechart as a state is strictly a shorthand for drawing a new state box inside the statechart and attaching the transitions to that.

4.5.9 Allowed events

There is yet another way of drawing the **Bottle** statechart of figure 4.19. In the textual part of the statechart we can specify that certain – or all – events are to be allowed if they are accepted by the event list but don't cause a transition. We have done this in figure 4.20.

By indicating that we wish to allow the **drain** event we are saying it is acceptable in any state; sometimes it will cause a transition, otherwise it will be ignored. Allowing an event is equivalent to:

- including an unguarded self-transition for the event for every state without an existing transition for the event; and
- including a guarded self-transition for all states with one or more existing guarded transitions for the event, with the guard set to be the logical 'not' of the logical 'or' of the existing guards.

The special 'allow' entry **<all>** is permitted, meaning all the events in the event list.

The facility to allow events is particularly useful because an allow statement can be included in the textual part of any state, not just the outermost one. An allow statement applies to the state in which it appears plus any nested states.

Allowing an event does not bypass any pre-conditions. If pre-conditions are given in the event list they must hold even if the event will be allowed[4].

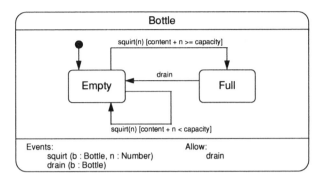

Figure 4.20 *Allowed events*

4.5.10 Event sequence validity

Having now introduced pre-conditions and allowed events, we can attempt a better definition of event sequence validity.

> *Every event in a valid event sequence that appears on the event list of a statechart must satisfy the pre-conditions (if any) and must cause a transition or be allowed.*

> *An event sequence is valid for the model as a whole if and only if it is valid for all statecharts in the model.*

A more complete and precise definition will be given later in the next chapter.

4.5.11 Post-conditions

Refer back to figure 4.18. To complete the description we ought to show that the **content** property has a new value after a **squirt** event. We do this by specifying *post-conditions*. A post-condition is a logical expression that is true after the event has occurred. Post-conditions formalise the textual consequences we discussed earlier, on page 88. The name space for these expressions is the same as that for guards. Since we frequently wish to describe a change in a property, we need a way of referring both

---

[4]This means there is a subtle difference between specifying a pre-condition in the event list and specifying the same condition using a guard. Pre-conditions are never affected by 'allow's, but guards can be bypassed by them.

to the value of a property *before* the event and the value of the property *after* the event. We append a prime character (') to the property to mean the new value of the property, the value after the event. Post-conditions have been added to the statechart in figure 4.21.

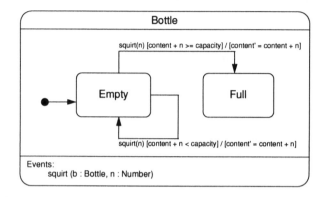

Figure 4.21 *Post-conditions*

The post-conditions are shown on the transitions, after the event name and guards, and after a separating '/' character. As with guards, they are enclosed by '[ ]'.

As a shorthand, post-conditions which always apply whenever an event causes a transition can be shown in the event list, as in figure 4.22. Such post-conditions will hold even if the event is 'allowed'.

As a general rule, post-conditions should not assert state changes in any object other than **self**. If an event causes a change in state of many objects the changes should be described separately for each object, on the appropriate statechart.

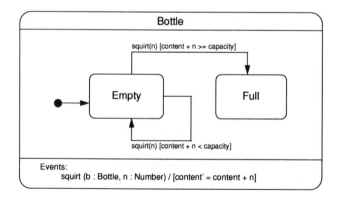

Figure 4.22 *Factoring post-conditions*

4.5.12 Creation operations

Objects are dynamically created and destroyed during the life-time of a situation. When we design state views we need to show how events change the state of the situation, including the creation and destruction of objects. At the time of creation a new object will typically take on properties and form associations using information already in the model or carried with the event. We need a way of showing how this information is made available to the new object. We do this by defining creation operations.

The act of object creation in the model, to be described shortly, invokes a creation operation. An object of a particular type cannot be created unless that type has a creation operation defined[5]. The simplest kind of creation operation is one that takes no parameters. For some types, we will want to define more sophisticated creation operations that have parameters, where the parameters represent information being made available to the object on creation. A type may have any number of these creation operations, distinguished by their parameter signatures. Creation operations do not have names; they are described by their parameter signatures.

We can attach post-conditions to the initial state arrow of the statechart, showing the initial values taken by properties (and associations) of the object created. In figure 4.23 we have defined a creation operation for bottles that takes a single numeric parameter and uses it to specify the value for the **capacity** property. It also specifies an initial value of 0 for **content**.

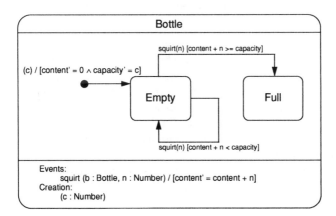

Figure 4.23 *Creation operation*

As you can see from figure 4.23, creation operations are listed in their own section within the outermost textual part of the statechart; again, formal parameter names are

---

[5]We might assume that an intelligent tool will automate the definition of creation operations.

given so that they may be referenced in the body of the statechart. Clearly, property and association names used in creation post-conditions must *always* be followed by a prime character, because they did not exist before the object was created.

As with other post-conditions, we can move the creation post-conditions into the textual part. In figure 4.24 two different creation operations for bottles have been specified, one that defines a default value for **capacity**. The post-conditions for each are specified separately.

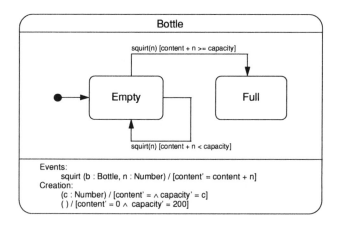

Figure 4.24 *Multiple creation operations*

An alternative to figure 4.24 would have been to show two explicit initial state arrows, one for each creation operation, labelled with the parameter signatures. We normally do that only when we want to point the arrows at different states: different creation operations may cause the object to adopt different initial states. We can even put guards on initial state arrows, to select a starting state depending on a creation parameter. An example of this is shown in figure 4.25. Such guards can reference *only* the formal parameter names of the creation operation, never the state of the object (because it has not yet been created).

Neither guards nor post-conditions can be attached to initial state arrows that appear inside enclosing states to indicate which of the enclosed states is the default, such as the one shown in figure 4.15.

The primary definition of creation operations is on statecharts. However, we can, if we wish, reproduce the signatures of creation operations on the type view. They are shown in the appropriate type box, under their own heading, as shown in figure 4.26. Formal parameter names are not needed.

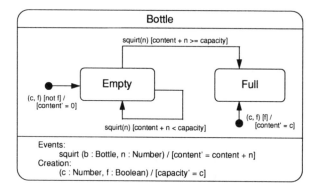

Figure 4.25 *Alternative initial states*

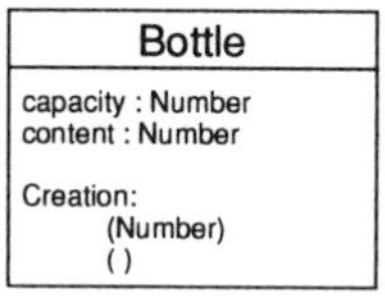

Figure 4.26 *Creation operations on type view*

4.5.13 Creating objects

Post-conditions can be used to show that a consequence of an event is the creation of one or more new objects. Consider the type view in figure 4.27.

Figure 4.27 *Type view for bottle–manufacturer example*

Imagine there is an event

makeBottle(m : Manufacturer, c : Number)

which occurs when a new bottle is made. The post-condition of this event is that a new bottle object, with capacity **c**, exists. We can write this as in figure 4.28.

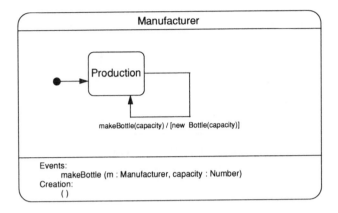

Figure 4.28 *Object creation*

The diagram shows how creation operations are invoked. For any type **X**, the expression:

new X

will yield a new object conforming to type **X**, having invoked a creation operation with no parameters. Parameters may be specified to select particular creation operations[6]. The use of expressions containing **new** is the only way of formally indicating the creation of objects. When we show the creation of an object in our models, we indicate the most specific type to which the object must conform.

In figure 4.28, we could write the post-condition in the event list. This would leave a degenerate body, with a single state and only unguarded self-transitions with no post-conditions. Such degenerate bodies can be omitted altogether. The absence of a body but the presence of an event list implies a single, unnamed, state with unguarded self-transitions for each event in the list.

4.5.14 Creating associations

Although figure 4.28 shows the creation of a new bottle object, it does not show that the new object becomes associated with the manufacturer. We do this in figure 4.29.

---

[6]In the essential model, which we are considering here, the idea that a new object is 'created' needs consideration. What we really mean is that an object previously unknown in the situation has now become known in some way and can subsequently be referenced by its identity.

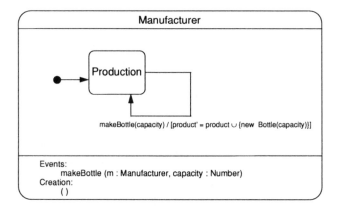

Figure 4.29 *Creating an association*

In the post-condition expression, **product** represents the set of bottles yielded by navigating the association to **Bottle** before the event and **product'** represents the set of bottles after the event. The new set is equal to the old set with the addition of a new bottle[7].

Although we have asserted in figure 4.29 that the new bottle is a member of the manufacturer's **product** set, we have not explicitly asserted the logical implication that the manufacturer is the **maker** of the new bottle. We could do so by passing the identity of the manufacturer as an argument to the bottle's creation operation and showing the consequential value of the bottle's **maker** association as a post-condition. Do we need to do that? Our position is that it is unnecessary. Either an association exists, and can be navigated freely in both directions, or it doesn't, and asserting the existence of the association from just one end is enough (although asserting it from both ends is not wrong, just unnecessary)[8].

It is useful to contrast this approach with the rule given earlier that each object should specify its own changes in state, on its own statechart. Value-typed properties belong to a single object, and managing their states is logically the responsibility of the owning object; associations belong equally to the two objects being associated, and can be managed from either end.

Creating initial object configurations

When the initial object configuration consists of more than one object, we can describe the configuration required by including object and association creations in post-conditions of the creation operation of the initial type.

---

[7]A more concise, but less rigorous, post-condition would be:

    [new Bottle(capacity) $\in$ **product']**

[8]You will recall from chapter 2 that we consider an association to be a pair of logically related functions. Given the result of one function we can deduce the result of the other. It is therefore unnecessary to define the results of both.

4.5.15 Finalisation

Some events will result in objects that were previously known in the situation becoming unknown.   We can think of this as object destruction or *finalisation*. Extending our earlier statechart for bottles, we might want to model the fact that bottles leave our sphere of interest when they are packed (in a container).   Figure 4.30 shows this.

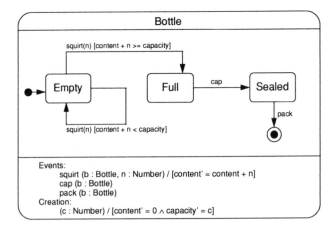

Figure 4.30 *Finalisation*

When an object is finalised it ceases to be known in the situation; any associations it had with other objects are destroyed[9].   Once finalised, an object can no longer participate in the situation.   The real-world concept represented by the object might subsequently re-enter the situation but it will appear as a different object, with a different identity.

4.6 Summary

- The static descriptions of models given by type views present only part of the story; they must be complemented by models of dynamic behaviour.
- *Events* denote happenings in the situation being modelled.   They cause objects to be created and the state of objects to change.   They have no duration and their effects can be described only in terms of consequential changes to the model.
- All events have parameters which define the information carried.
- An *event type* provides a formal description of the event and its parameter types.

---

[9]This is another example of associations being managed from just one end.

- Every model has an *initial object configuration*, which exists when an instance of the model is created.
- Every model has an *initial type*, of which there is only ever one instance. The model is created by instantiating the initial type.
- A systematic consideration of object and association creation, deletion and change will help identify events.
- An event is valid if its parameters do not violate model constraints and the objects referred to by the event are in the correct state.
- By definition, invalid events do not occur.
- The necessary state of the model for an event to occur can be specified in textual *pre-conditions*.
- The *consequences* of an event can also be specified using text.
- An *event table* can be used to bring together definitions of events.
- Specific example sequences of event instances, called *event scenarios*, can be constructed and their effects illustrated using object diagrams.
- All generic model behaviour is described on an object-by-object basis. We do not define generic model-wide event sequence views. Extra object types can be introduced to describe important event sequences.
- Although most objects can take an infinite number of different *states* (because they have properties with infinite domains), we distinguish and name those states which distinguish the possible orderings of events, or which relate to dynamically acquired properties and associations.
- The formalism used to describe event sequences is the *finite state machine*. The important elements of a state machine are states and *transitions* between states.
- The state changing behaviour of each object type is described in a *statechart*. The important elements of a statechart are a state machine and a textual part containing, among other things, a list of events (the *event list*) of interest to objects of the type.
- Transitions are triggered by the occurrence of events.
- States may be nested inside one another.
- Logical *pre-conditions* can be attached to events in the event list.
- Transitions may be *guarded* by logical predicates. A transition can be taken only if its guard is true.
- The whole statechart may be treated as an enclosing state.
- As a shorthand, events which may occur but do not cause a change in state of the state machine may be *allowed* by specifying them in the textual part of a state.
- Logical *post-conditions* may be attached to transitions to specify the consequences of an event precisely. An object should specify only those conditions which apply to its own properties and associations.
- Post-conditions may be associated with creation operations to define initial conditions.
- Post-conditions can describe the creation of objects and associations. The creation of an association needs to be defined at just one end.

- When an object enters a *finalisation state*, it loses all associations with other objects and ceases to exist in the model.

4.7 Bibliographic notes

That part of this chapter concerning statecharts derives from the original work by David Harel [Harel87]. His work is significant for setting out in detail two important techniques that simplify the specification of finite state machines. Harel's work has been popularised by the use of statecharts in the OMT method [Rumba91].

As we noted in chapter 2, our ideas for mathematical specifications, and the notations used to describe them, derive from the formal specification language Z. An excellent introduction to Z can be found in [Words92].

Derek Coleman and his colleagues used statecharts coupled with logical specifications to describe object behaviour in [Colem92].

4.8 References

[Colem92] D. Coleman, F. Hayes and S. Bear. Introducing Objectcharts or how to use Statecharts in object-oriented design. *IEEE Transactions on Software Engineering* 18(1) January 1992.

[Harel87] D. Harel. Statecharts: a visual formalism for complex systems. *Science of Computer Programming* 8:231–274, 1987.

[Marti92] J. Martin and J. Odell. *Object-Oriented Analysis and Design*, Prentice-Hall, Englewood Cliffs, New Jersey, 1992.

[Rumba91] J. Rumbaugh, M. Blaha, W. Premerlani, F. Eddy and W. Lorensen. *Object-Oriented Modeling and Design*, Prentice-Hall, Englewood Cliffs, New Jersey, 1991.

[Words92] J. Wordsworth. *Software Development with Z*, Addison-Wesley, Wokingham, Berkshire, 1992.

CHAPTER 5

Describing behaviour: adding more detail

5.1 The importance of behaviour

The preceding chapter discussed techniques that allow a lot to be said about object behaviour. However, there is still more that can be said. In this chapter we examine some specific technical areas where precise interpretation is extremely beneficial and revealing.

5.2 Statecharts and objects

In the same way that an object type in a type view is a generic description of all objects conforming to the type, so a statechart for an object type is a generic view of the behaviour of all objects conforming to the type. Just as each object will have its own values for its properties, it will also be in one particular state. We use the phrase *statechart instance* to mean the realisation of the generic statechart for a particular object. A particular statechart instance is in a particular state, reflecting the state of the object which owns it.

The event list in a statechart indicates the types of event that this type of object is interested in. But not all objects of the type will be interested in all instances of the listed events. We need to take this into account when deciding on the exact meaning of statecharts. In the following two sections we discuss how statecharts relate to individual objects.

5.2.1 The use of 'self'

Intuitively, when we think about a statechart we interpret it by considering one particular statechart instance, for one particular object. Of course, there actually exists simultaneously one instance of a statechart for each object conforming to the type described by the statechart. We don't normally try to consider all the instances of the statechart at once – mainly because it is nearly always unnecessary.

For any statechart instance, the object known as **self** is the object which owns that statechart instance. Guard and pre-condition expressions are always interpreted with respect to the object **self**.

Consider an event that transfers the contents of one bottle to another, whose signature is:

transferContents(source: Bottle, destination: Bottle)

An instance of this event type involves two bottles and has the following restrictions:

- The source and destination bottles must be different.
- The source bottle must be full.
- The destination bottle must be empty.

The consequences of the event are:

- The source bottle becomes empty.
- The destination bottle becomes full.

Our first attempt at a statechart for **Bottle** that includes this event might be similar to that shown in figure 5.1. We have included a pre-condition to show that the source and destination bottles cannot be the same.

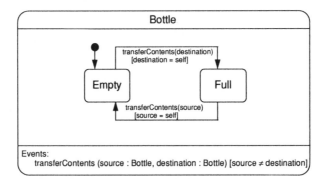

Figure 5.1 *Statechart with transferContents (1st attempt)*

To understand this statechart we must consider the statechart instance belonging to each object of the type. If the source bottle is in the **Empty** state it cannot take the transition because of the guard; the guard is satisfying the requirement that the source bottle not be empty. If the source bottle is in the **Full** state the guard is satisfied and the bottle becomes **Empty**. If the destination bottle is in the **Full** state it cannot take the transition because of the guard; the guard is satisfying the requirement that the destination bottle not be full. If the destination bottle is in the **Empty** state the guard is satisfied and the bottle becomes **Full**. The statechart seems to work.

But what about all the other bottles that might exist, those which are neither the source nor the destination? For all such bottles, irrespective of their state, the guards will fail and thus the event cannot happen. According to figure 5.1, a **transferContents** event can happen only if there are exactly two bottles and these bottles are the event parameters. Up until now, we have failed to take into account the effect of an event on *all* objects conforming to the type.

To take account of those bottles which are neither source not destination we must add extra transitions, as in figure 5.2.

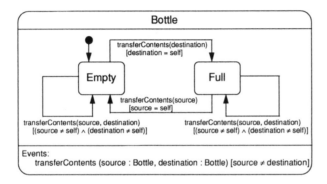

Figure 5.2 *Statechart with transferContents (2nd attempt)*

Now bottles that are not involved in the event simply take the new self-transitions.

5.2.2 Filters

Designing the statechart body to deal correctly with events for all statechart instances can become very tedious; it frequently requires the addition of many guarded self-transitions. In practice, most events affect only one object of the type described by the statechart, although we have just seen an example that affects two. To simplify the body of the statechart we can include *filter expressions*, or *filters*, in the event list that select which objects of the type are interested in an event. The event will be presented only to those statechart instances belonging to objects for which the filter evaluates to true.

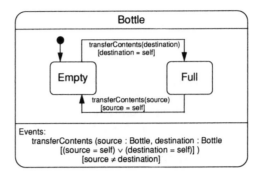

Figure 5.3 *Filters*

The statechart shown in figure 5.3 replaces the self-transitions of figure 5.2 with a filter. This has the effect of filtering the event stream, allowing only those events which satisfy the predicate to be applied to the statechart instance. In this example, a **transferContents** event will be presented only to those statechart instances which belong to the source or destination bottle. The filter appears just inside the closing parameter bracket to separate it from the pre-condition, to indicate that it is concerned mainly with selections based on parameter values, and to show that filters take precedence over pre-conditions.

We need to reconsider figure 5.4, which first appeared in the preceding chapter, in the light of our new understanding of statecharts.

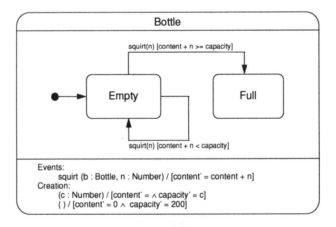

Figure 5.4 *Filling a bottle*

Let us assume that there are three bottles, which we will call **b1**, **b2** and **b3**, on the conveyor belt of our bottling plant, as shown in figure 5.5. Bottle **b2** is under the filling nozzle so the next **squirt** event will squirt into that bottle, and not any other. As you can see from the statechart in figure 5.4, the squirt event has a parameter denoting the bottle being filled.

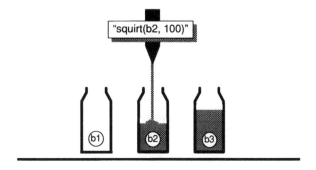

Figure 5.5 *A bottle being squirted*

We want our statechart to mean that a **squirt** event associated with **b2** affects only the statechart instance of **b2** and has no effect on **b1** or **b3**. The statechart in figure 5.4 doesn't mean that. It appears to say that all **squirt** events, irrespective of their parameters, are applied to all instances of the statechart, that is, all bottles. So the **squirt** event for **b2** will be applied to all the bottles, including **b3** – which is already in the **Full** state. Since the **Full** state has no transition for **squirt** we must assume that the event cannot occur. Thus, with the current statechart, it seems that no **squirt** events at all can occur once a single bottle has reached the **Full** state. We need a way of limiting the effect of the **squirt** event to the statechart instance representing the particular bottle being filled.

The solution is, of course, to include a filter. Filters allow each object to decide whether it is interested in any specific *instance* of the event, as depicted in figure 5.6.

A filter has been added to the statechart shown in figure 5.7, so that **squirt** events are applied only to the statechart instance belonging to the object specified as the **squirt** parameter.

More complex expressions than those shown so far can appear in filters, but to aid comprehension we place a limit on their complexity. They may refer to **self**, the event parameters, literal constants, plus any constant properties or associations (i.e. aggregations). They cannot refer to variable properties, such as **content** in the example above. Filters cannot be attached to creation operations.

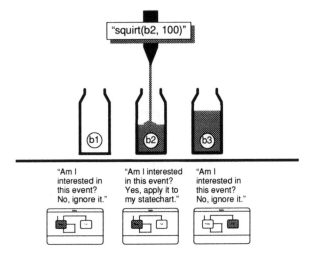

Figure 5.6 *Statechart instances*

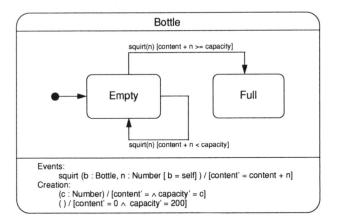

Figure 5.7 *Filter on squirt*

The default filter
Filters in event lists of the form:

[x = self]

where **x** is an object conforming to the type owning the statechart (or one of its super-types), are very common, because in most cases you want events parameterised by an object of the type being described in the statechart to apply only to the object that is the parameter. Indeed, these kinds of filter are so common that we make them the default. The rule is:

> *If an event appearing in the event list has exactly one parameter, p, of the type described by the statechart or a super-type there is a default filter of [p = self]. In all other cases an explicit filter must be shown.*

Therefore, the filter shown in figure 5.7 could be removed; it is the same as the default. So, it turns out that the statechart shown in figure 5.4 was correct after all!

We have already seen one example, the **transferContents** event, where the default filter does not apply. Another example appears in figure 5.8, and is concerned with radio buttons.

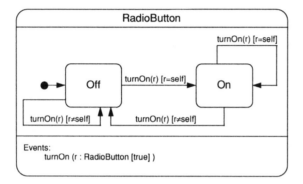

Figure 5.8 *Radio buttons*

Here, all buttons are interested in **turnOn** events, even if they are not the subject of the parameter, because they may need to turn off as a result. To avoid the default filter, which would prevent this, we have supplied a null filter. The two self-transitions are essential to ensure that a transition can be taken in all circumstances.

Filters and pre-conditions
A filter does not indicate in any way whether an event can or cannot occur. It merely indicates which object or objects conforming to the type being considered are interested in any particular event. As we have already seen, pre-conditions can be specified in the event list to indicate whether an event can occur.

In fact, pre-conditions are also specified on an object-by-object basis – this must be so because they can refer to properties of the object. It is not reasonable to require a pre-condition to hold when evaluated against a particular object if the object is not interested in the event. Therefore, pre-conditions need not hold if the event fails to pass through the filter.

Filters and post-conditions

Post-conditions are also, of course, specified on an object-by-object basis. References to properties and associations are implicit references to **self**. If an event affects the state of more than one object of the type being described by the statechart, the filter should be set to allow the event to be applied to the statechart instance of each. Placing post-conditions in the event list in no way affects the filtering of the events, and the post-conditions hold only if the event is accepted by the statechart instance.

5.3 Location of post-conditions

Often there is a choice about where to put post-conditions. If an event is detected by more than one statechart instance, post-conditions specifying its effect may be put in several places. The choice is up to the modeller. We suggest that events should be detected by all the types whose properties and associations it affects, and that the post-conditions specify all of the effects, even if they can be deduced from post-conditions specified elsewhere. Sometimes this is too cumbersome. For example, in the **Bottle** and **Manufacturer** example described by the type view in figure 5.9, the event **pack(Bottle)** takes a **Bottle** object into a finalisation state, as shown in the statechart.

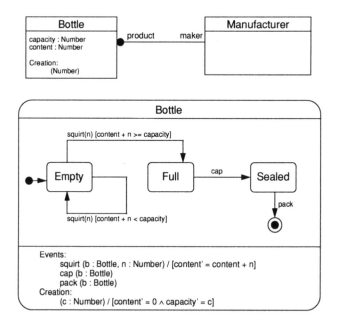

Figure 5.9 *Location of post-conditions*

The event could also be included in the **Manufacturer** statechart as follows:

pack(b: Bottle [b ∈ product]) / [product' = product – {b}]

Often, we omit such post-conditions because they add little to our understanding. A good design support tool should be able to deduce consequences such as the one above and make them available to the developer automatically.

Post-conditions could potentially be given globally, that is, at system level rather than at object type level. For example, we might write, in a global context:

pack(b: Bottle) / [b.maker.product' = b.maker.product – {b}]

Indeed, if all post-conditions were given globally in this way, the problem of post-condition redundancy would be eliminated. However, we reject this proposal because the dependency of behaviour on the states of individual objects would be more difficult to express and would not be localised with the object types. This would mitigate against re-using object types, because it conflicts with one of the basic tenets of object-orientation, which is to locate behaviour descriptions in object types, rather than separately. This is our major motivation for introducing the concept of initial objects: without root objects we may not always have a suitable object type in which to express all behaviour.

5.4 Variables

Any state may define local variables whose scope is that state and any nested states; they most commonly appear at the outermost level. Statechart variables are used to retain information between events, in much the same way as properties. Their values are established and changed by post-conditions. Unlike properties, statechart variables can never be referenced outside the statechart; for example, they cannot be used in a type view.

Statechart variables are defined in the textual part under the heading **Variables:**. The variable name and type must appear. It is not permitted to redefine variables defined in an outer scope.

5.5 State invariants

If desired, invariants can be specified inside states in a statechart to show the conditions that always prevail when the object is in that state. These invariants are called *state invariants*. Some state invariants have been added to the states in figure 5.9.

State invariants are logical expressions which are always true when the object is in the particular state. They must be consistent with the guards and post-conditions.

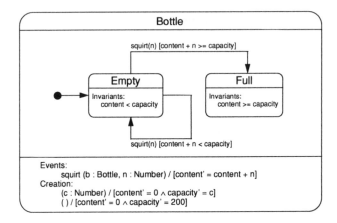

Figure 5.9 *State invariants*

5.6 Creation operations and sub-types

In the preceding chapter we introduced the idea of creation operations. We now wish to explain how creation operations are affected by the creation of sub-types. The bigger question of how sub-type statecharts are related in general is discussed in chapter 8.

The creation operations of a super-type do not apply to its sub-types. Every type must define its own creation operations. When an object conforming to a sub-type is created, all the appropriate creation operations of the super-types are applied first, starting with the most abstract type. Objects conforming to a sub-type cannot be created unless every super-type has a creation operation. The sub-type must explicitly nominate the appropriate super-type creation operation. Consider figure 5.10.

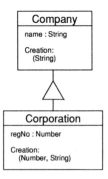

Figure 5.10 *Creation operations in sub-types*

We might expect an entry in the Corporation statechart of the form:

Creation:
    (n : Number, s : String) / [regNo' = n]

However, this is incorrect because it doesn't deal with the initialisation of the super-type property. We must propagate the string parameter to the super-type creation operation using a special syntax:

Creation:
    (n : Number, s : String) : (s) / [regNo' = n]

The second set of parentheses, following the colon, enclose a set of parameters to be used to invoke a super-type creation operation with that signature. It is an error if there is no such operation. The super-type operation is invoked before the sub-type operation. We would expect to find a definition of the Company creation operation that looked like this:

Creation:
    (s : String) / [name' = s]

Creation parameter propagation is not usually shown on type views, only on statecharts.

5.6.1 Propagation to multiple super-types

The situation becomes more complicated when there are multiple super-types. We can deal with this situation by naming the super-types explicitly. Consider the type view shown in figure 5.11.

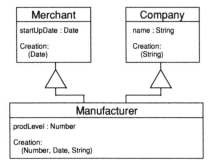

Figure 5.11 *Propagation to multiple super-types*

The creation section of the **Manufacturer** statechart would look something like the following[1]:

Creation:
  (n : Number, d : Date, s : String) : Merchant(d), Company(s)

The order in which the super-types are listed is not important and carries no meaning. Special care is needed when multiple super-types share a common ancestor, as in figure 5.12.

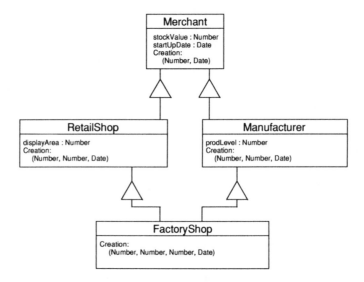

Figure 5.12 *Creation with common ancestor*

The creation section of the **FactoryShop** statechart would look something like the following:

Creation:
  (da : Number, pl : Number, sv : Number, sd : Date) :
    RetailShop(da, sv, sd), Manufacturer(pl, sv, sd)

The creation operations of both **RetailShop** and **Manufacturer** would look as follows:

---

[1] A sharp-eyed C++ programmer might notice that this is very similar to the way the C++ language deals with constructor initialisation lists.

Creation:
> (da : Number, pl : Number, sv : Number, sd : Date) : Merchant(sv, sd)

RetailShop and **Manufacturer** would both propagate **sv** and **sd** to **Merchant**. Will the creation operation of **Merchant** be invoked twice? Recall that we define this model to mean that a **FactoryShop** has only one **stockValue** property; that is, it inherits 'Merchant-ness' only once. Clearly, then, the creation of a **FactoryShop** object should invoke only one creation operation of **Merchant**. To deal with this, we define a rule:

> *When an object of a sub-type is created, exactly one creation operation is invoked for each super-type, even if there are two or more routes to it. If more than one creation operation were to be invoked, or if the same creation operation could be invoked with differing parameters (by virtue of alternative routes), the model is in error.*

The example given above complies with this rule, because the two routes to the **Merchant**'s creation operation both give the same parameters.

5.7 Orthogonal state machines

In the hypothetical bottling plant that we have used as a source of examples, bottles move along a continuously moving conveyor belt. When a bottle needs to be held stationary, for filling or capping, it is grabbed by vacuum operated clamps mounted adjacent to the filling and capping machines. Similar clamps, situated along the conveyor belt, are used to regulate the flow of bottles. We could capture this situation in a statechart, as in figure 5.13.

There are really two distinct state machines in operation here, one to do with filling, capping and packing, the other to do with clamping and unclamping. We can use another notational improvement provided by Harel statecharts, the idea of *orthogonal machines*, to capture this distinction. The revised statechart is shown in figure 5.14.

The dashed line separates the two machines. An instance of this statechart must, at all times, be in one state from the left-hand machine and one state from the right-hand machine. Notice how the states in the preceding statechart are made up from all the combinations of states in these two machines; using orthogonal machines greatly reduces the number of states required in complex models. The most common use of orthogonal machines is at the outermost level, as here, but any state can contain two or more orthogonal machines[2].

---

[2]We do not allow the statechart to be treated as a state, and thus a source for transition arrows, when it contains two or more orthogonal machines because it would no longer be meaningful to start the arrow from any point on the edge of the statechart. We could require the arrow to start at some point on the edge within the area of the appropriate machine but we dislike notations that use the exact positioning of graphical elements to convey meaning.

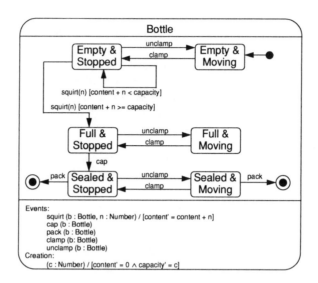

Figure 5.13 *A more complex Bottle statechart*

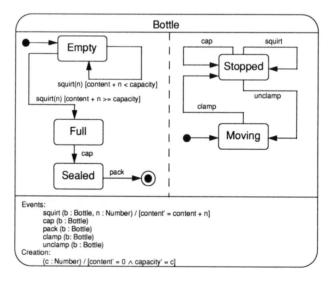

Figure 5.14 *Orthogonal machines*

We have put transitions for the **squirt** and **cap** events on the **Stopped** state to try to show that these events occur only when the bottle is stationary. The same events appear on both machines. We must determine how this affects our event sequence validity rule. The rule now becomes:

> *Every event in a valid event sequence which appears on the event list of a statechart and which satisfies the filter for an instance of the statechart must also satisfy the pre-conditions (if any) and must cause zero or one transition in each orthogonal machine, provided it causes at least one transition overall.*[3]

We can now see that, according to this rule, adding the self-transitions on the **Stopped** state has not had the desired effect. A **cap** event occurring in the **Full** and **Moving** states will cause a transition in the left-hand machine but not in the right-hand machine. The rule says this is fine, so we must conclude that **cap** events can occur while the bottle is moving.

There are two possible ways of changing the statechart to make it mean what we want. The first is to guard the **squirt** and **cap** events with a condition that the object must be in the **Stopped** state. This is fine in most circumstances but tends to clutter the diagram. The other possibility is to take advantage of the fact that the event sequence validity rule is really defined in terms of the event list (see below). If we wish, we can give each orthogonal machine at the outermost level its own event list; then the rules for event validity apply separately to each machine.

Figure 5.15 use both approaches; the **cap** event is guarded, the **squirt** event appears on both event lists. Since the **squirt** event is on both lists, it must cause a transition in both machines. Therefore **squirt** cannot occur in state **Moving**.

Finalisation is always an all-or-nothing event. An object that is finalised ceases to exist in the situation, so it doesn't matter that finalisation is shown in only one orthogonal machine.

5.7.1 Event sequence validity rule

The full event sequence validity rule can be stated as follows:

> A **statechart unit** is a group of state machines governed by a separate event list.

> An event sequence is valid for a statechart if and only if every event instance in the sequence, considered in turn, is valid for the statechart.

---

[3]For simplicity we ignore allowed events.

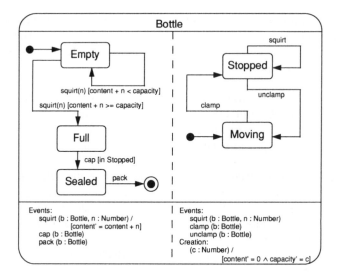

Figure 5.15 *Separate event lists*

An event instance is valid for a statechart if and only if it is valid for every unit in the statechart.

An event instance is valid for a statechart unit if and only if it is valid for the unit in every instance of the statechart.

An event instance is valid for a statechart unit in an instance of the statechart if and only if:
(a)   the event's type is not listed in the unit's event list; OR
(b)   the event's type is listed in the unit's event list but does not pass through the filter; OR
(c)   the event's type is listed in the unit's event list and passes through the filter and satisfies the pre-conditions (if any) and causes at least one transition in the unit; OR
(d)   the event's type is listed in the unit's event list and passes through the filter and satisfies the pre-conditions (if any) and is allowed in at least one machine in the unit.

So, in the simple case of a statechart with a single unit, an event sequence is valid if every event in which the statechart is interested triggers exactly one transition[4]. When there are two top-level concurrent machines governed by the same event list (i.e. one

---

[4]Bear in mind that a statechart is incorrectly constructed if it could allow an event to cause more than one transition in any one state machine. So, although the rule says *at least one transition in the unit*, this does not imply two or more transitions in any one machine. Remember that a unit can consist of more than one machine.

unit), as in figure 5.14, each interesting event must trigger a transition in one or both concurrent machines. When there are two top-level concurrent machines governed by different event lists (i.e. two units), as in figure 5.15, an event that is interesting to both units must trigger a transition in each.

5.7.2 Showing orthogonal state on type views

The states in orthogonal machines may be depicted in type views by using separate type extension triangles for each machine. The type view corresponding to the statechart in figure 5.15 is shown in figure 5.16.

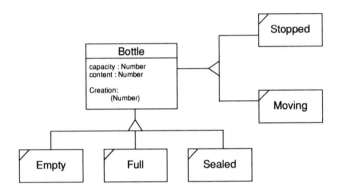

Figure 5.16 *Orthogonal states in the type view*

5.8 Summary

- Each object conforming to a type has its own instance of the type's statechart. The object that owns a particular instance of a statechart is called **self**.
- *Filters* may be added to the event list to select which statechart instances are interested in a specific event instance.
- In principle, all objects affected by an event should detect the event and the effects shown on the relevant statechart using post-conditions. However, post-conditions are sometimes omitted where they can be inferred from others.
- Statecharts may define their own local variables.
- A state may contain *state invariants* that describe conditions that hold when an object is in the state.
- Creation operations are not inherited by sub-types from super-types. Every type must specify its own creation operations.

- Creation operation parameters must be propagated from sub-types to super-types to ensure correct initialisation.
- A statechart may include two or more *orthogonal state machines*. An object must be in one state of each machine.

Part Three

Models of software

Software specification

6.1 The software boundary

Chapters 2–5 discussed techniques for describing situations in the world, by building essential models. In this chapter we discuss the extension of these techniques for specifying software – the *specification model*. At some point during a development (which may or may not be at the beginning), the interface at the boundary between the software and its *environment* must be specified, and the specification model provides a way to specify this interface precisely. Like the essential model it uses notations which describe object types and how their instances change state when events are detected.

It is a good idea to build an essential model in cases where the software boundary is not well-understood, in order to provide a systematic way of making decisions about that boundary. In other cases, the software boundary is sufficiently well-understood that there is no need to build an essential model, and the specification model provides the starting point for development. In yet other cases, especially for interaction domains, the level of abstraction offered by the specification model may be unnecessary, and development may proceed directly by considering the implementation model. The relationship between essential, specification and implementation models is discussed in detail in chapter 10, and the need to build the models in different circumstances is discussed in chapter 13.

The interface between the software and its environment is, in principle, a complete external specification of the behaviour of the software; but we are obviously concerned with the software's internal structure, too. There are an infinite number of possible software systems which would all yield the same externally visible behaviour, but some of them have a much more robust and flexible internal structure than others. The best way to design such a structure is to use a combination of expressive modelling techniques which permit a proper separation of concerns, their combination providing redundancy between techniques to enable cross-checking. We adopt the basic principle that the specification model is constructed from object types and statecharts, just as the other models are. Using this principle, we can strive for a seamless development in which the discontinuities between the different models are minimised as far as possible.

The techniques we use for the specification model build on those we have described already. We extend the notation for statecharts and also change the interpretation of this notation slightly. In chapters 2–5 we introduced the techniques in the context of essential modelling; in this chapter we start to take into account some of the problems of software development.

In the specification model, we describe the effects of incoming events in terms of the changes of state they cause, and any outgoing events generated as a result. So the specification model is a *stimulus–response* model of a software system, as illustrated in figure 6.1.

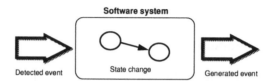

Figure 6.1 *A stimulus–response model*

The specification model is idealised because it assumes infinitely fast processing, and an infinite amount of totally reliable persistent storage with instantaneous random access. By making these assumptions the specification model leaves on one side issues such as distribution, concurrency, persistence, and error-recovery: these are addressed in the implementation model.

6.2 Agents

It is often helpful to think about the interface between the software and its environment in terms of *agents*. Agents are people, or other systems, which interact with the software. Agents are outside the software itself, but are an essential part of the whole situation. If an essential model is built, agents and their behaviour might be modelled in it. Some examples of agents are as follows:

- in a stock control system, the storeman who manages the arrival and departure of goods and enters information into the computer system;
- in a petrol station, the customers and attendants;
- in a branch system for a bank or building society, the customers and tellers;
- in a lift control system, the passengers, motors, sensors and actuators;
- in a remote controller for a video recorder, the operator and the remote recorder itself.

When agents are human, they correspond to roles played by people during interactions with the software. One person may play many roles and thereby act as many agents; conversely, many people may play one role and act as a single agent.

Figure 6.2 depicts a software system and agents – three people and one clock. It indicates stimuli going from the agents to the software system, and responses going from the software back to the agents. Note that the state of the software may always be assumed to be visible to observers, even when no events are explicitly generated.

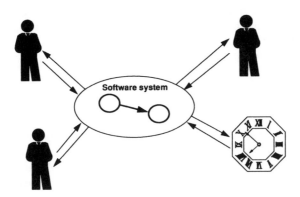

Figure 6.2 *Software system and agents*

In any situation, agents can be found at several different levels of abstraction. For example, when modelling the logic of stock control we will think of the storeman as an agent, whereas when modelling the user-interface to the stock-control software we may well think of the keyboard and touch screen as agents. Agents are chosen at the correct level of abstraction for the model being built.

The interface between software and its environment is a designed system. Often this interface involves interacting with a computer screen using input devices such as keyboard, mouse, touch screen or pen. Equally, the interface may involve sensors and actuators, such as bar-code readers, temperature or position sensors, clocks, valves, motors, embedded controllers, etc. Choosing the correct interface technology (from a rapidly evolving selection) and designing an effective interface are crucially important – although both are outside the scope of this book.

A *concept domain* is a portion of the software system responsible for maintaining a model of the state of its environment. Every software system has one or more concept domains, and a specification model for the concept domains is a very important part of any system development. This model is an idealised description of stimulus–response behaviour at the level of abstraction of the concept domains. It does not consider the mechanics of how stimuli are detected by the software, or how responses are translated into real occurrences in the world. These are the responsibility of other domains – which may, nevertheless, also be described using specification modelling techniques.

Agents may be represented by software objects in the specification model, often within interaction domains. The software agent understands how to communicate with the real agent, so that when, for example, the real agent causes an event that is to stimulate the concept domain, the software agent can detect the event and transform it appropriately. Some agents may themselves be modelled in a concept domain.

Except in the simplest systems, it is not possible to describe the stimulus–response behaviour of a system completely without describing its internal state, because the response to a particular stimulus depends in general upon the state at the time of the stimulus. Nevertheless it is often useful when building a specification model to describe the *typical* stimulus–response behaviour of a system, that is, its responses to a particular sequence of stimuli in normal operation, as well as under various special conditions. We give several examples of such *event scenarios* in this chapter.

6.3 Type views

Specification model type views use exactly the same notation as type views in the essential model, but are interpreted as describing types of object in the software, rather than types of object in the situation. All of the constructs of chapters 2 and 3 are used in the specification model without modification: types, properties, associations and invariants.

Figure 6.3 shows the specification model type view of an example system that monitors the prices of company shares. We use this example in this chapter and later in the book. Here we use it to illustrate some of the features of specification models.

Shares are associated with a particular sector, such as chemical or retail, and many sectors of shares are traded on a particular stock exchange, such as London or New York. A history of changes to share prices is kept using a sequence of **ShareChange** objects, each one representing a price change. Shares, sectors and exchanges have a **movement** property, the amount by which their price (or sum of prices for sectors and exchanges) has increased or decreased since the start of trading. **Minder** objects can be attached to shares, sectors and exchanges; minders generate an alarm if the movement exceeds a pre-determined limit.

To make it perfectly clear that the diagram in figure 6.3 describes the types of software object, we append **-S** to the type-names. In this book we adopt this convention for all specification models. We don't consider the **-S** to be an integral part of the type name, so it doesn't get used in declarations, event lists, etc.

The similarity between the techniques for type views in essential and specification models should not be misunderstood. It does *not* mean that the essential model and specification model type views for a given system are the same. An essential model is created for the purpose of understanding a situation, not for specifying software to operate in that situation. There may be an essential model describing associations between 'real' shares, sectors and exchanges, and there may well be a close correspondence between it and the specification model; but they are not the same thing.

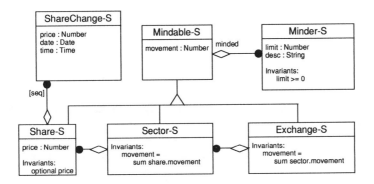

Figure 6.3 *Specification model type view of share system*

6.4 Events

Unlike in the essential model, detected events or *stimuli* in the specification model can cause events to be *generated*. These can be subsequently detected by the model (*internal* events) and/or manifested in the environment (*external* events or *responses*).

The syntax for all specification model events is the same as in the essential model. Like essential model events they are instantaneous and broadcast, that is, they may be detected simultaneously by many objects of many types. The effect of a detected event is to cause state changes in one or more objects. These state changes are specified by post-conditions on statecharts defined for object types.

Why do we propose that events are broadcast in an object-oriented specification? Many authors would argue that the very essence of object orientation is message-sending between objects, and would therefore argue that broadcast events violate this basic principle. We disagree, and believe that describing software in terms of message-sending is over-specification for the purpose of specifying stimulus–response behaviour. Descriptions of message-sending mix up specification issues with implementation tactics.

Consider, for example, the simple case of representing the employment of a person by a company, in a software system partially described by the type diagram given in figure 6.4.

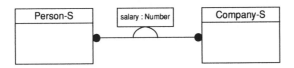

Figure 6.4 *Type view for employment*

To specify the effect of a stimulus to this software system which establishes a new employment association between a **Person** object and a **Company** object, we define an event:

hire(p: Person, c: Company, sal: Number)

and specify the consequence of that event for the types **Person** and **Company** by using post-conditions, for the **Company**:

hire(p: Person, c: Company, sal: Number) / [p ∈ person' ∧ salary'(p) = sal]

and for the **Person**:

hire(p: Person, c: Company, sal: Number) / [c ∈ company' ∧ salary'(c) = sal].

Specifying the results of this stimulus using messages would require us to choose between the following tactics:

1. Send a message to the **Company** object, which then sends a message to the **Person** object.
2. Send a message to the **Person** object, which then sends a message to the **Company** object.
3. Send a message to a third object, which then sends two messages to the **Company** and **Person** objects – in one order or the other.

Any one of these tactics is an acceptable implementation of the desired behaviour, but with broadcast events the designer may avoid choosing between them at specification time. Deciding about the order of these messages requires detailed consideration of implementation issues such as concurrency. Concurrency is necessary in an implementation when an external stimulus must be responded to while the consequences of a previous stimulus are still being processed. In the specification model we avoid thinking about this by assuming that all event processing is instantaneous, and that all of the consequences of an external stimulus (including the processing of any internal events generated as a result) are completed before any further external stimuli occur. The broadcast event model thus allows us to specify only the necessary logical consequences of a stimulus, without specifying any unnecessary sequencing. As a result it becomes easier to design a concurrent implementation to satisfy performance requirements than it would be if the design of message-sequencing had been pre-empted in the specification. In general, avoiding premature commitments is a most important strategy for successful software design.

Note that only one of the post-conditions given above is strictly necessary, because the other can be deduced from it. We give both for symmetry and clarity. With post-conditions there is a trade-off between clarity and minimality of expression. When using a specification model for the purpose of designing an implementation we often need to determine which events affect a type and how. As with essential modelling, we normally suggest that an event is detected by all the types whose properties and associations are affected by it, and that post-conditions are given for all the effects it has on the properties and associations of the type in question, even though many of these post-conditions could be deduced logically from the type diagram and each other[1].

6.4.1 Pre-conditions

Not all events can happen at any time. As with the essential model, there are pre-conditions for events to occur. However, the interpretation of these is rather different in the specification model.

In the essential model, the failure of a pre-condition is interpreted to mean that an event cannot happen in the situation being described, that is, it is logically impossible. By contrast, in the specification model the failure of a pre-condition means that the software's response to the event is *undefined*.

The basic principle behind this interpretation is design by contract. A pre-condition is part of the contract that a supplier makes to its clients: 'if you (the client) promise not to generate this event unless the pre-condition is satisfied, I (the supplier) promise to respond properly. However, if you generate it at some other time, I make no promises at all about what will happen.' This interpretation enables us to construct a robust story about sub-types, as we will see in chapter 8.

The implementor of a specification model needs to consider carefully how the pre-conditions are to be satisfied. It may be a physical or logical property of the situation that the event cannot happen unless the pre-condition is satisfied; in this case an undefined response is adequate, although a healthy implementation would normally produce some kind of error report should the event actually occur. On the other hand, it may be the responsibility of some part of the software, typically an interaction domain, to validate events, and to ignore or reject those that fail the pre-conditions. Whichever of these strategies is ultimately adopted, the specification model itself simply leaves the response undefined.

6.4.2 Event scenarios

It is often useful to show a typical sequence of events for the whole or part of a software system using *event scenarios*. The scenario tabulated below shows stimuli and responses during a customer's typical interaction with a petrol station[2] to dispense petrol. Three agents participate in this scenario: the customer, the attendant controlling

---

[1]Smart automated tools could either check the consistency of redundant logic, or deduce any consequences omitted by the designer.

[2]Gas station, for US readers.

the transaction and the physical pump. Stimuli, or events detected by the software, are indicated by a question mark '?' prepended; responses, or events generated by the software, are indicated by an exclamation mark '!'.

Customer	Attendant	Pump
?gunRemove(p)		?gunRemove(p)
	!alarmOn(p)	
	?activatePump(p)	
!zeroPumpDisplay(p)		!zeroPumpDisplay(p)
	!alarmOff(p)	
	!zeroConsoleDisplay(t)	
!motorOn(p)		!motorOn(p)
		?dispensePulse(p)
!updatePumpDisplay(p)		!updatePumpDisplay(p)
	!updateConsoleDisplay(t)	
		?dispensePulse(p)
!updatePumpDisplay(p)		!updatePumpDisplay(p)
	!updateConsoleDisplay(t)	
.	.	.
.	.	.
.	.	.
?gunReplace(p)		?gunReplace(p)
!motorOff(p)		!motorOff(p)
?pay(t)	?pay(t)	
?receiptRequest(t)	?receiptRequest(t)	
!receiptPrint(t)	!receiptPrint(t)	

Each column of the table is an event scenario, which describes the software system's overall behaviour from the perspective of a single agent. The three scenarios could be combined if required to produce a single scenario describing the overall composite behaviour of the software during this interaction.

Each scenario represents the events that an agent participates in, either by initiating or receiving it, or, in the case of human agents, by observing it as a necessary part of their interaction with the system. For example, the customer initiates the **gunRemove** event, which is a stimulus to the software and hence indicated by a '?'. The customer observes the **zeroPumpDisplay** response, but the customer does not normally observe the **alarmOn** response and hence this does not appear in the customer's column. The inclusion of a particular event in a particular agent's scenario might be a matter for argument. From the point of view of the specification, this doesn't matter: agents are not formal concepts in our notation, and the presence or absence of a particular event in a particular agent's scenario has no impact on the software specification. Scenarios should be thought of as a useful informal tool for reasoning about the software boundary.

Each event in the scenario has parameters, which are either values or the names of objects. These names are interpreted in an associated object diagram, shown in figure 6.5, which shows a **Pump** called **p** and a **Transaction** called **t**, associated with each other after the creation of the transaction (which occurs as a response to **activatePump**).

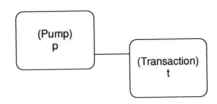

Figure 6.5 *Object diagram showing* **Pump** *object* **p** *and* **Transaction** *object* **t**

Often, object configurations change during scenarios; if this happens, more than one object diagram may be needed to interpret the scenario fully. For example, in the scenario above, only the pump object exists until the transaction is created.

Generated responses will eventually be manifested in the world, often by audible and visual signals, or by actuating a motor or other device. Specification modelling says nothing about the physical mechanisms used to create these manifestations. A generated event should be interpreted as a request to produce a manifestation, with the order of these requests defined by the order in which the events are generated.

It is important to note that the order of the actual manifestations themselves depends upon the nature of the physical mechanisms which create them. In some cases we know that the order of the manifestations will be the same as the order of the requests; for example we may safely assume that a request to switch something on followed by a request to switch it off again will cause it to be switched first on and then off. But in other cases we must be more careful. To land an aircraft automatically, we might generate an event which represents a request to put the wheels down, followed by an event which represents a request to land. It would be foolhardy to issue the second request immediately after the first, because the request to put the wheels down takes considerable time to fulfil. In such a case the software had better wait for a detected acknowledgement that the wheels really are down before issuing the request to land. Note that the ordering in event scenarios is the order of requests, not of their manifestations.

The choice of events to include in a scenario depends upon the purpose of the scenario. Often, a scenario is created from the perspective of a specific agent or a specific software object. Scenarios can be used to design and validate state views, which describe the complete behaviour of the software system as it is partitioned between objects.

6.4.3 The event table

For those events which are detected by the software it is often useful to draw up a table with a description for each event, showing its parameters and informally describing its pre-conditions and consequences, exactly as we discussed for essential model events in chapter 4, except that the consequences of an event may include the generation of other events.

6.5 State views

Every type in a specification model has a state view, defining how instances of the type respond to events. Syntactically, state views in the specification model are the same as in the essential model, with the addition of generated events as described below.

6.5.1 Generated events

A specification model statechart can specify the *generation* of events. Events can be generated from specific transitions, or from event list entries. An additional section in the event list of the statechart, headed **Generations:**, gives the types of events generated in the statechart.

The syntax for generating an event consists of naming the generated event, giving values for any parameters, after the '/' and any post-conditions on a transition or event list entry.

To illustrate event generation, consider the statechart in figure 6.6, which shows the behaviour of the type **Minder** in the model shown in figure 6.3.

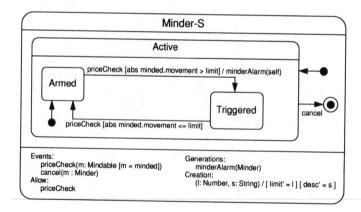

Figure 6.6 *Minder statechart*

The statechart responds to the **priceCheck** and **cancel** events, and allows the **priceCheck** event in any state. The **priceCheck** event carries as its parameter the identity of the relevant **Mindable**, which might be a **Share**, **Sector** or **Exchange**. The transition between the **Armed** and **Triggered** states shows the generation of an external event called **minderAlarm** with one parameter whose value is **self**, that is, the identity of the **Minder** object generating the event. The **Generations:** section in the textual part shows the type of all events generated on the statechart, in this case **minderAlarm**.

Figure 6.7 shows a possible sequence of events for this statechart, together with an object diagram corresponding to the state of affairs at the place in the scenario marked with an asterisk.

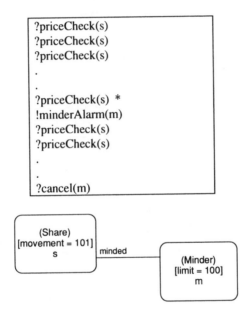

Figure 6.7 *Event scenario plus object diagram at point when the alarm occurs*

6.5.2 Entry and exit generations

Figure 6.8 shows an extended version of the **Minder** statechart, with an additional **Disabled** state. Events called **lightOn** and **lightOff** are generated on all of the entries and exits from the **Triggered** state. As a result the statechart is rather cluttered.

The clutter can be reduced considerably by using *entry* and *exit* event generations. Any state can have in its textual part a list of generations under the heading **Entry:**, which will be performed upon any entry to that state, and a list of generations under the heading **Exit:**, which will be performed upon any exit from that state. Using these

features the **Minder** statechart can be simplified as shown in figure 6.9, where the
Triggered state has entry and exit sections containing the event generations.

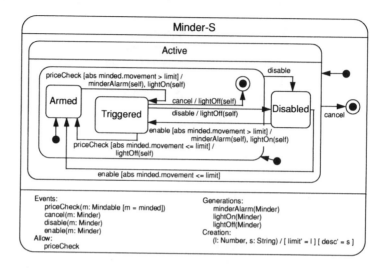

Figure 6.8 *Extended **Minder** statechart with clutter*

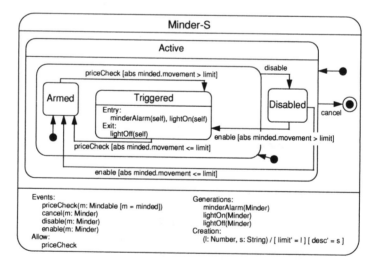

Figure 6.9 *Simplified statechart with entry and exit generations*

Entry and exit generations are triggered on any entry and exit from the state,
including transitions which explicitly begin and end with the same state. *Allowed*

events which do not cause transitions, such as **priceCheck** occurring in the **Triggered** state with **[minded.movement>limit]**, do not trigger entry and exit generations (although if **priceCheck** were to have any post-conditions or generations defined in the event list, these would still apply).

Event generations may also be shown in the event list of the statechart, after any post-conditions, meaning that the generation occurs whenever the event occurs.

6.5.3 Internal events

Often, the overall response to a stimulus can only be described as taking place in a number of discrete steps. Each of the individual steps moves the entire system from one valid state to another, but the overall response to the stimulus consists of all the steps taken together. We call this division into discrete steps *factoring* the stimulus, and we describe it using *internal events*, which are both generated and detected by the software (although they might also cause external effects)[3]. Figure 6.10 illustrates the statechart for the **Share** type from figure 6.3, and shows how **priceCheck** events detected in figure 6.6 are actually generated by a **Share** object. Similar statecharts, not shown, exist for the **Sector** and **Exchange** object types.

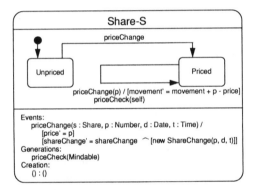

Figure 6.10 *Shares generate **priceCheck** events*

To understand figure 6.10 fully we need the statechart for **Mindable**, which although trivial, shows how the **movement** property is initialised.

---

[3]Internal events are one of several possible approaches to the factoring of a response. A second approach would be unstable states, with transitions guarded only by conditions. A third would be transitions guarded by statements about state changes in other statecharts. We discard these approaches in favour of internal events to avoid a proliferation of additional concepts (although we use unstable states to decompose transitions in the implementation model: see chapter 7).

Figure 6.11 *Mindable* statechart

In this example, the overall consequence of a **priceChange** event is in two well-defined stages:

1. Change the price of the share, sector and exchange.
2. Check that the movement has not exceeded the limit.

The first consequence is specified by the post-condition on the **priceChange** event, together with the invariants on the type view, and the second by the generation of the **priceCheck** events.

Note that all of the consequences of an external stimulus happen before any further external stimuli may happen. In other words, all of the internal events are generated and detected, and their consequences established, before any further external events. We may assert this because of our fundamental assumption in the specification model that all processing is instantaneous.

6.5.4 Event ordering

Events are generated from a transition after its post-conditions have been established[4] and the target state has been entered. In general, where the source state of a transition has exit generations and the target state has entry generations, the complete evaluation of the transition proceeds in the following order:

1. Establish all of the post-conditions and enter the target state.
2. Trigger exit generations on the source state, in order.
3. Trigger generations defined in the event list, in order.
4. Trigger generations on the transition, in order.
5. Trigger entry generations on the target state, in order.

If an event is allowed and has no transition defined for the current state, its complete evaluation proceeds by establishing the post-conditions and then triggering in order any generations defined in the event list.

The overall response of a given statechart instance to a single event may therefore be a sequence of events, generated in order after the post-conditions have been

---

[4]As with the essential model, the order of post-conditions is immaterial.

established. When one of these events itself gives rise to further events, all of these further events occur before the next event in the sequence.

An object changes state instantaneously at the same time as the post-conditions are established. This means that when any generations occur, the object is already in its new state. Note in particular that any exit generations in the source state happen after the object is in the target state. This interpretation, although somewhat strange at first sight, gives the cleanest and most intuitive meaning for event generations as a whole.

What about when the same event is detected by several statechart instances, each of which generates events as a result? We can definitely state that all of the post-conditions are established, and all of the state changes occur, before any of the generations. But note that we cannot determine the relative ordering of events generated by different objects in such circumstances. If these events are themselves detected within the model they could give rise to ill-formed specifications; we return to this point later in this chapter.

6.5.5 Events generated and detected by 'self'

Since a state change is completed before any events are generated, it is legitimate to generate an event from a statechart instance which is detected by the same instance. This can happen *directly*, as illustrated in the example below, or *indirectly* in cases where, because of the behaviour of other objects, a generated event results in an event detected by the original object.

Consider the type shown in figure 6.12, which specifies the operation of a type **Magazine**, controlling a magazine of slides in a slide projector. This statechart detects the event **moveTo(n: Integer)**, and generates a sequence of **up** or **down** events which will move the physical magazine step-by-step to the required position.

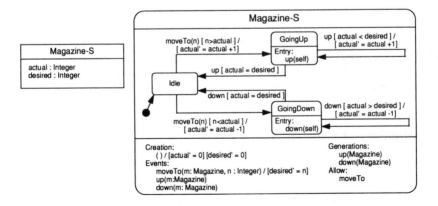

Figure 6.12 *Slide magazine with self events*

For example, if **actual = 0** and the event **moveTo(7)** is detected, then seven **up** events will be generated. In this example the generated events are detected internally as well as causing external manifestations (the physical movement of the slide magazine).

6.6 Object responsibilities

A crucial aspect of specification modelling is allocating the responsibility for overall system behaviour among individual objects. The way to determine where responsibilities belong is by considering the potential for change in the design. A properly partitioned system is much more resilient to changing circumstances than one where responsibilities have been poorly allocated.

Consider, for example, a simplified version of the system shown in figure 6.3, in which alarm processing were a responsibility of the share objects themselves. In such a system, there would be no scope for setting alarms on complete sectors or exchanges, and no scope for setting more than one alarm on any price. Perhaps the original requirements are such that a single alarm per share is all that is required. If, later on, the requirements change so that sector alarms are also required, the worst possible approach would be to retain responsibility for alarm processing in the share objects. All too often we see software systems modified in this way which rapidly become akin to unmanageable spaghetti.

Responsibilities can be divided informally into categories. Taking an anthropomorphic approach, that is, pretending that objects are people, an object can be thought of as having the following responsibilities:

- knowing (i.e. remembering or calculating) a value;
- listening for an event;
- telling other objects about an event;
- creating new objects.

In specification models these correspond to properties, event list entries, generations and object creations. Thinking about an object's responsibilities in anthropomorphic terms is often very helpful to beginners in object-oriented design, because it helps them to visualise how the system works.

6.7 Unordered events

Note: this section is rather specialised and may be omitted on a first reading.

Consider the somewhat contrived arrangement in figure 6.13, which shows three statecharts dealing with three events. Assume that a **start** event arrives. In consequence, the **Initialiser** generates an **initialise** event, and the **Resetter** generates a **reset** event. These are un-ordered with respect to each other. So what does the **Starter** do? If **initialise** is before **reset**, then it will go smoothly from **Starting** to **Initialised** to **Reset** to **Started**, whereas if **reset** is first, the behaviour is undefined.

The problem is that a set of unordered events is being detected by the same object. As a result, the overall specification is ill-formed.

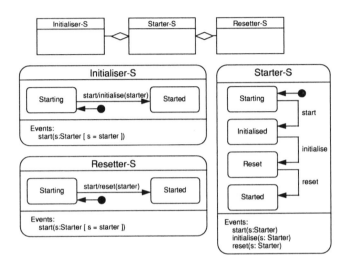

Figure 6.13 *An ill-formed specification*

A slightly more realistic, and more subtle, example is shown in figure 6.14. Here the **refresh** event is detected by all the **Window** objects, every one of which generates an **update** event. This is unproblematic as long as each **update** event is only detected by a single object, for example its own **Window**, as shown in the diagram.

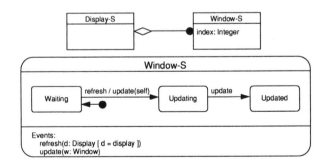

Figure 6.14 *Generating events with no order defined*

However, if the **Display** object were to have the **update** event in its own event list, the order of detection of these events by the **Display** would be undefined. For example, we might encounter something like figure 6.15. If we were to assume that the set of **update** events is actually processed sequentially, this statechart would generate a sequence of **reset** and **initialise** events in an arbitrary order. This would become a problem as soon as a statechart anything like the **Starter** in figure 6.13 were introduced into the system.

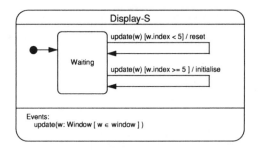

Figure 6.15 *A problematical statechart*

A set of generated events with no well-defined order does not present a problem. What does present a problem is if a single instance is capable of detecting more than one event in this set with different results, as with **Display** in this example. In practice, such situations rarely arise, and they can readily be avoided by using the following rule:

> *Whenever a set of generated events does not have a well-defined order, no instance may detect more than one of this set.*

A set of events without a well-defined order is generated when a single event is detected by several instances, each of which generates one or more events as a result. Once such a set has been generated, its consequences (i.e. events generated as a result of detecting any of the unordered events) remain unordered.

6.8 Summary

- The specification model is a stimulus–response specification of a software system.
- It is useful to think of the agents which interact with the software system.
- A specification model assumes infinite processing and memory resources.
- Specification model type views are very similar to essential model type views, but describe software objects rather than objects in a general situation.

- Specification model events can be detected, generated or internal.
- Events have broadcast semantics to avoid premature commitment to sequencing.
- Event scenarios are useful to describe typical event–response sequences.
- Detected events can be described using pre-conditions and consequences.
- Processing responsibilities should be properly allocated to objects for a robust design.
- Statecharts in the specification model define state changes and events generated when events are detected. *Entry* and *exit* sections can make the statechart more compact.
- The behaviour of the software is undefined for events with no transitions which are not *allowed*.
- Internal events are used to factor the overall effect of detected events.
- Events are partially ordered.
- Events may be both detected and generated by the same object.
- Unordered events may give rise to ill-formed specifications. These may be avoided by not detecting several unordered events in the same object.

6.9 Bibliographic notes

Some of the inspiration for our treatment of events in essential and specification models comes from Tony Hoare's work on Communicating Sequential Processes [Hoare85].

6.10 References

[Hoare85] C.A.R. Hoare. *Communicating Sequential Processes*, Prentice-Hall, Hemel Hempstead, Hertfordshire, 1985.

CHAPTER 7

Describing the implementation

7.1 The implementation model

In the implementation model we examine the flow of control in the software. We are not directly concerned with the way in which events are handled and generated but, instead, we design the message interactions between objects. The implementation model must deal with the 'edges' of the software; the points where the software interacts with its environment. The software must detect stimuli and cause messages to be sent; some messages will cause responses to be generated in the environment. A major concern of the implementation model is the mapping of stimuli to messages and messages to responses. We deal with this subject in chapter 11.

This chapter describes techniques that help to determine the correct sequence of message processing. Messages are not processed instantaneously, so we need to take into account the finite speed of computer hardware when producing an implementation model. To ensure an adequate response to stimuli, we may need to introduce multiple threads of control. This subject is covered in depth in chapter 9.

The implementation model is expressed using concepts that are familiar in object-oriented programming, namely objects and messages, but we are not necessarily assuming implementation in an object-oriented programming language. The abstract model of execution defined by the implementation model can be mapped into any number of different execution environments, although we cheerfully admit that the easiest mapping is to an object-oriented language; anything else is a compromise.

It is perfectly possible to design an entire software system using only the implementation model perspective. One might argue that since the detailed design of object and message interaction is an inevitable part of the development process one might as well do the whole job at that level. For some simple systems this view may be appropriate but we believe the separation of concerns provided by the distinctions between the specification and implementation models is well worth the extra effort in most cases. For that part of the software concerned with implementing the software's model of the world (called the *concept domains*; see chapter 11) we think it nearly always worth the effort.

The implementation model occupies the middle ground between specification and executable code. It shows how inter-object message sequences achieve the desired specification; it does not show the internal details of object implementation. However, the model does allow a complete description of implementation design, at a level of abstraction above that provided by programming languages such as C++ or Smalltalk. We see no reason why implementation models should not be directly executable in the longer term.

7.2 Mechanisms

In the implementation model, objects communicate using *messages*. A message is a point-to-point synchronous communication mechanism. One object, the *sender*, sends a message to another object, the *receiver*, which takes control when it receives the message, processes it and then allows control to return to the sender. Control is relinquished by the sender when the message is sent. The sender must know the identity of the receiver but the receiver does not automatically know the identity of the sender. The message always has a name, the name of the operation to be invoked; it may have parameters and may return a result. The fundamental semantics of a message are the same as those of a procedure call in a conventional programming language; the different terminology is used to show that messages extend the capabilities of procedure calling: the same message can invoke different behaviour in different types of object.

We need to distinguish between messages and *operations*. An operation is a piece of code triggered by a message. Many types may have an operation with the same name and parameter signature defined for them.

We show a message-send using a similar notation to that of model navigation, introduced in chapter 2. To send the message **x** to the object known by the name **a** we write:

a.x

If the message has parameters we show them in parentheses:

a.x(4)

For convenience we can send a set of messages in one statement. If the name **s** represents a set of objects, we can send each object in the set the message **x** by saying:

s.x

One of the most important views of the implementation model is the *mechanism*. A mechanism shows, for a particular arrangement of objects in particular states, the sequence of messages sent when one object receives a particular message. Each mechanism is an example; it shows the single sequence of messages that flow in the particular scenario. It is therefore difficult to use mechanisms to define the behaviour of a system completely because a very large number of mechanism diagrams would be required to represent all possible states of even a moderately complex system. Instead, we identify and construct *key mechanisms*, those which illustrate the most important and significant patterns of message interaction. The way we select key mechanisms is similar to the way we select test cases when testing a software system, or part of one. We choose a few cases that represent general behaviour and then several that explore special behaviour at the limits.

Mechanisms are used to explain or explore the design intention. In many development projects the construction of mechanisms is the primary technique for detailed implementation design. Everything that can be said in a mechanism can be said generically in a statechart and type view, but it is often easier both to create a design and to understand it using mechanisms. Mechanisms can be quite expressive, using their own syntax rules to show the results of computation, but in many cases mechanisms obtain most value when used more informally. Although a mechanism diagram can be checked for consistency against other, more formal views, it need not be fully understandable in isolation. We often describe mechanisms as an informal technique but they do have a well formulated syntax; they are informal in the sense that, as examples, they are only very rarely a complete description of behaviour.

Mechanisms use the basic syntax of object views, introduced in chapter 2. Each mechanism diagram contains the following:

- Two or more rounded-rectangles representing objects in a scenario.
- Lines between objects representing instances of associations (which may be temporary).
- Annotated arrows lying alongside associations representing messages sent using the communication path of the association.
- A single arrow unrelated to any association representing the initial message in the sequence. The sender of this message is unknown. The mechanism ends when control is returned to the sender of this message.

7.2.1 The anatomy of operations

Figure 7.1 shows the specification type view of an example system that monitors the prices of company shares, introduced in chapter 6.

Figure 7.2 shows statecharts for the **Share, Sector, Exchange, Mindable** and **Minder** types. Notice how **priceChange** events are detected by sectors and exchanges as well as shares so that they, too, can generate **priceCheck** events. This allows minders to mind sectors and exchanges. The **priceCheck** events are detected by minders as the trigger to recheck their movement limits[1].

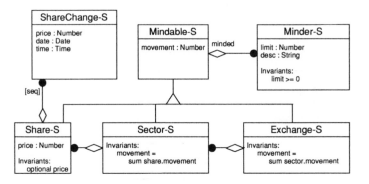

Figure 7.1 *Specification model type view of share system*

We are now going to use mechanisms to explore the implementation design of this system. A mechanism begins with the arrival of a specific message that triggers an operation. We will assume that the externally generated events shown as detected in the specification model become messages in the implementation model, sent to the appropriate concept domain object. This is an over-simplification, as illustrated in chapter 11, but it will suffice for these examples. The processing of **priceChange** messages, corresponding to **priceChange** events, is clearly a key mechanism, and we will focus on it. The **priceChange** message will be sent to a **Share** object; we need to determine the action of a share on its receipt.

In general, we can divide the necessary behaviour of an object on receipt of a state-changing message, such as **priceChange**, into six parts:

1. checking of guard conditions;
2. fulfilment of post-conditions;
3. fulfilment of system invariants (and determination of result, if any);
4. forwarding of the message to other objects;
5. invocation of subsequent behaviour of other objects;
6. return result (if any).

---

[1]The post-condition for the **priceChange** event in the textual part of the **Share** statechart shows the creation of a new **ShareChange** object and its concatenation on to the end of the sequenced association.

The minder could detect the **priceChange** event instead but this would complicate the specification of the minder because it needs to refer to the **movement** property of the object being minded, such as a share. This property is changed by the **priceChange** event and so its new value is not established until after the event.

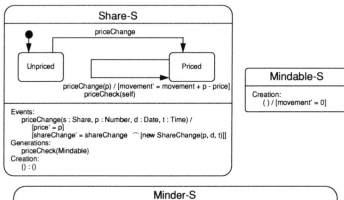

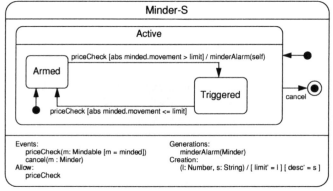

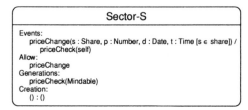

Figure 7.2 *Specification model statecharts for share system*

It is easy to see how these correspond to elements of the specification model:

1. transitions and guards on the statechart;
2. post-conditions on the statechart;
3. invariants on the type view;
4. more than one statechart detecting an event[2];
5. and (6) generated events[3].

This correspondence helps greatly with the construction of implementation models. Sometimes, the correspondence will really be as close as these lists imply, and we will be able to spot it easily. In other cases, the needs of implementation will demand a looser correspondence. These lists are a guide only.

Frequently, the same event is detected when the object is in different states and different things must happen. The question as to whether this is implemented as a single operation that checks the current state or as a family of operations that are selected in some way concerns the implementation of state machines and we will not consider this further at this point. We will assume that the same operation name applies in all cases and the mechanisms we draw will assert particular states and show the behaviour in a scenario where those states exist.

Filters will normally have no direct correspondence in the implementation model; we assume that messages will be sent only to the objects interested in them. This implies that consideration of filters is the responsibility of the client, not the supplier.

Checks that pre-conditions are valid may or may not be implemented as code. Depending on the implementation language, they are more likely to be implemented as assertions.

7.2.2 A simple mechanism

We know, from the specification model post-conditions, that when a **Share** object receives a **priceChange** message it must adjust its **price** and, if in the **Priced** state, its **movement** properties. This is likely to be accomplished by changing the values held in variables – possibly indirectly by invoking private operations – but these internal changes are a private, local matter and exactly how they are performed is not our concern in the implementation model. The main reason for this is that we still wish to be uncommitted to the exact way in which properties are implemented. Our mechanism that describes the processing of **priceChange** messages need not describe these internal changes.

---

[2]When an event is detected in more than one specification model statechart we must choose how to sequence the processing. Message-forwarding is one technique we can use, where the first object to be notified of a stimulus forwards the notification to others. This is discussed in more detail in chapter 11.

[3]We say that returning the result of a message corresponds to a generated event because, in the specification model, internal events are sometimes used to achieve information flow between objects.

We note from the specification model that sectors and exchanges have type invariants which depend on share **movement** properties. The implementation model must decide how to establish these invariants. Our starting point should be the assumption that one object cannot predict the implementation strategy of another, so **Share** objects cannot predict whether sectors intend to implement their **movement** properties as data or functions. This is important because if the sector implements **movement** as data it must adjust the value every time a share changes its price. In our first attempt at this mechanism, shown in figure 7.3, we show the share explicitly notifying the sector that its price has been adjusted.

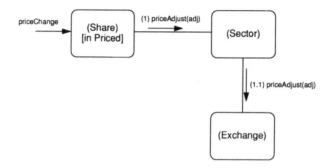

Figure 7.3 *Simple mechanism*

Figure 7.3 shows a scenario involving three objects, a share, a sector and an exchange. In the mechanism we show only those objects in which we are interested: the sector might have more than one share associated with it; either we don't wish to show the effects of those other shares or they don't make any difference to the mechanism. We assert, using a logical constraint, that the share begins the scenario in the **Priced** state. Of course, we know that shares never leave the **Priced** state but we are making the point that constraints shown on mechanisms show the state of the scenario at its commencement. The lines between the share, sector and exchange represent associations that exist between the objects. We can predict that such associations will exist from the specification model; they are confirmed by our need to send messages along them in the mechanism. The message flow is shown in annotations alongside arrows, showing the direction of flow. The annotations begin with a sequence number, showing the order in which the messages flow; the predominantly left-to-right flow is unintentional and has no significance.

The mechanism begins with the arrival of a **priceChange** message at the share. This message has a parameter but we haven't shown it; this is fine provided it is unambiguous. There might be several implementations of **priceChange** for the **Share** type, with different parameter signatures, and this would make the mechanism ambiguous. When we have a more complete implementation model we can compare our mechanism against the type view to check this. The second message is a **priceAdjust** message sent by the share to its sector. This time we have shown the parameter, using the name **adj**. We deduce the meaning of this name by considering the name-space of the sending object. It has no properties or associations called **adj**; therefore, we conclude that **adj** is a variable introduced into the name-space of the receiver (the sector object) for the purposes of this mechanism. The variable has not been bound to any particular value – it should have a value equal to the change in price[4]. The mechanism would be in error if the sector was using the name **adj** for a property or association role. Mechanism variables, like **adj**, have no meaning outside the mechanism.

The sector can do what it will with this **priceAdjust** message; if it is implementing its **movement** property as data it can use the message parameter to recompute it. We must also establish the exchange's invariant in the same manner, either by getting the share to send it a message directly or, as here, by getting the sector to pass on the **priceAdjust** message. This message is the third and final message in the mechanism. The **adj** variable is used by the sector to pass the required adjustment to the exchange[5].

7.2.3 Object creation and variable assignment

The mechanism just discussed is concerned with item 3 in the list above, fulfilment of system invariants. Can we use a mechanism to illustrate item 2, the fulfilment of post-conditions? We have said that we will not consider in mechanisms any internal messages sent (to **self**) for the purpose of modifying properties. But we can, and should, show the creation of new associated objects, such as **ShareChange** objects, indicating the moment of their creation in the message flow. Figure 7.4 shows this.

Now we show the parameters of the **priceChange** message because we wish to reference them in the mechanism. The mechanism shows that the new **ShareChange** object is created before the **priceAdjust** message is sent. We have annotated the arrow with the parameters of the creation operation invoked, using the keyword **new** to show that it is a creation operation. The dashed association line between the **Share** and the **ShareChange** indicates that the association did not exist at the beginning of the mechanism. We have also shown the binding of the **adj** variable, using an assignment expression. These expressions allow us to give a name, for use by the receiver, to an expression written using names taken from the sender, such as **price**.

Expressions in message parameters can contain any names in scope for the sender:

- the names of the sender's properties;
- the role names of the sender's associations;

---

[4] A clever tool should be able to spot unbound variables and warn the designer.

[5] If we knew that sectors and exchanges computed their **movement** properties on demand, rather than holding them as data, we might decide, as an optimisation, not to notify them of price changes. This needs careful consideration because it might affect other parts of the mechanism.

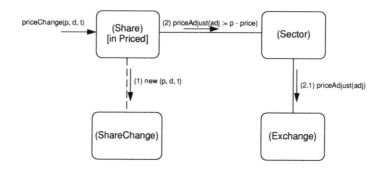

Figure 7.4 *Mechanism with object creation*

- the names of any variables introduced into the sender's name-space during the mechanism up to that point.

In particular, note that they cannot include navigation expressions that represent message-sending; complicated expressions must be broken down into their constituent message-sends.

7.2.4 Forwarding

We note from the specification model that sectors and exchanges also detect **priceChange** events. In our implementation model design, it is the share which is told about this event, by being sent a **priceChange** message. Therefore, the share must forward notification of the event to the sector and the exchange. We can extend our mechanism to show this, as in figure 7.5.

In the specification model, sectors and exchanges have filters to select the relevant **priceChange** events. In the implementation model, the share uses its association link to identify the relevant sector; the sector does the same to identify the relevant exchange.

7.2.5 Subsequent processing

We must now consider how we will implement the generated **priceCheck** events shown in the specification model. The most common implementation is as a single message, sent to the interested object. In this case, there may be more than one minder for each share, sector and exchange (the association from **Mindable** to **Minder** is multiple), so we will need to send a series of messages, one to each minder. A mechanism is an example scenario, so we have to *decide* how many minders there will be in it. We could decide to show none but it would be pointless; that is really what we have done in figure 7.5. We could decide to show a hundred minders for each of the share, sector and exchange but the diagram would be impossibly large and it wouldn't tell us anything more than we could learn by considering just two or three. We could draw a whole family of mechanisms, showing different numbers of minders; this would be appropriate if the behaviour differed depending on their number. In figure 7.6 we have chosen to show two minders for the share, one for the sector and none for the exchange.

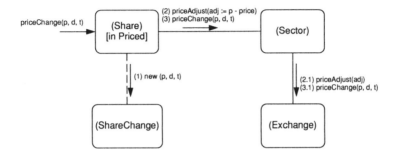

Figure 7.5 *Forwarding notification*

7.2.6 Message ordering

We generally design our implementation so that operations such as **priceChange** carry out their processing in the order of the items in the list shown earlier, on page 155. We can see how the behaviour of the share in figure 7.6 corresponds to items in this list:

1. checking of guard conditions: none (local processing only);
2. fulfilment of post-conditions: creation of new **ShareChange** object;
3. fulfilment of system invariants: **priceAdjust** message sent to the sector;
4. forwarding to other objects: **priceChange** message sent to the sector;
5. invocation of subsequent behaviour: **priceCheck** messages send to minders;
6. return result: not applicable.

Thus, the sending of the **priceCheck** messages by the share to its minders is done after sending the **priceAdjust** and **priceChange** messages[6]. The same logic applies to the sector and the exchange, so they will send **priceCheck** messages to their minders (if they have any) after doing any other processing associated with **priceChange**. The order in which the messages are sent to the minders is quite arbitrary because their

---

[6]At first sight it seems excessive to send two messages to the sector (**priceAdjust** and **priceChange**) when just one would do. The design could be optimised to send just one message but this needs care because, as we will see in chapter 9, the capability of the share to respond to further messages is not the same at the moment it sends **priceAdjust** as it is when it sends **priceChange**.

association with the share forms a set. Since message-sending *is* a serial activity we have to indicate some order[7]. Although we haven't used them in the mechanism, we have given the minders 'names': **m1, m2 and m3**. Of course, objects don't have names, they are distinguished by their identities, but it is often useful to attach these informal names to objects in mechanisms so that they can be used to identify objects as the subjects of message parameters, for example[8].

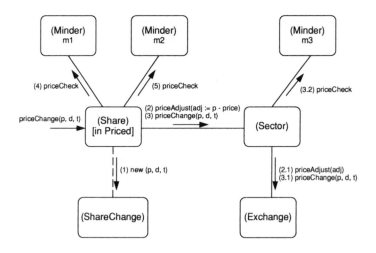

Figure 7.6 *Implementing the generated events*

7.2.7 Partitioning mechanisms

Figure 7.6 is useful and correct even though it doesn't say everything that could be said; in particular, it doesn't show how minders react to **priceCheck** messages. A mechanism doesn't have to show every message sent; a mechanism showing hundreds of message-sends would not be useful. Instead, we break down lengthy sequences into more manageable parts, each part being triggered by one message. This also gives us the flexibility to show variations in the message pattern without reproducing the entire mechanism many times. In figure 7.7 we show two mechanisms in which a minder receives the **priceCheck** message.

In the first (top) mechanism, we assert that the minder is in the **Armed** state and has a **limit** of 10, while the object being minded, shown only as conforming to the **Mindable**

---

[7]This illustrates clearly why we think message-sending is an inappropriate concept for more abstract models, such as specifications and models of the world.

[8]We know they are 'names' because they are not enclosed in square brackets.

type, has a **movement** of 8. Referring back to the specification model statechart for the minder, shown in figure 7.2, we can see that it becomes triggered and generates an alarm event only if the movement exceeds the limit. The implementation of the **priceCheck** operation for the **Minder** type must first check the guard condition, which involves interrogating the minded object to ascertain its **movement** property. This is itself a message-send: we obtain the values of properties (and associations) by sending messages, with the same name as the property, to the relevant object. The message numbered **(1)** in the mechanism is this message. In the first mechanism the conditions for generating an alarm are not met, but the minder doesn't know that until it has found out the **movement** value.

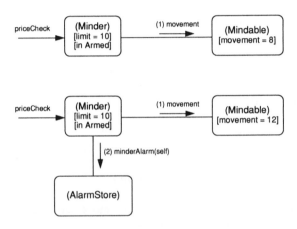

Figure 7.7 *Two scenarios for price checks*

In the second (bottom) mechanism the conditions for generating an alarm are met. 'Generating an alarm' translates into sending a message to another object, in this case an **AlarmStore**. The identity of the minder, written as **self**, is sent as the parameter. By passing the identity of the minder, the **AlarmStore** object has full access to the properties of the minder and, indirectly, its associated objects. Passing the identity of the object rather than specific properties is often preferable in situations like this because it gives the receiver more flexibility; the interface is less likely to require change if the requirements of the **AlarmStore** change. The disadvantage is that it increases the coupling between the two types. Figure 7.8 shows an alternative interface, and also illustrates some other features of mechanisms.

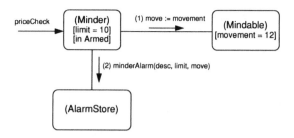

Figure 7.8 *Sending particular information to the alarm store*

7.2.8 Assigning message results

We have already shown variables being assigned to parameter expressions in order to make the parameter available in the name-space of the receiver. In figure 7.8 we are using an assignment to bind the result of a message-send – the **movement** message – to a variable in the name-space of the sender. If the sender has not used that name before, the variable is also introduced[9]. The minder is then using this variable to forward the result of the **movement** message, together with two of its own properties, to the **AlarmStore** object. Note that we cannot write this message-send as:

> minderAlarm(desc, limit, mindable.movement)

because this implies a message-send – the very **movement** message shown in the mechanism. Sending the **minderAlarm** message introduces the names **desc, limit** and **move** into the name-space of the **AlarmStore** object as variables. What we have written is really a shorthand for:

> minderAlarm(desc := desc, limit := limit, move := move)

and the usual rules for name uniqueness apply.

7.2.9 Using associations

Sometimes we use association lines on mechanism diagrams to show structure, rather than paths for messages.

In figure 7.9 we invent a scenario where a share is told to adopt a 'suspended' state by sending it a **suspend** message. It is the duty of the share to inform its exchange that it is suspended but it has no direct association with the exchange. It obtains the

---

[9]Although mechanism variables are not formally declared anywhere, their type can be deduced and, in principle, their use can be checked for consistency.

identity of the exchange by asking the sector, to which it *does* have a direct association. By sending the **exchange** message to the sector the share obtains a temporary association with the exchange, an association that did not exist at the start of the mechanism and one not shown on the type view. It is indicated in the mechanism by a dashed line. The association line between the sector and the exchange is drawn to indicate that the **Exchange** object with which the share has its temporary association is the same object as that known by the sector.

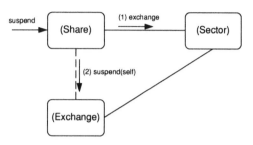

Figure 7.9 *Mechanism with temporary association*

7.2.10 Showing results

For a moment, let us assume that sectors do not hold their **movement** property as data but compute it on demand. Figure 7.10 shows a mechanism where a sector has two associated shares and receives a **movement** message. The results of sending the **movement** messages to the shares are assigned to two variables, in the scope of the sector, called **x** and **y**. The result passed back to the sender of the original **movement** message (message **(1)**) is shown in terms of **x** and **y** by placing an expression after the message name, separated from it by a colon. This expression can use any names in scope for the receiver.

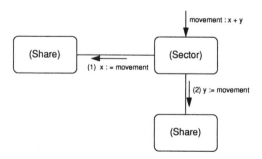

Figure 7.10 *Showing message result*

7.2.11 Message-sequence diagrams

Another way of representing a mechanism is to use a *message-sequence diagram*. In these diagrams, each object in the scenario is represented by a horizontal line, with message-sends being shown by vertical lines and message-processing by horizontal lines[10].

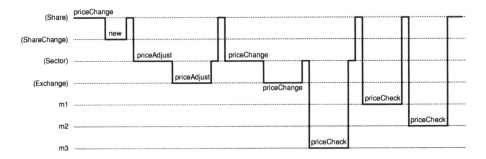

Figure 7.11 *Message-sequence diagram*

Figure 7.11 describes the same mechanism as shown above in figure 7.6. Notice how the objects are identified either by their type or by their 'name'. These diagrams are not quite so expressive because they lack the idea of associations. On the other hand, they do make the message flow and control passing very clear.

Message-sequence diagrams are not usually drawn to any scale – the horizontal axis does not accurately represent time – but they could be used in that way if desired.

Messages sent to **self** appear infrequently in mechanisms because we don't usually show how an object modifies its own state. The most common need to show messages to **self** is when a message implements a generated event that is detected by the same object. Such messages can be shown easily in either the standard or message-sequence form of mechanism diagrams. In the standard, object view form, they are shown using arrows that both leave and enter the same object; in the message-sequence diagram, they are shown by a line slightly displaced from the object's main horizontal line.

7.3 Type views of the implementation model

As with essential and specification models, an implementation model can be expressed through type views that depict object types and their relationships. Type views in the implementation model are similar to those in the specification model. The same general ideas and notations apply but the detailed interpretation is different.

---

[10]Some people prefer to rotate these diagrams, with message-sends being horizontal lines.

7.3.1 Observers and updaters

The most important difference between the specification model and implementation model type views is that the concept of properties, as listed in the lower part of the type box, is replaced by listings of the *observer* and *updater* operations defined for the type.

An observer operation is one which does not change the state of the system in any way, it merely obtains information for the sender. An updater operation can change the state of the object executing it and, indirectly, the state of other objects. We distinguish observers and updaters for two reasons. First, it is updater operations that will take the place of events as the triggers for transitions in statecharts, as we will see shortly. Second, having a clear distinction is a great help in designing multi-threaded systems, as explained in chapter 9. Unlike some authors, we do not require updaters to be procedures rather than functions; that is, we allow updaters to return a result. So an updater with a return type is that much denigrated animal, a function with side-effects. While we accept all the arguments concerning their conceptual impurity, we, along with most people we've met, find them very useful.

Figure 7.12 shows the implementation model type view for the share monitoring system described earlier. Comparing it with the specification model type view shown in figure 7.1, we see that the properties have become observer operations, whereas the updaters reflect events. This correspondence is examined in more detail in chapter 10. Also, note that the suffix -I is appended to the type names to indicate an implementation model.

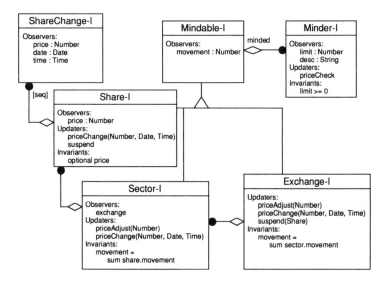

Figure 7.12 *Implementation model type view of the share system*

7.3.2 Observing associations

We assume that an object can navigate all its associations, unless they end with a cross or a question mark. Therefore, an object may use freely, within updaters and observers, the results of navigating such associations.

This does not imply that the results of navigating associations from an object are available to the object's clients, that is, they are not observable by default. If we wish to make an object's association visible to its clients we must include in the type box an observer operation specifically for that purpose. The name of this observer is frequently chosen to be the same as the role name of the association being observed, as with the **exchange** observer of the **Sector** type in figure 7.12.

We can extend the **Sector** type, as in figure 7.13, to define an observer that returns the set of shares in a sector. If we choose the name of the observer to be the same as the role name, as here, we do not need to specify the return type, nor an invariant linking the observer with the association[11]. The return type of the observer operation for an association is determined by the multiplicity constraints. For a single-valued or optional association the return type is the destination object type – for an optional association the result might be **nil**, so the observer has an implicit **optional** invariant. For multiple associations the return type will be a collection (set, sequence or bag) of the destination type.

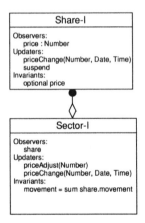

Figure 7.13 *Observing associations*

---

[11]If we had chosen a different name we would need to specify the return type and an invariant, for example:

    Observers:
        theShares : set of Share
    Invariants:
        theShares = share

7.3.3 Navigation expressions and messages

Navigation expressions through the implementation model represent message-sending sequences. For example, given **s : Share**:

> **s.sector.exchange**

means 'send the **sector** message to the share and send the **exchange** message to its result.'

> **s.minder.priceCheck**

means 'send the **minder** message to the share and send the **priceCheck** message to each object in the resulting set, in some undetermined order.' If **s.minder** yielded a sequence, the messages would be sent in the sequence order. All the navigation expressions discussed in earlier chapters can be interpreted in this way. Where no receiver is specified for a message, **self** is assumed.

7.3.4 Super-type name clashes

In chapter 3 we pointed out the possibility that there may be name clashes between super-types. This applies equally to the implementation model, with the further complication that there may be clashes in the names of updater operations as well as observers and role names. As before, we take the simple position that name clashes are not permitted, and the design must be changed to eliminate them. In practice, we need rather more flexibility than that, and we outline possible approaches to this problem in chapter 12.

7.3.5 Structural conformance

The rules for structural conformance between a type and its sub-types given earlier in the book apply equally to the implementation model. The general principle is that an object which sends a message to another object conforming only to the super-type will be able to send the same message to an object conforming to a sub-type and will never be 'surprised' by the result. To be more precise:

1. The sub-type must provide the same observers as the super-type, or a superset thereof.
2. The sub-type must provide the same updaters as the super-type, or a superset thereof.

3. The return type of a sub-type operation must be the same as, or a sub-type of, the return type of the super-type operation[12].
4. The parameter types of a sub-type operation should be the same as the parameter types of the super-type operation[13].

A discussion about behaviour conformance between types in the implementation model appears in chapter 8.

7.3.6 Meaning of invariants

When we place an invariant on a type in an essential or specification model we mean that the invariant holds at all times. This is reasonable because all state changing in these models is considered to be instantaneous. In an implementation model we need to take into account the time taken to process messages. State changing is not instantaneous. Consider the share monitor example used earlier, whose type view is shown in figure 7.12. If we took a snapshot of this system during execution the type invariants of **Sector** and **Exchange** might not hold because one or more share objects might be in the process of changing their prices.

Type invariants in the implementation model can only show intention. If we were to cut off the stream of events being detected by the software system and wait until all the outstanding events had been processed completely, then the type invariants should hold. We cannot expect them to hold at all times during operation.

7.3.7 Visibilities

Mechanisms and, as we will see shortly, statecharts show messages being sent to objects. To send a message to an object we must know its identity. An operation knows the identity of an object to which it wishes to send a message either by:

- being passed the identity as a parameter;
- obtaining it by navigating an association;
- obtaining it as a result from an updater or observer;
- itself creating the object.

---

[12]The principle of *co-variant* result types.

[13]We don't feel so strongly about this rule. Although perfectly type-safe, this rule might be considered overly restrictive. It would be equally type-safe to allow *contra-variant* parameter types, where the parameter type in the sub-type is a super-type of the parameter type in the super-type. In the Eiffel programming language, parameter types can be co-variant but not contra-variant; this might not be theoretically type-safe but is claimed to be more useful in practice. Requiring the types to match exactly at least makes it clear when an operation is being overridden.

If any operation of an object type obtains an identity by navigating an association we say that the association is *visible* in the direction navigated. If we want, we can show this visibility by annotating the type view with an arrowhead on the association.

Figure 7.14 shows a simple mechanism and the related type view. In the mechanism the share object sends a message to a minder using the association called **minder** that exists between them. The share must be navigating this association to find the identity of the minder: it requires visibility of the association. This is shown on the type diagram. What should we infer from the lack of an arrowhead at the other end of the association? It would be wrong to infer that no visibility will exist between minders and mindables. All we can say is that, given the sole mechanism shown in the diagram, visibility is not needed. The lack of an arrowhead means we haven't decided yet.

As we add new mechanisms we can say more about the necessary visibilities. When we extend the mechanism of figure 7.14 we introduce an additional visibility, as shown in figure 7.15.

It is useful to have a clear picture of the necessary visibilities because they influence the implementation techniques considerably. Sometimes we might want to revisit visibility decisions in the light of performance trade-offs or concurrency constraints.

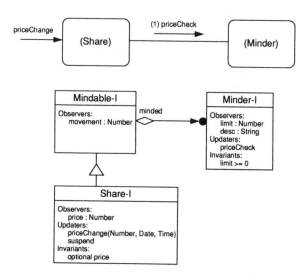

Figure 7.14 *Association visibility*

Having discovered (or defined) the necessary visibilities we must ensure that the creation operations are sufficient to create them. Figure 7.15 tells us that each minder must know the identity of its **minded** object and each mindable must know the identities of its set of minders. This knowledge will not be acquired automatically so

mechanisms must be designed to achieve it.   In figure 7.16 we show a creation
operation for minders with the object to be minded as a parameter and add an updater
to the **Mindable** type to allow a minder to be added to the set.   The mechanism shows
how this works.

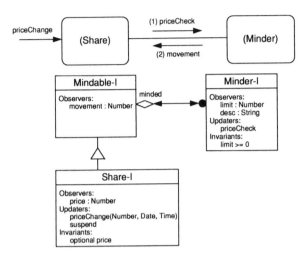

Figure 7.15 *Bi-directional association visibility*

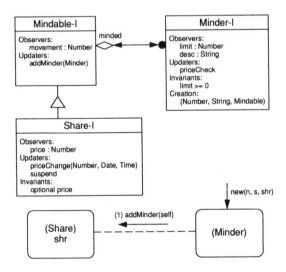

Figure 7.16 *Implementing associations*

It is necessary to consider how each association is to be created, and to add creation operations and other updaters to support their creation. While we recognise this necessity, we don't needlessly complicate our examples by making such considerations in every case. For that reason some of our examples may be incomplete in this respect.

The addition of arrowheads to associations is a useful, but relatively informal, way of annotating design decisions and discoveries. We do not claim that their use is essential; we suggest that it may be helpful. The addition of arrowheads can be treated as an intermediate step towards further refinement of associations: at some stage we may wish to place question marks at the ends of associations with no arrowhead, and then to remove the arrowheads completely.

7.4 State views of the implementation model

The dynamic state behaviour of every object type in an implementation model can be described using a separate statechart. We interpret the absence of a statechart for an object type to mean that all of its operations are valid at all times[14]. Our interpretation of statecharts in the implementation model is very different from that in the specification model.

Transitions in implementation model statecharts are triggered by the arrival of updater messages. An unguarded transition for a message leaving a state means that it is valid for objects of that type to process that message in that state. It is invalid for an object to process a message in a state where there is no transition for the message or the guards on transitions prevent any transition from being taken. As with events in the specification model, the behaviour of an object that attempts to process an invalid message is undefined[15].

It is a design error to construct a statechart that would allow a message to trigger more than one transition.

The messages that trigger transitions will always be updaters because only updaters may change the object. It is assumed that observers are valid in all states but this may be modified using the 'allow' feature, as described later in this chapter.

In figure 7.17 we show an implementation model statechart for the **Share** type used in the earlier examples. We know it is an implementation model statechart because it has **-I** after the type name.

As in the specification model, the share has two states; the **priceChange** message causes a transition between them. Post-conditions are shown in the normal way, but in the implementation model they are specifying the relationships between the results of observer operations, not properties. The term **price** means the value that would have been returned by the **price** observer at the time message-processing began, and the term **price'** means the value that will be returned by the **price** observer after this message has

---

[14]But their instant availability might be limited by concurrency constraints – see chapter 9.

[15]Later in the chapter we will discuss the use of exceptions to signal invalid messages, but this does not alter our fundamental position that the behaviour is undefined.

been processed.   Notice that the textual part of the statechart contains no list of messages being handled. This list already appears in the type view and there is no need to repeat it here.   We only list updaters in the textual part when we wish to add information.

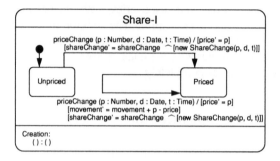

Figure 7.17 *Implementation model statechart*

7.4.1 The processing sequence

As we saw earlier in this chapter, the action of an updater operation can be divided into the following six parts:

1. checking of guard conditions;
2. fulfilment of post-conditions;
3. fulfilment of system invariants (and determination of result, if any);
4. forwarding of the message to other objects;
5. invocation of subsequent behaviour of other objects;
6. return result (if any).

The purpose of the first three parts is to process the message sufficiently to bring the system into a consistent state.   We call the section of the updater that performs these three parts the *secured section*.   The remaining parts of the updater we call the *relaxed section*[16].   Since message-processing is not instantaneous, we need to define exactly when the state change indicated by a transition occurs.   When the operation reaches the end of the secured section the system is in a consistent state; all post-conditions and system invariants will hold.   We define the state change to occur at the end of the secured section. The relaxed section is performed once the object has entered its new state.   To ensure system integrity, it is important that once an object has begun processing an updater, it does not begin processing another message until it has at least entered its new state.   The concurrency rules described in chapter 9 ensure this, and

---

[16]It will become clear why these names have been chosen when you read chapter 9.

guarantee synchronous behaviour of implementation model statecharts, even in the presence of multiple threads of control. They ensure that on object will never begin processing another message while executing a secured section. Therefore, we can validly claim that a state machine can never be processing more than one transition at a time.

Imagine that a share object in the **Unpriced** state receives a **priceChange** message. The object will begin the **priceChange** operation but it is still in the **Unpriced** state. Once it has completed the secured section of the updater it enters the **Priced** state and the relaxed section is executed.

7.4.2 Showing message-sending on statecharts

We can simplify figure 7.17 by factoring-out the common post-conditions and placing them in the textual part of the statechart, under an **Updaters:** heading. Messages appear under this heading only if we want to attach post-conditions or other information to them. We can also show on the statechart more details of the processing of **priceChange** messages, using information taken from the mechanisms designed earlier, such as the one in illustrated figure 7.6. The resulting statechart appears in figure 7.18. Notice how the messages sent in the secured section of an updater appear *before* the post-conditions, while those sent in the relaxed section appear *after* the post-conditions. This reinforces the idea that the purpose of the secured section is to establish a consistent state for the system.

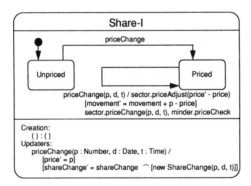

Figure 7.18 *Statechart showing processing details*

Although event generation and message-sending are clearly different, the intention here is to make the overall behaviour of an implementation model statechart comparable to (but not necessarily in direct correspondence with) that of a specification model statechart. The effects of sending messages after the post-conditions mirror that of generating internal events. In both cases the events/messages that are generated/sent can cause further transitions in the same chart.

If a transition shows only message-sends after the slash, with no post-conditions, we assume that all the messages are sent in the secured section, and that there is no relaxed section. Empty brackets can be used to delimit the secured and relaxed sections if there are no post-conditions.

7.4.3 Pre-conditions

Pre-conditions may be shown against updaters in the textual part of the statechart, using the same syntax as for events in the specification model. If an object receives a message and the pre-conditions fail to hold, the behaviour of the object is undefined. Pre-conditions in the implementation model often indicate expectations of objects in other domains.

7.4.4 Guards

As we remarked earlier, it is a design error if a statechart makes it possible for a message to trigger more than one transition. Therefore, the guards on transitions for the same message from the same state must not be constructed so that they could both be true.

There are limits on the expressions that can appear in guards. They cannot use updater operations, only observers. Even so, care must be taken when writing expressions that contain more than one observer on other objects because we do not require guards to be computed atomically; because of concurrency the other objects might change state during guard evaluation.

If all the guard expressions on transitions for a message from a state are false no transition can be taken and the behaviour of the object receiving the message is undefined[17].

7.4.5 Variables

Statechart variables may be declared in the outermost textual part of an implementation model statechart, as with statecharts in other models. In the implementation model, variables can also be declared on a transition, when their scope and life-time is the single transition on which they appear.

---

[17]Unless the message appears in a relevant 'allow' list.

Variables are useful because, uniquely in statecharts, they can be assigned the results of expressions. This commonly arises when the result of one message-send is used as a parameter to several others. For example:

> **var := obj1.getValue,**
> **obj2.setValue(var),**
> **obj3.setValue(var)**

Variables can be used in post-conditions:

> **var := obj1.getValue,**
> **obj2.setValue(var),**
> **obj3.setValue(var)**
> **[v' = var']**

The prime character on **var'** is important. It shows that the result returned by the observer **v** after executing the secured section of the operation to which this fragment relates will be equal to the new value of the variable **var**, that is, the value of **var** at that time. Without the prime character we would be referring to the value **var** had when processing began, which is undefined for variables declared on a transition.

Assignment to *transition* variables can appear anywhere in the transition. Assignment to *statechart* variables cannot be permitted in the relaxed section because the new state of the object must be fully established before leaving the secured section.

7.4.6 Post-conditions

Post-conditions in implementation model statecharts are logical assertions of the state of an object after executing the secured part of an operation. They are not executed, so the idea of sending updater messages or creating objects as part of their expressions seems very strange. Sending updater messages that do not return a result is never permitted, but we often see updaters which do return a result used in post-condition expressions. Given that **setValue** is an updater, what should we make of:

> **[v' = obj.setValue(v)]** ?

We conclude that this is a shorthand for using a transition variable:

> **temp := obj.setValue(v) [v' = temp']**

Things become more complicated when we consider[18]:

>   [v' = obj.setValue(v)] [x' = obj.setValue(v)]

This could mean either:

>   temp := obj.setValue(v)
>   [v' = temp'] [x' = temp']

or:

>   temp1 := obj.setValue(v),
>   temp2 := obj.setValue(v)
>   [v' = temp1'] [x' = temp2']

or even:

>   temp1 := obj.setValue(v),
>   temp2 := obj.setValue(v)
>   [v' = temp2'] [x' = temp1']

These alternatives would give different results if **obj.setValue(v)** gave a different answer each time it was called. Ambiguous constructions such as this are not allowed. If the order matters, it should be stated explicitly. Updaters (and object creations) can be used in post-conditions only if either:

1. there is only one in the expression; or
2. it doesn't matter in which order they are performed.

Since the post-condition:

>   [v' = obj.getValue]

is really equivalent to:

>   temp := obj.setValue(v) [v' = temp']

we must not expect that **v** will be equal to the result of **obj.getValue** from the moment the message establishing the post-condition has finished until another updater changes **v**. Another thread might change the state of **obj** immediately after the **getValue** observer has been called.

---

[18]Bracketed terms in post-conditions are logically 'and'ed together.

Since updaters can return results, we need a way of representing the value to be returned in a post-condition. We represent the returned value using the message name with a prime character appended:

msg / [msg' = 6]

Using the message name *without* a prime character has no meaning.

7.4.7 'Allow'

Often we want to show that messages are valid but don't cause a change in state. One way of doing this is to use self-transitions but a better way is to use the 'allow' feature discussed in earlier chapters. Individual states or entire statecharts may include 'allow' lists in their textual parts to show that the messages listed are always valid in the state where they appear and any nested states. For an 'allow' list in the outermost textual part this means the whole statechart. A message may appear on transitions and in an 'allow' list; where a message is 'allowed' but would also cause a transition the transition is taken. An updater that appears neither in the body of the statechart, nor on an 'allow' list, can never be valid, so we must show updaters that can occur in any state in the outermost 'allow' list.

Even if an 'allowed' message doesn't cause a transition, any message-sends and post-conditions shown in the updaters list in the textual part do apply. The message is *not* being ignored, it just isn't causing a transition.

An 'allow' cannot override pre-conditions. If the pre-conditions do not hold, the object's behaviour is undefined, even if the message is 'allowed'.

Statecharts for the **Sector** and **Exchange** types appear in figure 7.19.

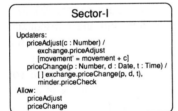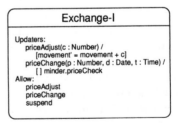

Figure 7.19 *Allowing updaters*

These statecharts have no body parts, so we must show the **priceAdjust, priceChange** and **suspend** updaters in the 'allow' lists. If we did not, they could never happen.

Observers are, by default, assumed to be valid in all states. If an observer is valid in only some states it must be included in an 'allow' list for those states; by showing an observer in an 'allow' list anywhere on the statechart we change its default to be invalid. Restricting the validity of observers is useful when certain properties can be observed only in certain states. In figure 7.20 we have modified the statechart for shares to show that a share's price can only be observed in the **Priced** state.

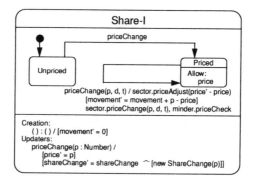

Figure 7.20 *Restricting the availability of observers*

7.4.8 Entry and exit actions

Any state in an implementation model statechart can contain entry and exit actions. These appear in the textual part of the state under the heading **Entry:** or **Exit:** and consist of one or more message-sends. The use of entry and exit actions is a shorthand. Defining an entry action is equivalent to sending the messages at the end of the relaxed section of each incoming transition. Defining an exit action is equivalent to sending the messages at the start of the relaxed section of each outgoing transition.

This seems reasonable enough for entry actions but the consequences for exit actions needs to be considered carefully. Exit actions are not performed until the object *is in the next state*. This seemingly bizarre interpretation makes perfect sense when you consider it logically: exit actions mustn't be performed until you are sure a transition will be taken; by that time the object will be executing in a secured section and you don't want them to be performed in that condition. Therefore, they must wait until the next relaxed opportunity, which is on entry to the new state. This interpretation is also in line with that taken in the specification model.

We can show the use of an entry action on the statechart for the share price minder used in the earlier examples, shown in figure 7.21.

Whenever the minder enters the **Triggered** state it sends a message to the alarm store to post an alarm. Notice in particular what happens if a **priceCheck** message is received in the **Triggered** state and **minded.movement** is greater than **limit**. The message is valid, because of the entry in the 'allow' list, but it does not cause a transition and would not cause either an exit or entry action to be performed. Entry and exit actions are really attached to transitions, not states. Notice also how the creation mechanism has been shown.

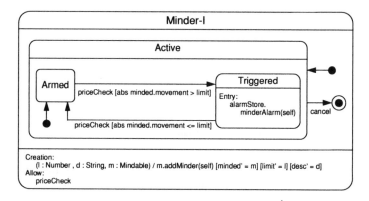

Figure 7.21 *Entry actions*

7.4.9 Combining the textual and body parts

As we have already shown, it is possible to attach post-conditions and other information (but not guards) to messages shown in the **Updaters:** list in the textual part of the statechart at the outermost level. Such lists can only appear at the outermost level. We need to consider the way in which information shown in these lists is combined with other information shown on the transitions themselves. Figure 7.22 shows a stylised statechart with all the possible features that can be combined, together with exit and entry actions.

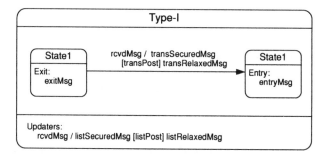

Figure 7.22 *Separate body and textual parts*

The principle of combination is that elements in the list entry take precedence over elements on the transition. The combined equivalent is shown in figure 7.23.

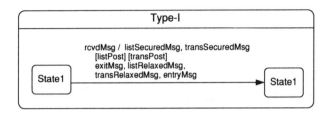

Figure 7.23 *Equivalent combined body*

Although the post-condition from the list has been shown before the post-condition from the transition, this is not meaningful; the post-condition clauses are just 'and'ed together, as usual, and no order of satisfaction is implied.

7.4.10 Finalisation

Implementation model statecharts can have finalisation states. As before, we define an object as having no associations with other objects on entry to its finalisation state but in the implementation model we must ensure this rather than just require it. If other objects are holding the identity of the object being finalised, and are not themselves going to drop its identity, the object being finalised must send the messages necessary to force associations to be broken as part of the secured section of the finalisation transition. These transitions cannot have any relaxed actions.

An object is eligible for destruction when it has no associations with other objects. The exact moment when an object is destroyed will depend on the implementation environment.

7.4.11 Transition decomposition

Note: this section is rather specialised and may be omitted on a first reading.

Earlier we drew a mechanism that showed a **Minder** sending a **minderAlarm** message to an **AlarmStore** object. As you can see from figure 7.24, an alarm store holds a queue of minders with pending alarms. The **minderAlarm** message adds a minder to the queue and the **nextAlarm** message removes one. There is also a **clear** updater which empties the queue. Note also that minders have been given a **priority** property.

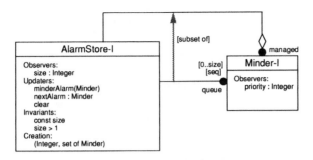

Figure 7.24 *Alarm store*

The statechart for **AlarmStore**, given in figure 7.25, shows how the queue is manipulated.

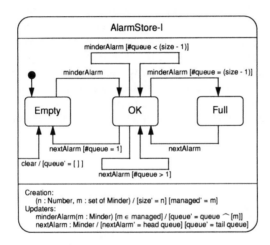

Figure 7.25 *AlarmStore statechart*

Imagine we had an object with an updater called **process** that took an **AlarmStore** as a parameter. This object wishes to move to one of two states depending on the priority of the minder at the head of the alarm store queue. We might try to describe the behaviour of this object with the statechart fragment shown in figure 7.26.

This statechart fragment is incorrect, because we do not allow updaters, such as **nextAlarm**, to be sent in guard expressions. This is because, conceptually, if not actually, all guard expressions for a message are evaluated when the message arrives. Thus, in figure 7.26, **nextAlarm** would be sent twice.

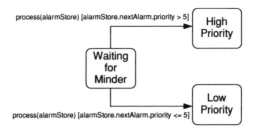

Figure 7.26 *Attempting to send updaters in guards*

Instead, we allow a transition to be decomposed, and to end conditionally at different states. We can replace the two transitions of figure 7.26 with one decomposed transition, as in figure 7.27.

Although there are three arrows, figure 7.27 really contains just one transition, with varying end states. The state **Testing** is not a stable state; it represents an intermediate point in the transition decomposition. When a transition is decomposed, the first arrow will carry the name of the message; subsequent arrows will have no message name but they may have guards, as in figure 7.27. The transition ends when a stable state is reached, such as **HighPriority** or **LowPriority**. An unstable state, such as **Testing**, can have only unnamed arrows leaving it; stable states can never have unnamed arrows leaving them. Names introduced into a decomposed transition, such as the formal parameter name **alarmStore** and the transition variable **theMinder**, are in scope throughout the transition.

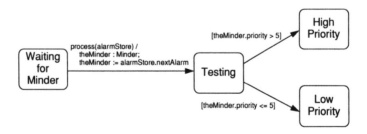

Figure 7.27 *Transition decomposition*

Transition decomposition is essential when, as in this example, we want to select a destination state according to the result of an updater message sent to another object.

We need to consider how, in a complex decomposition, messages sent and post-conditions specified in each part combine to form the behaviour of the entire transition. Consider the transition at the top of figure 7.28. In the transition from **A** to **B**, the secured messages **sec1**, **sec2** and **sec3** are sent, the post-condition **p** is established and the relaxed messages **rel1**, **rel2** and **rel3** are sent.

Now consider the decomposed version of the transition shown in the bottom part of the diagram. We assume that the secured messages are sent at the point where they appear. In a situation like this, where no transition variables are declared, the post-conditions must all hold at the end of the whole transition, so

p1 ∧ p2 ∧ p3 = p

In the usual way, relaxed messages are sent on entry to the new stable state, that is, **B**, *irrespective of where they appear in the decomposition*. However, they are sent in the order described by the decomposition.

Another use for decomposed transitions is when we wish to show repeated behaviour in a loop. In figure 7.29 we show the design of a new updater for alarm stores, called **clearTo**, that takes a minder as a parameter and empties the queue until the specified minder is at the head of the queue.

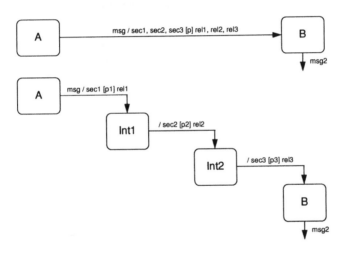

Figure 7.28 *Post-conditions in decomposed transitions*

We saw a similar example to this in chapter 6, where internal events were used to position the magazine of a slide projector. The natural implementation model form of this would be to send messages to **self**; using transition decomposition is an alternative.

Figure 7.29 illustrates a very important point: assignments to transition variables, or, as here, post-conditions that imply changes to transition variables, apply to the arrow on which they appear. So the post-condition on the looping arrow:

[tmpQ' = tail tmpQ]

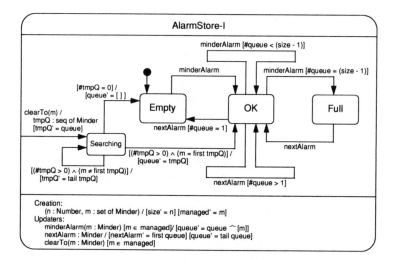

Figure 7.29 *Looping using a decomposed transition*

means 'the value of **tmpQ** at the end of this arrow is equal to the tail of the value of
tmpQ at the beginning of this arrow'. By contrast, post-conditions that mention the
values of observers, associations or statechart variables must hold over the entire
transition. We could not have written, as an alternative:

> **[queue' = tail queue]**

because **queue**' is describing the state of queue at the end of the whole transition.

7.5 Exceptions

Note: this section is rather specialised and may be omitted on a first reading.

Nearly every worthwhile programming language supports exception generation and
handling. Exceptions break the normal call and return behaviour of message-sending
by suspending the flow of control and passing control to a nominated point.
Unfortunately, every programming language has its own way of treating exceptions.
Rather than follow any particular language, we use a simple abstract model of
exceptions that can be mapped into any language which supports them, or, if the
chosen language does not support them, into an equivalent error handling structure.

In our abstract model of exceptions, each possible exception is identified by a
unique textual symbol. Exceptions are raised explicitly by placing the exception name
after the slash on a transition on the statechart. We assume that some exceptions, such

as divide-by-zero, are raised implicitly by the run-time system. Exceptions are handled by adding transitions where the message name is replaced by the exception name.

7.5.1 The 'wrongState' exception

We have said that when an object receives a message and the pre-conditions fail to hold or no transition can be taken (and the message is not 'allowed'), the behaviour of the object is undefined. However, we assume that these situations will be detected in some way, at least whilst the software is executing in development mode, and will cause an exception to be raised, nominally an exception named **wrongState**. But, since this behaviour is not formally mandated – indeed, an object conforming to a sub-type might do something different – it would be incorrect for a client to trap and handle **wrongState** exceptions as a matter of routine.

7.5.2 The exception hierarchy

Exceptions have an implication hierarchy. We can define one exception to imply another; for example:

> **divideByZero** $\Rightarrow$ **numericError**
> **numericError** $\Rightarrow$ **any**

This says that the occurrence of a divide-by-zero exception implies a numeric error, and a numeric error implies the occurrence of a general exception that we have called **any**. Having an implication hierarchy makes it simple to detect a group of related exceptions without having to specify each of them. It is useful to require that all exceptions ultimately imply a general exception, such as **any**, because then we can look for the general exception if we want to detect any sort of exception. We can either specify these implications when we introduce the exception, on a statechart where it is raised or generated, or in a separate formalism.

Although we will not deal with it further here, it is useful for exceptions to be able to pass parameters to the exception handler. The syntax for this is straightforward but we need to consider how parameters match-up in the implication hierarchy.

7.5.3 Exception handling

We will deal with exception handling first. Consider the transition from **Armed** to **Triggered** on the statechart for the **Minder** type shown in figure 7.30. Any number of things could go wrong during this transition but let's just pick two: the sending of the **movement** observer to the minded object might fail, due to some unspecified fault, as might the attempt to notify the alarm store by sending the **minderAlarm** message, due to the alarm store being full.

In the diagram we are detecting the occurrence of any exception while in the **Active** state, and terminating the minder. The entry action, part of the relaxed section, executes in the **Triggered** state where we are detecting the **alarmFull** exception and returning to the **Armed** state so that we can try again on the next price change. If any other exception were to occur while executing the entry action we would detect it and take the **any** transition. When there is a choice of exception transition to take, the most specific exception is handled.

Unhandled exceptions are passed up to the sender of the message being processed at the time of the exception, so that they may detect it if they wish, and so on. For example, exceptions occurring during processing of the **cancel** message are unhandled by minders; they will be passed to the sender of the **cancel** message. Exceptions ultimately unhandled must cause a system failure of some sort, but we do not try to define the consequences.

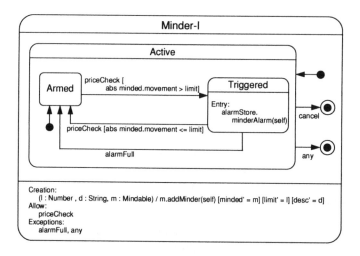

Figure 7.30 *Exception handling*

Complex transitions can be decomposed to allow specific exception handling at various stages. Consider figure 7.31, which shows a fragment from the **Share** statechart. The upper part of the diagram shows the transition as it appears earlier in the chapter. The lower part decomposes the transition to allow specific exceptions to be handled at specific points. For example, exception **ex1** is handled during the sending of the **priceAdjust** message. We have introduced a new stable state, **Int3**, to allow specific handling of **ex3** exceptions during the relaxed section, when the

priceCheck and **priceChange** messages are sent. A new updater, **endPriceChange**, is introduced to allow escape from **Int3**.

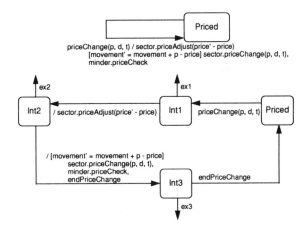

Figure 7.31 *Exception handling in decomposed transitions*

Exception handling transitions, such as those just discussed, may be guarded. If the exception occurs and the guard fails, the exception is passed up the sender stack just as if the transition were not there. These transitions can also have actions and post-conditions. In particular, they can include a post-condition defining the resulting value of an updater.

7.5.4 Raising exceptions

The statechart for **AlarmStore** shown in figure 7.32 has been extended to show how exceptions are raised. It raises the exception **alarmFull** when it tries to process a **minderAlarm** message when the queue is full. *Exception raising transitions* can be guarded but must have only the exception name after the slash. They behave similarly to normal transitions except for the following:

- They must be self-transitions and must not cause a change of state.
- None of the post-conditions, secured actions, relaxed actions, entry actions or exit actions normally associated with the message that caused the exception apply and are not performed.

If an alarm store tries to process a **nextAlarm** message when the queue is empty it will raise a **wrongState** exception. We could have designed it to raise a more specific exception but this brings up the question of what exceptions are for. We believe exceptions should be used only for truly exceptional conditions, not to resolve routine design errors. It seems reasonable to use a specific exception to indicate that the alarm queue is full if, in normal operation, the queue is not intended to become full but if we must take some sensible action in the unlikely event that it does. On the other hand, we should not use a specific exception to indicate that the alarm queue is empty because we don't want clients to use exception generation as a way of simulating a 'queue empty' result from **nextAlarm**. If, as a matter of course, we expect clients to want to be able to send **nextAlarm** when the queue is empty, we should design the message interface to return a result code or **nil**. We have sometimes seen exceptions used to indicate 'end of file' during file reading operations; this is sloppy programming and resembles the discredited use of the **goto** statement.

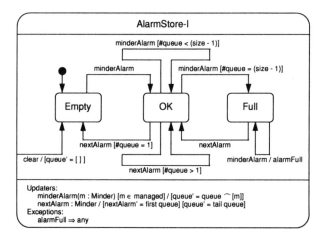

Figure 7.32 *Raising exceptions*

7.5.5 Exceptions and conformance

When building a sub-type of a type that raises exceptions, the following general principles must apply:

1. A message that *does not* cause an exception when sent to an object conforming only to the super-type must not be designed to cause an exception when sent to an object conforming to the sub-type[19].
2. A message that *does* cause an exception when sent to an object conforming only to the super-type need not cause an exception when sent to an object conforming

---

[19]Of course, an exception might still occur, due to some unexpected failure.

to the sub-type, and, if it does, the details of the exception, such as its name, may be different.

Remember that an message processed in the wrong state causes an implicit **wrongState** exception. So, according to principle (2) above, it is valid for a sub-type to show explicit handling of a message which was not handled (that is, was invalid) in the super-type. This is necessary if we are to be able to produce conformant sub-types that extend the capabilities of the super-type in meaningful ways. But it severely limits the usefulness of exceptions to indicate 'routine' errors because the client cannot assume that an exception will be raised by sub-types. For example, we might create a sub-type of **AlarmStore** which ignores **minderAlarm** messages when the queue is full, rather than raising an exception. Given our views on the correct use of exceptions, we do not consider this a serious problem.

7.6 Summary

- The *implementation model* provides a description of the chosen implementation design, and takes into account the limitations imposed by the physical execution environment.
- In the implementation model, objects communicate by sending point-to-point messages, following the model used in object-oriented programming languages.
- Stimuli received from the software's environment trigger message-sending sequences, which may, in turn, generate responses that manifest as events in the environment.
- The most important technique used in the construction of implementation models is the construction of *mechanisms*, which show object interaction message sequences in particular scenarios. Mechanisms are examples, and so cannot be a complete description of system behaviour.
- Messages invoke *operations*, and the organisation of operations can be structured to follow a regular pattern. This pattern is related to the organisation of statechart transitions in the specification model.
- Mechanisms can be broken into segments to avoid repetition of common parts.
- We divide the operations of an object into *observers* and *updaters*. Observers do not change the state of the object (or any part of the system); updaters may change the state of the object.
- Each updater has two parts: the *secured section* comes first and contains that code which establishes the new state of the object and ensures that the system is in a consistent state; the *relaxed section* comes last and contains code which forwards the stimulus to other objects and invokes consequential processing.
- Associations cannot be observed by clients unless specific observer operations are provided.
- The principle of structural conformance applies to the implementation model in the same way as in the specification model.

- Type invariants in the implementation model show intent; because processing is not instantaneous they will not hold at all times.
- Associations can be annotated by arrowheads to show required visibilities.
- Transitions on statecharts in the implementation model are triggered by the arrival of updater messages. If no transition can be taken or the defined pre-conditions do not hold, the behaviour of the object is undefined.
- The syntax of transitions is arranged so that processing in the secured and relaxed sections can be shown separately.
- Statecharts may be extended to show the generation and handling of *exceptions*. The receipt of an invalid message is assumed to cause a *wrongState* exception.

7.7 Bibliographic notes

The inspiration for our work on mechanisms, and the name itself, comes from the work of Grady Booch [Booch91].

The numbering scheme for messages in mechanisms is adopted from Fusion [Colem94]. With Booch's original, simpler, numbering scheme it is impossible in general to determine how far one invocation returns before the next starts.

For information on exceptions in programming languages see [Barne84], [Meyer88] and [Strou91].

7.8 References

[Barne84] J.Barnes. *Programming in Ada*, Addison-Wesley, London, 1984.

[Booch91] G. Booch. *Object Oriented Design With Applications*, Benjamin/Cummings, Redwood City, California, 1991.

[Colem94] D. Coleman, P. Arnold, S. Bodoff, C. Dollin, H. Gilchrist, F. Hayes and P. Jeremaes. *Object-oriented Development: The Fusion method*, Prentice-Hall, Englewood Cliffs, New Jersey, 1994.

[Meyer88] B. Meyer. *Object-oriented Software Construction*, Prentice-Hall, Hemel Hempstead, Hertfordshire, 1988.

[Strou91] B. Stroustrup. *The C++ Programming Language*, 2nd edition, Addison-Wesley, Reading, Massachusetss, 1991.

CHAPTER 8

Sub-types, inheritance and conformance

8.1 Sub-typing and inheritance: what is 'is'?

Claiming that something is something else is a risky business. Some time ago, one of the authors claimed in public that 'there is no doubt that an employee is a person.' After the presentation, one of the audience came up and said 'You know you said that employees can always do what people can do? Well, what about being unemployed?' It was difficult to find a good answer. Clearly, if we say that an employee is a person, we aren't saying that an employee can do or be everything a person can do or be. So what are we saying?

As software practitioners, we are not really interested in the fundamentals of linguistics or metaphysics, fascinating though they may be. Instead, we want a practical and precise interpretation of what it means when we say that one type is a sub-type of another – the relationship often interpreted as 'is-a'. Without such a precise interpretation, we are always at the mercy of disputes about whether a such-and-such is *really* a so-and-so, and our analysis and design sessions are in danger of being bogged down in unresolvable argument.

A diagram which shows one type as a sub-type of another, such as figure 8.1, is making a particular kind of formal statement, depending upon the interpretation – essential, specification or implementation – in use at the time. Ideally, we want to preserve the structure of our type diagram between all three interpretations, because then we can claim to have a seamless development. Hence when we have an 'is-a' relationship in the essential model, we would like the same relationship to apply in the other models as well.

The vital point about an 'is-a' relationship is that it always occurs with respect to a given set of expectations. Whenever I say 'an Employee is a Person', what I really mean is 'with respect to the following set of expectations about Persons: ... anything that is an Employee is a Person.' With this stipulation, we avoid the 'being unemployed' problem simply by leaving the ability to be unemployed out of our set of expectations. In normal conversation, we rarely expect such precision; but when building software, we must insist on it.

So sub-typing is a relationship of *substitutability with respect to a given set of expectations*. The expectations are different depending on the modelling perspective adopted. In the implementation and specification models, we are specifically interested in substitutability of software components during software construction and execution, and we need to define as accurately as we can what the expectations are for this substitutability, and how the substitutability principle corresponds from one model to the other. In the essential model, we are not building software, so some thought is needed about exactly what we want sub-typing to mean; we certainly want to preserve our concept of seamlessness, that is, preserving the structural correspondences between types where possible.

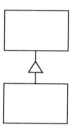

Figure 8.1 *A sub-type*

As we discussed briefly in chapter 1, we often call the set of expectations that a client has of a supplier its *contract*. A contract is a crucial aspect of the design of an object-oriented software system because contracts establish the 'plugs and sockets' which make software component reuse possible. We call the activity of establishing these re-usable interfaces *design by contract*.

Inheritance is not the same as sub-typing. Inheritance is a mechanism adopted by programming notations for sharing descriptions between types. If one type inherits from another, the inheriting type uses, modifies and extends the description of the inherited type. There is no guarantee that inheritance in a particular language or notation will produce a sub-type. In the Smalltalk language, for example, inheritance can be used freely to define classes as arbitrary modifications of other classes, which will not in general be type-conformant except as a result of the programmer's discipline. In C++ and Eiffel, the rules for inheritance are defined to give a certain level of type-conformance, although in each language there are loopholes which allow the creation of classes which inherit from, but do not strictly conform to, their parent classes. The same is true of our modelling notations, although we believe the loopholes are fairly small.

It is important to realise that type-conformance is a theoretical ideal. There are no practically useful programming languages in which the concept of sub-type is defined and enforced with complete accuracy and rigour. In this book, too, our logic simply isn't strong enough to ensure complete substitutability under all conceivable circumstances. The best we can (and do) claim is that our techniques provide a lot more ability to reason about the structure and behaviour of a software system than is provided by programming languages alone, or coupled with informal documentation.

There are three main concepts which must be taken into account when considering the relationships between super-types and sub-types, as follows:

- *Structural conformance*: the structure of the sub-type conforms to the structure of the super-type, as defined by the type view. Structural conformance expresses those aspects of the contract between a supplier and its clients which describe the clients' ability to access the supplier's properties and navigate its associations. The principles of structural conformance apply to implementation, specification and essential models in almost exactly the same way, and have already been described in detail in chapters 2, 3 and 7.
- *Behavioural conformance*: the behaviour of the sub-type conforms to the behaviour of the super-type, as defined by the type's statechart. Behavioural conformance expresses those aspects of the contract between a supplier and its clients which describe the clients' ability to cause the supplier to change state.
- *Inheritance*: the description of the sub-type inherits some or all of the description of the super-type, possibly with additions or modifications.

In this chapter we focus on behavioural type-conformance, and in particular how the statecharts of super-types and sub-types are related in each modelling perspective. We start with specification models, because these establish the principles for behavioural type-conformance in both specification and implementation models. Essential models, being unconcerned with software, have different rules for behavioural type-conformance, which we discuss later.

8.2 Specification model sub-typing

In the specification model, sub-typing describes substitutability of one type of object for another as an *event detector*. Client–supplier relationships are not explicitly expressed, because events are broadcast; nevertheless there are implicit client–supplier relationships between the generators and detectors of events.

So we require that sub-types conform to super-types in the way that they respond to events. More precisely, if an instance of a super-type responds to a particular sequence of events, ending up in a particular state, we would like an instance of any of its sub-types to respond to the same sequence of events and end up in the same state. Note that specification model sub-typing does not mean complete substitutability in a system, only substitutability as an event receiver.

We do not require sub-types to *fail to respond* to event sequences that super-types fail to respond to – in fact, sub-types often define additional behaviour which super-types leave undefined. Neither do we require that events generated by sub-types correspond in any way to those generated by super-types. If we also required these aspects of a type to correspond, we would be left with so little room for manoeuvre that the concept of sub-type would be practically useless.

As a consequence of the above, and as we saw in chapter 6, the interpretation of pre-conditions in the specification model is subtly different from that in the essential model. In the latter, the failure of a pre-condition implies that the event *cannot happen* under these circumstances. In the specification model, the failure of a pre-condition implies that the software's response to the event is *undefined*. There may in fact be a defined response in the ultimate implementation, typically ignoring the event altogether, or generating an error message; the specification model just says nothing about this.

There is a similar difference of interpretation concerning the meaning of absent transitions on statecharts. In the specification model, the absence of a transition means that if the event happens, the behaviour of the software is undefined. This interpretation allows a sub-type to extend the behaviour of a super-type so that the response to an undefined event becomes defined in the sub-type.

A proper discipline for type-conformance is essential to achieve reuse. Within certain limits, discussed later in this chapter, type-conformance means that an object can be guaranteed to satisfy a certain set of expectations without having to belong to a single specific type. As a result we can construct type hierarchies of abstract definitions intended for use in a variety of concrete configurations.

To illustrate the main ideas we use a detailed example from the field of interactive user interfaces, which we build up step-by-step using type-conformance as the 'glue' to fit the steps together. Imagine that the software being specified is a graphical editor for manipulating geometric shapes on a display screen using a pointing device (e.g. a mouse) with a single button. The first step is shown in figure 8.2, which defines two types called **Interactor** and **SelectableShape**. In this example we assume that the co-ordinate system and basic geometric shapes are pre-defined using the value types **Point**, **Line** and **Rectangle** whose specifications can be found in figure 8.4; in several of the diagrams we avoid clutter by not duplicating the details of these value types.

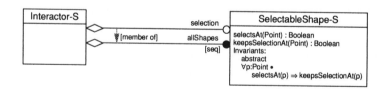

Figure 8.2 *Interactor and SelectableShape*

Interactor is an abstraction for the control of the complete display area in which the shapes are to be manipulated. **SelectableShape** is an abstraction for all selectable shapes. The sequenced association with the role name **allShapes** establishes all of the shapes being manipulated in this area. The sequence of the shapes determines the front-to-back ordering. At most one shape is selected at any time. **SelectableShape** defines two parameterised properties called **selectsAt** and **keepsSelectionAt**. The **selectsAt** property determines whether a shape can be selected at any point. When no shape is selected, by pressing the mouse button at a point, the frontmost shape for which **selectsAt** is true will become selected. The **keepsSelectionAt** property determines whether selection will be retained, that is, if a shape has already been selected then if the button is pressed anywhere where **keepsSelectionAt** is true, the same shape will remain selected.

The idea is that **selectsAt** describes the area of the shape itself, and **keepsSelectionAt** describes the area of the shape plus the additional control handles that it sprouts when it is selected. For example, if **selectsAt** describes a rectangle, as shown on the left in figure 8.3, then **keepsSelectionAt** could describe the rectangle plus control handles at its corners, as shown on the right.

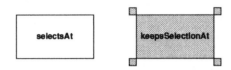

Figure 8.3 *The relationship between **selectsAt** and **keepsSelectionAt***

The invariant within **SelectableShape** specifies that any point which causes **selectAt** to be true also causes **keepsSelectionAt** to be true, that is, the area described by **selectAt** is contained within the area described by **keepsSelectionAt**. At this stage, because the properties have not been specified any further, nothing has been said about the actual shape; below we work through the example in detail for the cases of a line and a rectangle.

Figure 8.5 is the statechart for **Interactor**. It has two orthogonal parts. The right-hand part listens for **mouseDown** events, and if there are any shapes the **select** event is generated with the complete sequence of shapes as a parameter. The left-hand part responds to the resulting **confirmSelect** event and generates events up, **down** and **move** when a shape is selected. Note that the **Interactor** oscillates between **NoSelection** and **Selection** even when the selection doesn't change.

Figure 8.6 is the statechart for **SelectableShape**, and shows how selection and de-selection are controlled. The **select** event is detected by the shape at the head of the sequence. If this is already selected, and **keepsSelectionAt** is true at the selection point, the shape will stay in the selected state and generate the **confirmSelect** event (which is detected by the **Interactor**). If the front shape is not selected, and **selectAt** is true at the selection point, the shape will become selected, and generate the **confirmSelect** event as well as the **deselect** event for all the remaining shapes. The reader is invited to study all the transitions in the diagram in order to understand how it works in detail. One point to note is that the events **down, up** and **move** are all allowed to happen at any time in the **Selected** state. This ability must be retained in any sub-types of **SelectableShape** to ensure conformance.

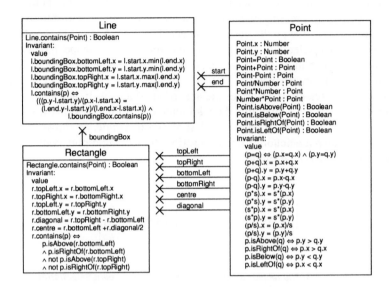

Figure 8.4 *Value types for geometrical shapes*

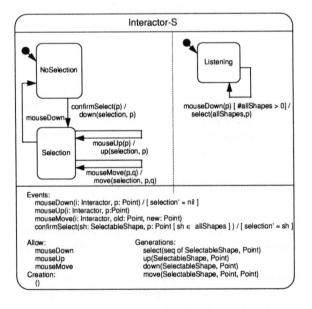

Figure 8.5 *Statechart for **Interactor***

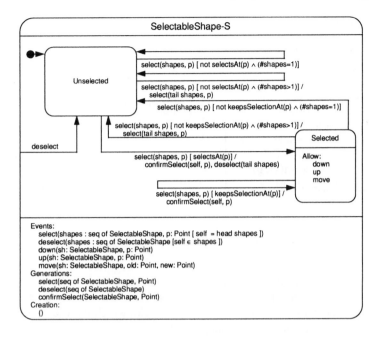

Figure 8.6 *Statechart for **SelectableShape***

We can illustrate the co-operative working of these two statecharts using an event scenario. To make the scenario more expressive, we allow specific objects to be named for each generation and detection shown in the scenario: thus **?i.mouseDown(p)** means 'object i detects the **mouseDown** event with parameter p'. The scenario commences in the object configuration shown in figure 8.7, which shows three **SelectableShape** objects associated with one **Interactor**. The **mouseDown** event parameter **p** is a point such that the following conditions prevail:

s1.keepsSelectionAt(p) = false, s2.keepsSelectionAt(p) = false,
and s3.selectsAt(p) = true.

At the beginning of the scenario, shape **s2** is selected; at the end, **s2** has been de-selected and **s3** selected. Indenting is used to clarify cause and effect: all the generations resulting from detecting a given event are shown indented at the same level as the detected event[1].

---

[1]Note that all the consequences of an event at one level of indentation occur before the next event at that level (in this case **s3.selected** and **s3.deselect**). As we pointed out earlier, the ordering of events is not always totally defined. In cases where orderings are only partially defined, linear event scenarios such as this can only describe relationships between the mutually ordered events.

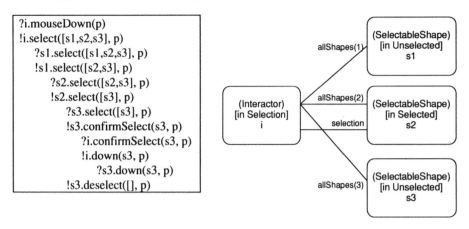

```
?i.mouseDown(p)
!i.select([s1,s2,s3], p)
   ?s1.select([s1,s2,s3], p)
   !s1.select([s2,s3], p)
      ?s2.select([s2,s3], p)
      !s2.select([s3], p)
         ?s3.select([s3], p)
         !s3.confirmSelect(s3, p)
            ?i.confirmSelect(s3, p)
            !i.down(s3, p)
               ?s3.down(s3, p)
               !s3.deselect([], p)
```

Figure 8.7 *One interactor and three shapes*

In figure 8.8 we take the next step by creating an abstract sub-type of **SelectableShape**, called **MovableShape**. Structurally, the only difference between this and its parent is the addition of a property called **origin**, which represents a fixed point which can be used to specify how the shape moves.

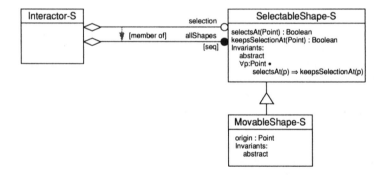

Figure 8.8 *Introducing* **MovableShape**

MovableShape has the statechart shown in figure 8.9. Because this is a specification model, the statechart of the super-type is *inherited*. So **MovableShape** inherits the statechart of **SelectableShape**, and specifies just the differences, which occur in the **Selected** state. The events **up, down** and **move** are still allowed at any time in this state, because the allow is inherited. However, in the **Down** sub-state the **move** event generates a **moveShape** event, which can be detected in the **Down** sub-state and which will cause the shape to be moved, as indicated by the post-condition in the event list. Detecting the **moveShape** event is not allowed in the **Up** sub-state.

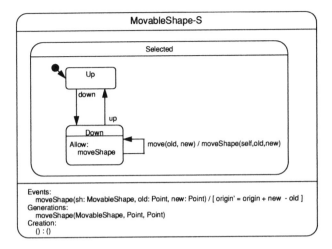

Figure 8.9 *Statechart for* **MovableShape**

You might propose that the same effect could be achieved by putting the post-condition on the **moveShape** event onto the transition for the **move** event in the **Down** state, and forgetting about the **moveShape** event. This would indeed have the same behaviour for the current example. However, it would prevent the behaviour in the **Down** state from being specialised further, to have effects other than moving the shape around. Once we have specified a post-condition for an event in a state, all sub-types must establish the same post-condition for that event in that state: otherwise we cannot ensure that all event sequences will be detected in a conformant way.

Also notice that the event list only contains entries for the new event introduced in this type; the other entries are inherited from the super-type and need not be repeated.

Extending the behaviour of a statechart by introducing nested states into a state defined in the super-type, as in this example, is one of the most common and useful ways of specialising a type.

Figure 8.10 is a composite statechart showing the overall results of the inheritance of **MovableShape** from **SelectableShape**. Notice the following:

- states **Up** and **Down**, shown inside the **Selected** state;
- the total event list built up from the separate event lists;
- the *allow* clause, inside the **Selected** state;
- the super-type statechart becoming a state inside the sub-type statechart;

Of course, one of the main motivations for inheritance is to avoid the necessity of drawing, or even looking at, complex statecharts such as figure 8.10.

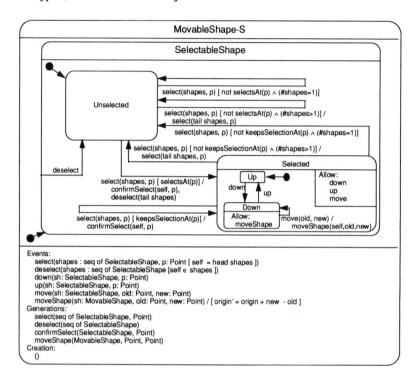

Figure 8.10 *The results of **MovableShape** inheriting **SelectableShape***

Our next refinement is shown in figure 8.11, which defines a further specialisation to **MovableShape**, this time introducing **ResizeableShape**. A **ResizeableShape** has a set of rectangular handles which can be grabbed and used to resize the shape. The invariants on the type diagram specify that the handles are all of the same size and do not overlap, that the **grabsAt** property is defined to be true when its parameter is within one of the handles, and the **keepsSelectionAt** property is only true within the **selectsAt** area or within the grab handles.

Figure 8.12 is the corresponding statechart. It shows how the **Down** state is specialised by sub-states called **Moving** and **Resizing**. The **down** transition is split, using guards, into transitions into the two sub-states. A **move** event in the **Moving** state generates the **moveShape** event, whose effect is inherited from the super-type; a **move** event in the **Resizing** state generates a **resize** event. This event is only allowed in the **Resizing** state, but its effect is not specified because we still do not know what specific shape we are dealing with. Note that we can specify the effects of moving a shape at a considerably more general level of abstraction than we can specify the effects of resizing one.

There is no need to show the **up** transition from the **Down** to the **Up** state, because all transitions not explicitly added or overridden are inherited from the super-type.

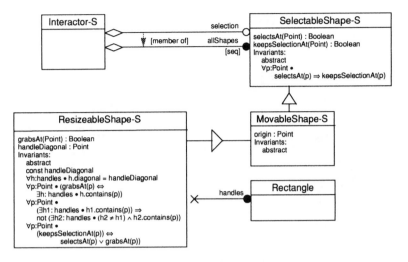

Figure 8.11 *Introducing* ***ResizeableShape***

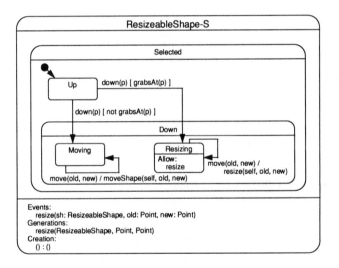

Figure 8.12 *Statechart for* ***ResizeableShape***

Our final step in specialising this specification to describe the behaviour of a particular shape is shown in figure 8.13, which introduces the concrete type **EditableLine** as a further specialisation of **ResizeableShape**. The invariants in this type specify the **origin** and **selectAt** properties in terms of properties of a **Line** value associated with the **EditableLine** object. Note that the handles are carefully arranged so that they cannot overlap, even with a line of zero length. Checking the consistency of the invariants of a type with those of its super-types is an important aspect of ensuring type-conformance.

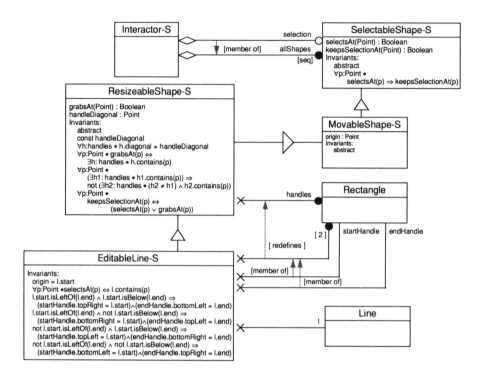

Figure 8.13 *Introducing EditableLine*

The statechart for **EditableLine** in figure 8.14 shows using post-conditions how the resize event causes the ends of the line to follow the mouse.

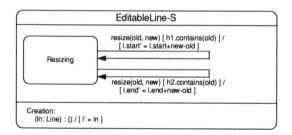

Figure 8.14 *Statechart for EditableLine*

Figures 8.15 and 8.16 show a similar extension of **ResizeableShape** to specify an **EditableRectangle** type.

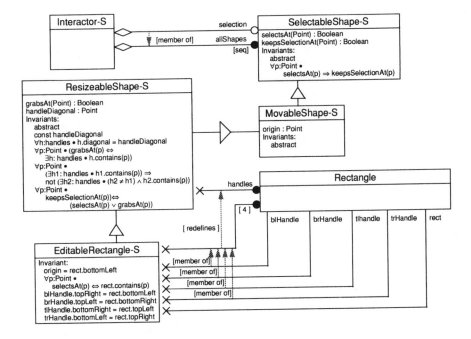

Figure 8.15 *Introducing EditableRectangle*

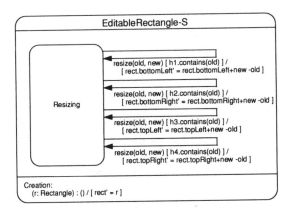

Figure 8.16 *Statechart for EditableRectangle*

8.2.1 Type-conformance rules

Having illustrated the main ideas through an extended example, we present the rules for conformance in the specification model. First remember that all of the rules about structural type extension introduced in chapters 2 and 3 apply to the specification model as well. The rules particular to the specification model are those which define how statecharts can be extended. These rules are designed to make sure (as far as is possible) that a sub-type is behaviourally conformant to its super-types, that is, that every event sequence accepted by an object of a super-type, leaving it in a particular state, will be accepted by an object of the sub-type and leave it in the same state. Another way of thinking about this is that all possible paths around the state space defined by the super-type are preserved in the sub-type. The general principle is that any number of new states and transitions may be added in a sub-type, but all states and transitions in the super-types must be preserved or refined:

1. Whenever a sub-type is defined, the statecharts from the super-types are inherited. This means that, in the absence of any defined extensions, the statechart for the sub-type is an orthogonal combination of statecharts, one for each super-type, each containing a single state with the name of the super-type.

   Each orthogonal section has a separate event list, which is the same as the event list for the corresponding super-type, including allow entries, but excluding creation entries. Creation on the sub-type invokes creation on all of its super-types, as described in chapter 4; creation post-conditions related to a super-type belong to the initial state arrow(s) entering the state representing the super-type in question.

   Figure 8.17 illustrates statechart inheritance for some symbolic types called **A**, **B** and **C**. The statechart called **Resulting C-S** denotes the result of inheriting **A** and **B**, without defining any extensions or refinements in **C**.[2]

2. When we draw a statechart for a sub-type we do not reproduce all of the statecharts for the super-types; we reproduce only the parts needed to define extensions and re-definitions.

3. A statechart for a sub-type which includes only states with different names from the statecharts of the super-types defines an additional orthogonal statechart with a separate event list. This is illustrated by figure 8.18.

4. By naming one or more states with the same names as states in the super-type statechart (including the state representing the super-type itself), we indicate that the definitions of the states are being extended. Super-type states which appear on the sub-type statechart are called *extended states*. The sub-type can embellish

---

[2] Note that all the principles of inheritance apply even if A and B are themselves non-disjoint sub-types of a common super-type.

the extended states by adding new transitions and states, redefining existing transitions and adding new nested states or concurrent machines within the extended states. The target of initial state arrows cannot be changed. All states and transitions not shown or overridden in the sub-type statechart, and the event list, are inherited. Extension is illustrated by figure 8.19, in which the extended state **b1** is embellished in several ways, while the state **b2** and the original transitions are inherited.

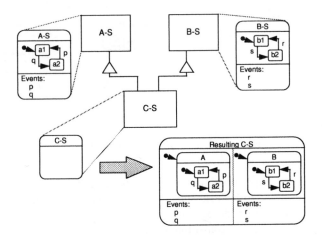

Figure 8.17 *Inheritance with no extension*

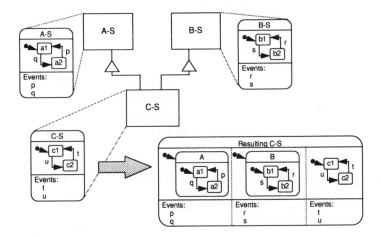

Figure 8.18 *Inheritance with orthogonal extension*

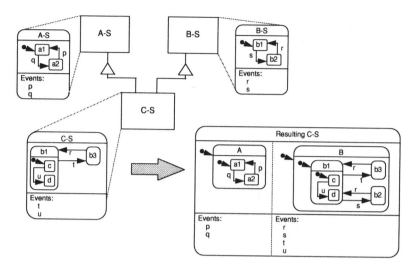

Figure 8.19 *Inheritance with embellishments*

5. An event with a pre-condition or incomplete guards (i.e. a set of guarded transitions with guards whose sum is not *true*) may be refined in a sub-type by weakening the pre-condition or guards, that is, by broadening the set of conditions under which a transition will be taken.

6. Transitions can be refined in a sub-type by *re-targeting* and by *splitting*. A re-targeted transition is one which is refined to enter a new sub-state of its original target state. This is shown in figure 8.20, in which the transition labelled **r** from **b2** to **b1** is re-targeted to the state **d** in the type **C**. Note that the transition labelled **s** from **b1** to **b2** is still inherited.

   A transition is split by dividing it into two or more transitions which take place under different circumstances, where the combination of the circumstances is equivalent to the circumstances for which the original transition was defined. Figure 8.21 shows two kinds of transition splitting: *target-splitting* (splitting by guards) and *source-splitting* (splitting by states). Target-splitting is illustrated by the transition labelled **r** from **b2** to **b1**, which is split into two transitions guarded on the value of the property **x**. When this kind of splitting is done, the logical 'or' of the guards on the split transition must be equivalent to the guard on the original transition (i.e. true in the example), and all of the new transitions must target either the original target or one of its sub-states.

   Source-splitting is illustrated by the transition labelled **s** from **b1** to **b2**, which is split into two transitions from the sub-states of **b1**. When this kind of splitting is done, there must be a transition with the same guard as the original from every sub-state of the original source state. The purpose of this kind of splitting is to be able to generate different events (and possibly different post-condition extensions) on the new transitions.

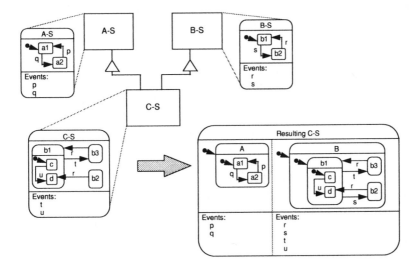

Figure 8.20 *Re-targeting*

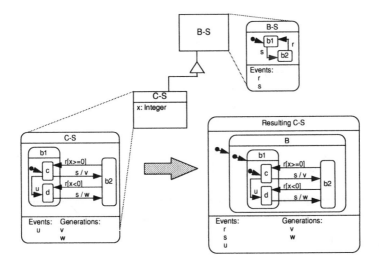

Figure 8.21 *Splitting*

7. Transitions can also be refined by tightening their post-conditions, that is, by adding more terms to the post-condition which are logically 'and'ed with the post-condition in the super-type. Only the new post-conditions need be stated in the sub-type. If a transition is split, the inherited post-condition applies to all the resultant transitions, which may separately tighten the post-condition.

State invariants can be tightened in sub-types by adding more terms. Only the new terms need be stated. Most often this is done by introducing invariants into nested states introduced in the sub-type.

The invariant in a state must be consistent with the guards and post-conditions on all of the incoming transitions; that is, there may not be any incoming transitions whose post-conditions (including post-conditions specified in the event list) do not logically imply the state invariant, assuming their guards to be true.

8. Normally, post-conditions in event lists are inherited. They may be refined by tightening, in which case the inherited post-conditions need not be re-stated, and the new post-conditions are logically 'anded' with the inherited ones.

However, if any new transitions are defined in a sub-type for events which have a post-condition in the super-type event list, the post-condition is not inherited[3]. In this case the sub-type statechart must show explicit post-conditions for all of the transitions defined for this event in the super-type; it may have additional transitions for the same event to which the post-condition in the super-type's event list does not apply.

Event list filters for refined transitions cannot be changed, and must be re-stated exactly as in the super-type.

9. If no generations are specified in the sub-type for an explicitly described transition, the generations specified in the super-type are inherited. However, any transition may be overridden in a sub-type to generate different events from those generated in the super-type. If generations are explicitly shown in the sub-type, the super-type generations are not inherited. The super-type generations may be invoked with the keyword **super** if required.

10. All the entry and exit generations shown on the super-type statechart apply automatically to the sub-type, without needing to be restated. If they are restated, they are being redefined, in which case the principles of rule 9 apply.

For an example of the application of rule 10, consider the type diagram shown in figure 8.22, which shows an extension to the **Minder** type introduced in chapter 6. The **UrgentMinder** type describes objects which will keep generating alarms while the minded object is outside its limit.

---

[3]Because there is no reason why it should apply to the new transitions.

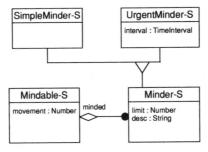

Figure 8.22 *Type view for* **UrgentMinder**

The statechart for **UrgentMinder** is shown in figure 8.23. It illustrates the extension of the state **Triggered** with a new nested state, and the overriding of the entry and exit generations, using **super** to refer to the generations in the super-type.

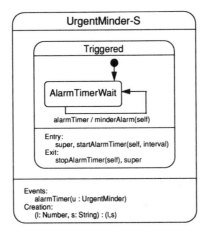

Figure 8.23 *Illustrating rule 10*

11. *Allowed* events are inherited. Allowed events may be overridden by explicitly defined events, which may be guarded and may introduce post-conditions and generations. There are several examples in the shape editing system, for example the **up, down** and **move** events which are allowed in figure 8.6 and overridden in figure 8.9.

12. Finalisation states are not true states for the purposes of inheritance. Any transitions which end in a finalisation state in a super-type can be re-targeted by

the sub-type to end at any state. The post-conditions of the original transition will be inherited, and must be consistent with the new target.

13. The above rules constrain the state structure of sub-types to match that of their super-types very closely. Whenever state types are shown explicitly on the type view in the specification model, they must exhibit the same structure as the corresponding statechart.

8.2.2 Conformance is an ideal

The set of rules given above will usually ensure that an object of a sub-type may be substituted for an object of a super-type, in the sense that it will respond to the same sequences of events. However, there are some situations in which the rules break down.

1. **Behaviour which updates restricted properties**. By far the most important kind of conformance breakdown may occur when a property or association is over-ridden to restrict its range of values in a sub-type. Consider the simple situation illustrated in figure 8.24, where a type **X** with an integer property **i** is extended by a type **LimitedX** with an invariant limiting the value of **i**.

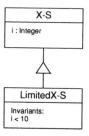

Figure 8.24 *Restricting a property*

Now consider the statechart for **X** shown in figure 8.25, in which repeated detection of the event **increase** will violate the invariant in the sub-type. This problem is readily detected; how may it be solved?

We avoid the problem by using a different strategy in designing **X**. Instead of responding to **increase** by always increasing **i**, the type is designed so that the detected event is a *request* to increase **i**, which may be *ignored* by the detecting object. Figure 8.26 shows the preferred statechart for **X**.

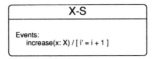

Figure 8.25 *A dangerous statechart*

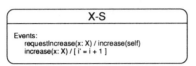

Figure 8.26 *A safer statechart*

With this statechart for **X**, the **LimitedX** sub-type can readily design a behaviour for the event **requestIncrease** such as that shown in figure 8.27, which is conformant with respect to this event and which also respects the constraint on the property **i**.

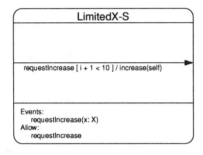

Figure 8.27 *A statechart which conforms to the safer statechart*

In fact we used exactly this strategy earlier when designing the behaviour for the event **move** in figure 8.9. This particular strategy is very common, both in specification and implementation models, in designing types for flexible extension.

2. **Self-detected events**. But what about the event **increase** in figure 8.27? Although we have solved the problem for **requestIncrease, increase** itself remains a problem because it could still be generated too many times by another object.

   In fact, when a statechart defines the generation of events which are detected by the same object, as in many examples in this chapter, the conformance rules fail for the self-detected events. However, when defining a sub-type under these circumstances, if the relationship between the generation and detection of the self-detected events is left undisturbed, conformance still applies for the other events.

3. **Behaviour dependent on properties of other objects**. A transition may be guarded by an expression which refers to one or more properties of another object. A simple example is shown in figure 8.28 (repeated from chapter 6), where the guard **[abs minded.movement > limit]** refers to the **movement** property of the object called **minded**.

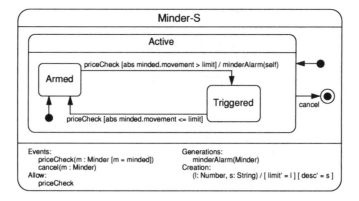

Figure 8.28 *Guards referring to other objects*

In such a case, the overall behaviour of the object given a particular sequence of events depends to some extent upon the behaviour of the other object. When a sub-type is created, the association named in the guard (**minded** in the example) could be over-ridden to refer to another object with different behaviour, thus affecting the overall response to certain sequences. Such over-riding should be avoided.

8.3 Implementation model sub-typing

In the implementation model, the sub-typing principle deals with substitutability of an object in the client–supplier relationship as a receiver of messages.

As discussed in chapter 7, structural conformance in the implementation model follows the same rules as the other models, except that the rules are interpreted in terms of reception of messages.

The rules for behavioural conformance in the implementation model are the same as the corresponding rules in the specification model set out in the preceding section, again except that the rules are interpreted in terms of message reception rather than event detection.

As with the specification model, the principle of client–supplier substitutability is strictly limited. Because one type conforms to another in the client–supplier relationship, it certainly does not follow that instances of the conforming type can be substituted successfully in a complete software system. Type-conformance says nothing at all about the messages sent by instances of a type. If we were to insist that type-conformance included a complete specification of the messages sent by instances of a type, and thus ensure total substitutability within a complete software system, we would have such a strong definition of sub-type as to be almost useless in practice.

Most object-oriented programming languages' definitions of sub-type are purely structural, based solely on the static properties of types, that is, if an operation exists in a super-type, the existence of a corresponding operation in a sub-type is sufficient to ensure conformance. Our definition is considerably stronger, because we also require that the state structure conforms, that is, that all sequences of messages accepted by the super-type will be accepted by the sub-type and leave it in a corresponding state. In our experience, designing this level of conformance is an excellent discipline for implementing reliable software.

Note that even in programming languages which offer no support for reasoning about the state structure of a type (such as C++), it is still essential for instances of a sub-type to respond to all sequences of messages (member function calls) accepted by a super-type, otherwise the program will fail. Using our techniques the designer can reason *explicitly* about the necessary properties of the client–server sub-type relationship.

The Eiffel language provides some support for documenting and reasoning about the state structure of a type, using pre- and post-conditions. There is a correspondence between pre- and post-conditions and state structure: the pre-condition for an operation describes the set of states in which invocation of that operation is valid, and the post-condition describes the state of the object resulting from the invocation. In Eiffel, type-conformance for assertions on an operation is formulated according to the following rules:

- Pre-conditions may be weakened (i.e. the sub-type may respond to a message in more states than the super-type).
- Post-conditions may be strengthened (i.e. the sub-type promises to ensure the same results as the super-type, and possibly more).

The statechart formalism allows us to say more than this about the logic of type-conformance. Weakening pre-conditions is equivalent to providing more transitions for a given message, or weakening guards on existing transitions, provided all existing transitions are preserved. Strengthening post-conditions on existing transitions is equivalent to promising to ensure the same result as the super-type, given the client's expectations. New transitions for an operation can have any post-conditions they like, provided they are consistent with the type's invariants, since these transitions do not form any part of a client's expectations about the super-type.

8.3.1 Sub-type statecharts

When we define a sub-type in the implementation model it inherits the statecharts of its super-types, in the same way as it does in the specification model. New orthogonal state machines may be added, and inherited machines may be refined.

The basic principles of sub-type conformance and the consequential rules for statechart composition described in detail in the preceding section for the specification model apply almost unchanged in the implementation model, and we will not repeat them here. However, there are a few differences to be noted.

As in the specification model, the statecharts of super-types become states inside orthogonal state machines in the sub-type. Since orthogonal machines in implementation model statecharts must partition the updater operations, it follows that no two super-types may have an updater with the same name.

Implementation model statecharts do not have event lists or generation lists, but the rules concerning the contents of event lists (pre- and post-conditions) apply equally to updater lists, and the rules about event generation apply to message generation.

8.4 Essential model sub-typing

The essential model describes the states of a system in terms of its structure, and possible changes in the system's state in terms of possible sequences of events. A sequence of events is accepted by an essential model if it is accepted by all of the model's state machines; otherwise it is rejected.

Structural type-conformance in the essential model is simple and helpful, and encourages seamless development. Clearly, structural type-conformance in the essential model can map very straightforwardly into the specification and implementation models, because the rules for all three interpretations are effectively the same. What about behavioural conformance?

In the essential model, the set of expectations to which a sub-type would intuitively conform behaviourally would be the set of sequences accepted and rejected by the super-type. For example, if a **Switch** accepts the sequence **<on,off,on,off, ...>**, we might expect a sub-type of **Switch** to accept some other events as well, for example **<on,off, count, on, off, count, ...>**, but we probably would not regard something that accepted **<on,on,on,on, ...>** as a **Switch**. Here is a considerable difference between things in the world and objects in the software, because our definition of sub-typing in software would certainly allow us to have a **Switch** component able to accept an infinite sequence of **on** events (and presumably ignore all but the first).

We might have proposed a theory of type-conformance for essential models based on the idea of keeping the set of sequences over the same event types fixed, but allowing the introduction of new event types. However, for reasons too complex to go into here, this proposal turns out to have theoretical problems. More importantly, we don't think that much would be gained by enforcing this kind of conformance in essential models. So our conclusion is that essential model conformance is simply structural. The consequence of this conclusion for statecharts is that we need only ensure that a sub-type has a state *structure* conformant with its super-types; there is no need for event lists or transitions to match in any way. An object of the sub-type may be interested in different events from its super-types, and is free to move between its states in any way its wishes, possibly in a way totally different from its super-types.

We complete our story on type-conformance in essential models (1) by showing how state-types are inherited, and (2) by describing the relationships between sub-type and super-type statecharts.

8.4.1 Inheritance of state types

Imagine we drew state types for **Bottle**, as in figure 8.29.

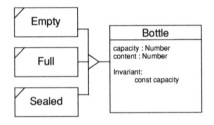

Figure 8.29 *State types for Bottle*

We must consider how to treat those state types when there are sub-types of **Bottle**. In figure 8.30 we show a sub-type of **Bottle**, called **PressureBottle**, which introduces new states. Because none of the states of **PressureBottle** have the same name as states of **Bottle** they are independent, or *orthogonal*, and **PressureBottle** inherits the states of **Bottle**. That is, a **PressureBottle** object can be in any one state taken from **Bottle** and simultaneously in any one state taken from **PressureBottle**. Orthogonal states were described in detail in chapter 5.

In figure 8.31 the states of **PressureBottle** have the same names as the states of **Bottle**, and therefore replace, or override, the inherited states. This is permitted provided the structural relationships between the states are the same in the sub-type as in the super-type. Here, the three states of **Bottle** are mutually exclusive; they remain mutually exclusive in the sub-type, although new states have been inserted. Therefore, **PressureBottle** is structurally conformant with **Bottle,** as it must be.

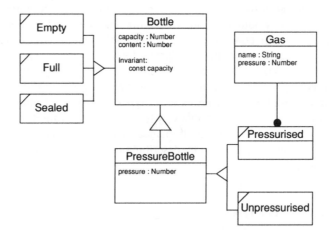

Figure 8.30 *Orthogonal states in sub-type*

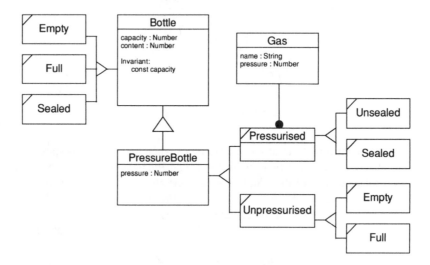

Figure 8.31 *Overridden states*

In figure 8.32 not all the **Bottle** states have been overridden in the sub-type. Therefore, the non-overridden states, the state **Sealed** in this example, are inherited in the simplest way possible that maintains structural conformance. The effective position of the **Sealed** state is shown by the grey box.

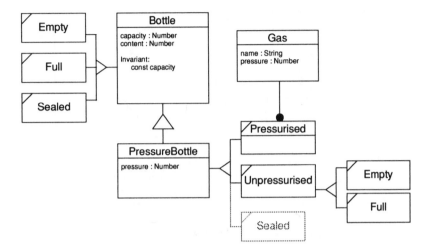

Figure 8.32 *Partial inheritance*

8.4.2 Sub-type statecharts

Consider again figure 8.30, which shows a type view of a situation involving bottles and, as a specialisation, pressurised bottles, which add additional properties and associations. The states of **PressureBottle** are orthogonal to those of **Bottle**, implying separate state machines. The state machine for **Bottle** appears as figure 8.33.

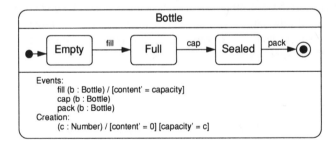

Figure 8.33 **Bottle** *statechart for* **PressureBottle** *example*

The simplest situation is where **PressureBottle** wishes to use the state-changing behaviour of **Bottle** without modification; this occurs frequently when sub-types introduce only orthogonal states. Rather than reproducing the statechart for **Bottle** in the statechart for **PressureBottle**, we can just include it, as in figure 8.34.

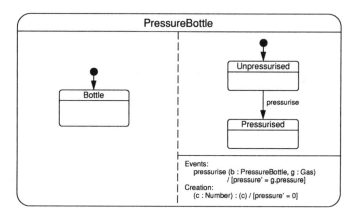

Figure 8.34 *Simple **PressureBottle** statechart*

The state named **Bottle** represents the entire statechart of that type, in line with the idea that a statechart can be used as a state[4]. Since the **Bottle** statechart includes its own event list, this **PressureBottle** statechart has two independent units. As a shorthand, we might omit the left-hand side of the statechart altogether, since it is implied by the type view[5]. If we now modify the type view to make **Unpressurised** and **Pressurised** states that enclose the super-type states, as in figure 8.35, we must modify the statechart[6].

Now we cannot simply include the **Bottle** statechart; it has been superseded by that of **PressureBottle**, which must include all details. The new statechart is shown in figure 8.36[7].

To summarise, in the essential model our options for sub-type statecharts are either explicitly to include the super-type statechart unchanged or to replace it with a full description of states and transitions, ensuring that the state structure remains conformant with the super-type.

---

[4]Note that the creation operation of **Bottle** is not included in the **PressureBottle** statechart by using this notation.

[5]This is largely a tool issue.

[6]This rearrangement of states is still structurally conformant because the super-type states are still mutually exclusive.

[7]Notice that, even though this statechart is completely separate from that defined for **Bottle**, we do not need to show all the creation post-conditions. The forwarding of creation parameters to the super-type indicates that the post-conditions of the **Bottle** creation operation apply.

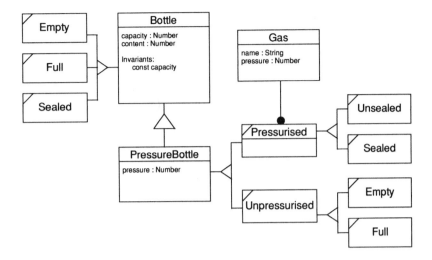

Figure 8.35 *Extended type view*

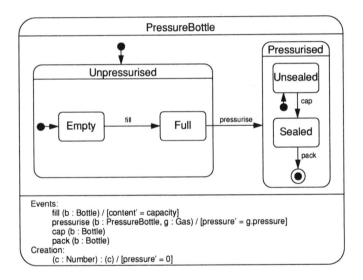

Figure 8.36 *PressureBottle statechart*

8.5 Summary

- The sub-typing relationship is relative to a given set of expectations.
- This set of expectations is called a contract.
- Inheritance is not sub-typing.
- Type-conformance is a theoretical ideal, which cannot be completely satisfied in practice.
- There are three aspects of sub-typing: structural type-conformance, behavioural type-conformance, and inheritance.
- In the specification model, type-conformance is both structural and behavioural.
- Specification model sub-typing means substitutability of components as event detectors.
- Absent transitions and pre-condition failure mean behaviour is undefined in the specification model.
- The structure of statecharts is inherited in sub-types.
- New states and transitions may be added in sub-types, and existing transitions redefined, according to rules which preserve the response to sequences of events.
- Conformance rules may break down under certain circumstances.
- The request technique may be used to design types which may be extended more flexibly.
- In the implementation model, type-conformance is both structural and behavioural.
- Implementation model sub-typing means substitutability of components as message receivers.
- The notations here can say more about sub-type relationships than popular programming languages.
- The rules for statechart inheritance for the implementation model follow the specification model very closely.
- Essential model sub-typing is only structural.
- The statechart of an essential model sub-type must conform to the statecharts of its super-types by preserving their state structure. It need not conform in terms of events or transitions.

8.6 Bibliographic notes

Good discussions about type-conformance can be found in the literature about the Eiffel programming language, notably [Meyer88] and [Meyer92]. There have been many research papers written about the semantics of data types with particular reference to sub-types and polymorphism; [Carde84] is among the most influential of these. A more general and somewhat more accessible treatment of the theory of data types can be found in [Carde85]. An interesting discussion of extension and restriction in sub-types can be found in chapter 4 of [Rumba91].

8.7 References

[Carde84] L. Cardelli. A semantics of multiple inheritance. *Semantics of Data Types*, pp 51–68. Lecture Notes in Computer Science no. 173, Springer-Verlag, 1984.

[Carde85] L. Cardelli and P. Wegner. On understanding types, data abstraction and polymorphism. *ACM Computing Surveys* 17(4), 1985.

[Meyer88] B. Meyer. *Object-oriented Software Construction*, Prentice-Hall, Hemel Hempstead, Hertfordshire, 1988.

[Meyer92] B. Meyer. Applying 'Design by Contract'. *IEEE Computer*, 25(10): 40–51, 1992.

[Rumba91] J. Rumbaugh, M. Blaha, W. Premerlani, F. Eddy and W. Lorensen. *Object-Oriented Modeling and Design*, Prentice-Hall, Englewood Cliffs, New Jersey, 1991.

CHAPTER 9

Concurrency

9.1 Threads of control

The implementation model must take account of the finite speed of the computer. Unlike events, messages cannot be considered to be instantaneous. Real-world occurrences won't wait for the software to be ready; the software must be able to detect stimuli at the rate they occur and must have policies to decide how to sequence the processing. This involves understanding and solving the problems inherent in the design of concurrent, multi-threaded software.

Concurrency occurs when there is more than one thread of control executing through the software. Unless the computer has more than one processor, we should more correctly refer to this phenomenon as pseudo-concurrency, or multi-programming. In a pseudo-concurrent environment, the language run-time system or the operating system will decide when to stop executing one thread and begin executing another. It is very likely that even if the computer has more than one processor, the allocation of work to the processors will be outside the control of the software designer and programmer. In some environments, threads can relinquish the processor only at specific points in their execution, typically when they access system resources (co-operative multi-tasking); in others, a thread's execution may be interrupted at any point (pre-emptive multi-tasking).

Concurrency is required in any software system which needs to begin processing a stimulus before having finished processing the preceding one(s). The techniques associated with concurrency are also extremely useful when the system needs to be ready to react to one of a number of stimuli coming from different sources, because each source can be considered as a different thread and dealt with independently. Systems with this architecture are called *event driven*. Concurrency is not always required in event-driven systems; it may be that each stimulus can be processed completely before processing of the next begins.

Popular belief is that concurrency is of concern only to people who design systems software or real-time systems – such as operating systems, signal switching or process control applications – and of no concern at all to those who design business and information systems. This may have been true in the past but it is certainly untrue now. The days when all business applications were data transducers, reading an input file and producing an output file, are over. Today, a typical business application might have an event-driven graphical user-interface, data feeds over communication lines coming from several sources and shared access to a multi-user database. Developing these systems demands knowledge about concurrency and the techniques needed to control it.

A thread of control is defined by its execution context. An execution context defines a thread's current point of execution and, for object-oriented programs, the message-sending sequence by which it reached that point (often called its *stack*).

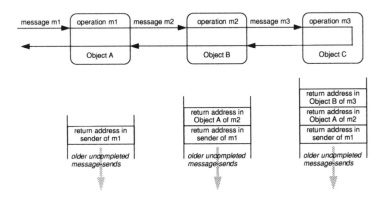

Figure 9.1 *Execution stack*

Figure 9.1 shows an example of a thread of control and its associated stack. When **Object A** gets control as a result of receiving message **m1** and running operation **m1**, the most recent item on the stack will be the address in the sender of **m1** to which control must return[1]. As **Object A** and **Object B** send further messages the stack builds up until **Object C** returns control and the stack unwinds. Each thread of control in the system has its own stack.

It must be recognised that the most popular object-oriented programming languages of today, C++ and Smalltalk, do not have anything approaching full support for concurrency. They were designed as strictly sequential languages, with a single thread of control. In particular, C++ has no standardised support at all, while Smalltalk has some limited standard support via its class library. This is in contrast to languages designed from the outset with concurrency in mind, such as Emerald [Black86], POOL [Ameri87], DRAGOON [Atkin91] and the Actor languages[2] [Agha86].

---

[1]In practice, the stack is used to hold other context-related information, not just return addresses. Such information includes message parameters and space for temporary variables.

[2]Not to be confused with the C-like language called Actor.

9.2 Strategies for concurrency

There are two basic strategies for supporting concurrency in object-oriented (or object-based) programming languages, called *orthogonal* and *integrated* by [Atkin91]. In the *orthogonal* strategy the threads of control are independent of the encapsulation boundaries of objects, weaving their way in and out of objects as they please, as suggested in figure 9.2, where we can see a thread initiated in object **A** (but not really belonging to it) making its way through objects **B**, **C** and **D**[3]. This happens because object **A** sends the message m1 to object **B**, moving the execution context into **B**. Then **B** sends the message **m2** to **C** and the same thing happens again. Notice that the operations invoked by the messages execute in the thread of the message-sender.

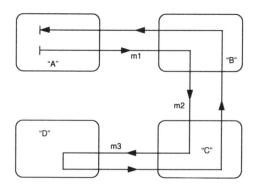

Figure 9.2 *Orthogonal concurrency*

Since in the orthogonal strategy the concept of threads is in no way integrated with the sequential programming language, the programmer must decide for his or her self how to ensure the integrity of the system in the presence of multiple threads.

In the *integrated* strategy the threads are, in some way, owned by objects and their effects beyond the object boundary are closely controlled. The Actor languages generate a new thread to process each message, making message processing asynchronous; we can try to represent this style in a process flow diagram, as in figure 9.3. When message **m1** arrives at object **B** it causes a new thread to be forked to execute the operation. Control passes back immediately to the caller, preventing the use of messages to return results. The same thing happens with **m2** and **m3**.

The proposed mechanism for concurrency in Eiffel [Meyer93] allocates a thread to a set of objects and all their operations execute in that thread rather than in the thread of the caller. In the simple case each object has its own process and execution behaves rather as in figure 9.4.

---

[3]This diagram, and others like it that follow, are not intended for formal interpretation; they merely give an impression of the actions of threads.

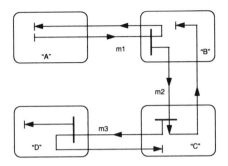

Figure 9.3 *Actor-style concurrency*

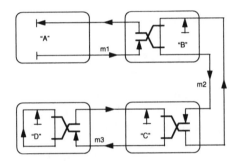

Figure 9.4 *Eiffel-style concurrency*

When the process allocated to object **A** sends the message **m1** to object **B**, one of two things can happen: if the message needs an immediate result **A**'s thread is blocked until **B**'s thread has processed the message; if no immediate result is required, **A**'s thread can continue and the message will be processed sometime later by **B**'s thread. If and when **A** needs to rely on the result of **m1**, it must wait until **m1** is complete[4].

Other languages, such as DRAGOON, use the concept of *active objects*: an active object is an object which owns a thread of control. To use the terminology of Booch [Booch91], active objects may be *actors*[5], providing no services to others but initiating actions by sending messages to other objects, or *agents*, both providing services and initiating actions. Although the operations provided by active objects execute in the thread of the caller, as in the orthogonal strategy, they can queue the message content for later processing by their thread, thereby providing a form of asynchronous

---

[4]The scissor-like symbol used in the diagram to represent synchronisation between threads is the symbol we have used elsewhere to represent Ada-style rendezvous. This is not to imply that the proposed Eiffel scheme has anything at all to do with Ada – or rendezvous. We have used this notation to help give a sense of the processing involved.

[5]Also not to be confused with the C-like language called Actor.

messaging.   Not all objects in the system need be active; some may do all their processing in the thread of their caller. The execution flow using active objects might be like that shown in figure 9.5.

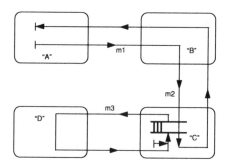

Figure 9.5 *Active objects*

Object **A** is active: it has its own thread of control, which is used to send the **m1** message to **B**. The **B** object is not active and the operation invoked executes entirely in **A**'s thread. During the processing of **m1** the **B** object sends the message **m2** to **C**, which is active.   **C** has decided to buffer the contents of **m2** messages for asynchronous processing so it places information in a queue. **C**'s thread empties the queue and sends an **m3** message to **D**, which is not active.

Each of these ways of integrating concurrency with object-oriented programming has its benefits; they are all much superior to the *ad hoc*, orthogonal approach because they provide a framework for reasoning about and managing concurrent processing. We favour the active object approach as combining both simplicity and flexibility.

Active objects can readily be simulated in languages such as C++ and Smalltalk using the *ad hoc* concurrency and synchronisation facilities found in class libraries. It then becomes a matter of programmer discipline to ensure success. Here we will concentrate on the abstract design of concurrent systems, using a set of well-formulated techniques and notations.

9.3 Serialisation

Concurrency is an implementation problem because it can endanger the integrity of objects. Two threads may simultaneously execute the same operation on an object, leading to corruption of the object's state data. We say the operation is being *multi-threaded*. Similar problems occur in single-threaded systems when there is unexpected or uncontrolled recursion (re-entrancy). The serialisation techniques described here are useful as a way of ensuring the correctness of single-threaded systems, as well as multi-threaded ones, although we might use the techniques more as a design guide than as an implementation strategy.

The main technique for avoiding corruption or erroneous behaviour as a consequence of multi-threading is *serialisation*. The code areas which might cause corruption if multi-threaded are identified and measures are taken to ensure that only one thread at a time executes those areas. Such areas are often called *critical sections*.

What, then, happens to a thread of control which attempts to execute a critical section when another thread is already executing it? The thread must wait. We say that the thread is *blocked*; it cannot proceed until the other thread has finished executing the critical section. Threads may be allocated a priority. Priorities are used by execution environments to decide on the allocation of resources (typically critical sections but also processors when the number of threads exceeds the number of processors) to threads. So if two or more threads are blocked waiting to enter a critical section, we might assume that the thread with the highest priority will gain access first. We don't state this as a fact, merely as an assumption, because the scheduling of threads may be outside the designer's control. Thread priorities should never be used to ensure correct program logic, only to express the desired allocation of resources. Neither do we specify the order in which threads with equal priority will be allocated resources, except to say that we expect threads to be treated fairly. In practice, it is usual for threads with equal priority waiting to enter a critical section to be held in an queue ordered by time of arrival.

9.3.1 Observers and updaters

In chapter 7 we distinguished between operations on objects which do not affect their state (or the state of any object on the system), called *observers*, and operations which do, called *updaters*. We will now set out the rules which apply to the execution of observers and updaters. Initially, we will set out the basic principles, then we will discuss three extensions that simplify designs and improve their quality.

9.3.2 Basic concurrency rules

To ensure integrity we require that, for every type of object, all the updater operations are critical sections. Furthermore, we require that the updaters of any object are *mutually exclusive*: no two updaters may ever execute concurrently. A thread attempting to execute an updater when another updater is in progress will be blocked. This means that not only will it be impossible for any updater operation to be multi-threaded but no two threads can ever be active inside updaters *in the entire object*. These rules are necessary because an updater, by definition, is changing the internal state of an object. The object is not in a consistent state until the updater has finished.

Observers are not critical sections and do not need to be mutually exclusive, but they must never execute concurrently with an updater. We can be more lenient with observers because they do not change the object's state and thus it can never be made inconsistent by their execution. On the other hand, attempts to observe an object's state while it is being changed by an updater must, obviously, be prohibited.

This is the familiar *one writer, many readers* protocol, which underpins most concurrency schemes. Any object may have many simultaneous readers but only ever one writer at a time, and an object cannot be read and written at the same time.

These rules explain why we chose a particular implementation strategy for dealing with price changes in sectors in the share minding system that appeared in chapter 7. Imagine we were to design a mechanism in which the share sent a **priceAdjust** message to the sector *without sending a parameter*, as shown in figure 9.6.

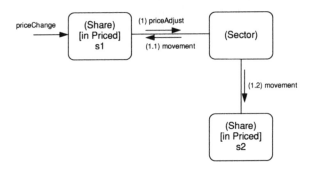

Figure 9.6 *Concurrency conflict*

If, as we chose in chapter 7, the sector is storing its **movement** property as data it would be forced to recompute the property by sending **movement** messages to all its shares, but this would not work because the share **s1** cannot respond to a **movement** message (an observer) while in the middle of executing **priceChange** (an updater). Assuming that the concurrency rules described here are implemented explicitly, the result would be a deadlock, or deadly embrace. The software would hang. If the concurrency rules are used only as a design guide, the result of execution would be undefined.

9.3.3 Invoking local observers

Although rigorous enforcement of the rules given above will guarantee integrity, they can be overly restrictive in practice. One particular problem is that it is often useful when coding an updater to access the object's state using observers. The rules just outlined would result in a deadlock because the observer cannot execute until the updater has finished and the updater cannot finish until it has executed the observer. We have said that the reason for prohibiting the execution of observers during updaters is to ensure that the observed state is consistent. We take the view that the implementor of an updater can reasonably be assumed to be aware of what they are doing and to know the risks of calling observers. Therefore, we ease the rules so that observers invoked *directly* from updaters (i.e. invoked by messages sent to **self**) will not cause deadlock[6]. Note that this easing of the rules does not extend to other objects because our encapsulation principles mean that we must never allow one object to observe another that is in an inconsistent state, even intentionally.

9.3.4 Secured and relaxed sections

The sharp-eyed reader may notice that we appear already to have broken the rules detailed above in an example in chapter 7, reproduced here in a slightly different form as figure 9.7.

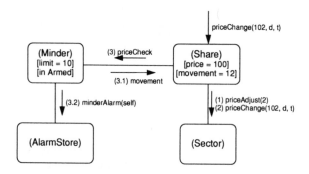

Figure 9.7 *An apparent concurrency conflict*

The share has sent the **priceCheck** message to its minder as part of the processing of **priceChange**, an updater. The minder, needing to evaluate its guard condition, sends the **movement** message, an observer, to the share. Apparent result: deadlock.

The traditional solution to this problem (e.g. as in HOOD [ESA89]) is to accept the restriction and devise a software architecture that acknowledges it. Recognising that problems of this kind occur only when message-sending forms a cyclic pattern, we might decide to organise our objects into a *service hierarchy*, where higher-level objects may only send messages to lower-level objects, as illustrated in figure 9.8.

A consequence of adopting this kind of architecture would be that all information about higher-level objects needed by lower-level objects must be passed as parameters because the lower-level objects cannot 'call back' the higher-level objects to obtain it. This leads to a programming style that sits uneasily with many object-oriented

---

[6]This can readily be implemented by coding two functions for each observer: one, used by other clients and subject to the usual concurrency rules, which calls the other, private, version, used directly from within the updaters. This second version contains the code for the operation and is not subject to the concurrency rules.

programmers; a style that leaves little flexibility in the interfaces. Any change in the information needs of a lower-level object must result in a change to its interface. Although the use of service hierarchies will clearly solve the problem, we wish to find a solution more in tune with the goals of object-oriented software development.

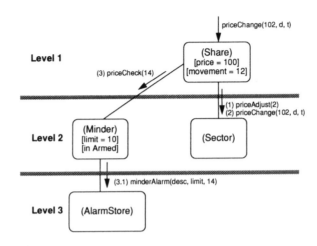

Figure 9.8 *Service hierarchy*

As we pointed out in chapter 7, the three messages **priceAdjust, priceChange** and **priceCheck** sent by the share in the previous examples meet different needs. The **priceAdjust** message is sent to establish a consistent state, to ensure that the sector's invariant can be met. The **priceChange** and **priceCheck** messages are sent to trigger some consequential but independent action once a consistent state has been established. It is clear, therefore, that we must certainly not allow the sector to execute observers (or updaters) of the share as a result of receiving **priceAdjust** because the share might not be in a consistent state. But since the share does not send **priceCheck** until it has ensured that the system is in a consistent state, why should we prohibit the minder from executing observers (or updaters) of the share?

You will recall from chapter 7 that we divide the processing of an updater into two sections: the *secured section* followed by the *relaxed section*. All messages sent to establish system consistency, and all other code to establish the operation's post-conditions, must be in the secured section. Messages that trigger subsequent, independent actions, that is, those which forward notification of stimuli or correspond to generated events, are sent from the relaxed section.

The relaxed section is so called because we can take a more relaxed view of the concurrency rules when executing that section. But relaxed does not mean unconstrained.

Consider an updater operation containing the following message-sends:

```
-- secured section
a.fixup
b.fixup
-- relaxed section
c.action1
-- point x
d.action2
```

Although the object is in a stable and consistent state by the time it reaches the relaxed section, it still requires that **action1** and **action2** are performed strictly in that order. However, if we make the relaxed section completely free of concurrency constraints the thread executing the updater could be suspended at **point x** and another thread could begin executing the updater. The consequences of this might be that a second action1 is performed before the first **action2**. This might be disastrous if the operation were to exchange the positions of two sets of control rods in a nuclear reactor[7]:

```
-- secured section
...

...
-- relaxed section
firstSetOfRods.moveOutBy(3)
secondSetOfRods.moveInBy(3)
```

So what does 'relaxed' mean? We define it to mean that the critical section and mutual exclusion rules are lifted *for the current thread only*. Other threads still cannot begin execution of any updater or observer until the current observer has finished completely. The current thread can execute, directly (using **self**) or indirectly (from another object), another updater or an observer (or even the same updater). When an object is 'relaxed' (i.e. has a current updater executing its relaxed section) and it begins executing an updater or observer for the current thread the normal concurrency rules apply during that execution. So, on entry to the second updater the object becomes 'secured' again, until the relaxed section is reached, when it becomes 'relaxed'. When the second updater ends and control returns to the first updater the object is still 'relaxed'.

Figure 9.9 might help to clarify what is going on. **Object 1** has no active updater or observer when it begins executing **updater1**. It immediately becomes 'secured', and none of its updaters or observers may begin execution, with the single exception of observers invoked directly from within **updater1**. **Object 1** then enters the relaxed section of **updater1**, in which it sends the **updater3** message to **object 2**. As part of its

---

[7]This example is somewhat fanciful because everyone knows that the system would always be designed to push the first set of rods in before pulling the second set out... .

relaxed section, **object 2** sends the **updater2** message to object 1. Because **object 1** is 'relaxed' and because the call is in the same thread of control, **updater2** can be executed and the thread is not blocked. **Object 1** immediately becomes 'secured' again, until it enters the relaxed section of **updater2**, when it becomes 'relaxed' again. Control passes back to **object 2** and, from there, back to the relaxed section of **updater1**. Finally, **updater1** ends, **object 1** become unrestricted once again and control returns to the original sender.

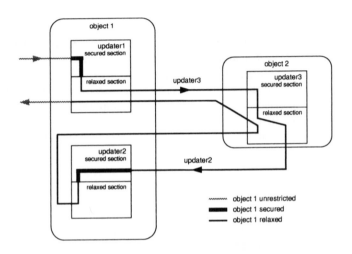

Figure 9.9 *Secured and relaxed sections*

We must never place in the relaxed section of an updater code that changes the state of the object, other than by sending updater messages to **self**. All state changes implied by an updater's post-conditions must be completed in the secured section; the secured section must ensure that all post-conditions and system invariants have been established prior to the object becoming relaxed. Since the return value (if any) of an updater is specified as a post-condition, it follows that this value cannot be determined in the relaxed section.

In our discussion of statecharts in the implementation model in chapter 7, we said that the relaxed section of an updater executes once the new state has been entered. Since other updaters on the same object can validly be activated from the relaxed section, it is perfectly possible for another transition to be triggered, from the new state, during execution of the relaxed section. If that happens, the second updater will execute completely, together with all its consequential effects, before control returns to the original point. This is exactly what was illustrated in figure 9.9. The object might change state several times before the original relaxed section is completed. Each time an updater message is received by the object it is interpreted in the context of the object's current state.

9.3.5 Invoking local updaters

Objects are frequently designed to have several layers of abstraction. Simple operations, often inherited from super-types, are combined to form larger, more powerful, operations. For example, we might want to define an updater operation for shares, called **changeAndSuspend**, that both changes their price and suspends them. This operation could be implemented by sending successive **priceChange** and **suspend** messages to **self**. Our serialisation rules do not prevent the creation of this operation. The sending of the **priceChange** and **suspend** messages must be done in the relaxed section to avoid deadlock; the secured section will be empty.

The difficulty comes when a new, composite, updater must return a result based on the results of messages sent to **self** within it. In chapter 7 we considered the behaviour of the alarm store used by minders; we reproduce the **AlarmStore** statechart here as figure 9.10.

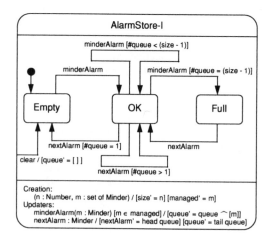

Figure 9.10 *Alarm store*

Now imagine we wish to define a new operation for alarm stores, called **nextAndClear**, that returns the next alarm and cancels the rest. The obvious way to design this is using successive **nextAlarm** and **clear** messages sent to **self**, as follows:

nextAndClear / [nextAndClear' = nextAlarm] clear

Since this new operation returns a result we must send **nextAlarm** in the secured section, but that will cause deadlock. We resolve this difficulty with the third and last of our extensions to the serialisation rules. We allow updaters to be partitioned into independent groups, and for an updater in one group that is executing in its secured section to invoke, directly using **self**, an updater in another group. There are limits to this. Updaters invoked in this way, by sending a message to **self** in the secured section of an updater from another group, cannot have relaxed sections[8]. Also, each group cannot be executing more than one updater in a secured section, so calling backwards and forwards between groups is not possible.

Orthogonal state machines

We use orthogonal state machines in implementation model statecharts to partition updaters into orthogonal groups. Each orthogonal machine describes a group of updaters, and the secured sections of one group may directly invoke updaters in another by sending a message to **self**.

Figure 9.11 shows a revised statechart for **AlarmStore**. The **nextAndClear** updater must be in a separate group to **nextAlarm** and **clear**; this is specified by placing it in an orthogonal state machine.

It is important to note that the presence of orthogonal machines does not mean that updaters are being multi-threaded. The orthogonal state machines do *not* operate independently, each with its own separate concurrency controls. The controls that serialise threads apply to the whole object. If a thread is already executing an updater, no other thread can begin executing a second one, even if it is in a different group. An object can be processing updaters on behalf of only one thread at a time.

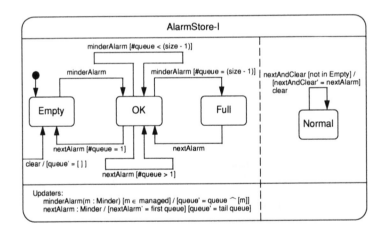

Figure 9.11 *Orthogonal machines*

---

[8]This is because it would be difficult to determine the meaning of a relaxed section under such conditions. The object as a whole is certainly *not* relaxed, because it has an updater executing in a secured section.

9.3.6 Creation operations

Creation operations affect the state of the object. Therefore, they must be treated in exactly the same way as updaters and be subject to the same rules. They have secured and relaxed sections. Some things are just not possible for creation operations; for example, they can never be re-entered. But it is possible for them to cause updater messages to be sent to the new object, so we must take the normal precautions.

9.3.7 Rules and pragmatics

Since we are unaware of any programming language that offers the above-described concurrency semantics directly, it is the responsibility of the implementor to realise them in the chosen language using whatever facilities are available in the operating system, language run-time system or libraries.

We want to make it clear that the concurrency rules we have arrived at are not foolproof. The foolproof rules are those which never allow any concurrent execution of updaters, but we reject those rules as too restrictive. If you want to observe foolproof rules, put all your code in the secured section. The rules we suggest are not foolproof because the action ordering error described in the reactor control rods example, when two threads simultaneously execute in the relaxed section, can still occur within a single thread if the same updater is re-entered. We defend our rules by pointing out that if they do cause erroneous behaviour, the same error would have occurred in a non-concurrent environment, because the error has occurred within a single thread, unaffected by others. Our rules do not prevent you from writing erroneous sequential programs but they do prevent concurrency from causing extra problems.

Although we recommend that you design your software in strict accordance with the rules specified here, you may wish to optimise the implementation by omitting critical sections where it is possible to reason that they are redundant. For example, you may choose an implementation architecture that limits the number of threads executing in a particular area of the system to just one. Within this area serialisation controls could be omitted[9].

9.4 Synchronisation specifications

In our consideration of concurrency so far, our aim has been to ensure the integrity of individual objects in the presence of multiple threads of control. We now need to consider the impact of concurrency on the contract between a *supplier*, an object

---

[9]Subject to the earlier remarks about re-entrancy.

providing services, and a *client*, an object making use of those services by sending messages.

Imagine that a client object is given, somehow, the identity of a supplier object conforming to the type **AlarmStore**, whose statechart appears in figure 9.11. The statechart tells us that **minderAlarm** messages add a minder to the queue and **nextAlarm** messages remove one. The client might therefore assume that it would be perfectly safe to send the message sequence:

> **minderAlarm(...)**
> **minderAlarm(...)**
> **minderAlarm(...)**
> **nextAlarm**
> **nextAlarm**
> **nextAlarm**

It isn't safe because the client has no idea whether other threads of control are also interacting with the supplier. The supplier might actually see the following sequence:

> **minderAlarm(...)**
> **minderAlarm(...)**
> **minderAlarm(...)**
> **nextAlarm**
> *nextAlarm [from another client]*
> **nextAlarm**
> **nextAlarm ['wrongState' exception]**

The final **nextAlarm** message is invalid because the alarm store is empty. If there is more than one thread interacting with the supplier, it is pointless for any client to try to reason about the state of the supplier. Reference to the supplier's statechart won't help a bit. The whole notion of 'programming by contract' has broken down. In this example, and this is typical, there is no way in which the client can use the supplier without being prepared to handle the possible exceptions. It is important to realise that this is entirely the client's problem; the supplier is just behaving correctly, according to the way it was designed.

9.4.1 Exclusive and non-exclusive suppliers

Fortunately, in the vast majority of client–supplier relationships the client can be confident that it is the only user of the supplier. This confidence has to be based on the knowledge that the supplier's identity is not known to anyone other than the client[10].

---

[10]Practically speaking, the supplier's identity will frequently be known to entities other than the client, such as object managers, without jeopardising the client's confidence in this matter.

The most usual way for the client to gain this knowledge is itself to create the supplier and not give away the supplier's identity to anyone. Under these circumstances the client can reason about the state of the supplier, with reference to its statechart, even if the system has many threads of control. This is because all access to the supplier by the client must be from the client's updaters, which are themselves serialised under the rules discussed earlier. So within any one updater the supplier must be being accessed sequentially. Within a single updater it would be perfectly safe to write the first of the message sequences shown above.

We can usually determine quite simply whether a client has *exclusive access* to a supplier by examination of the type view. Consider the relationship between a share object and its associated **ShareChange** objects, as shown in figure 9.12. The **ShareChange** objects are created by the share as a result of price changes and we have devised no interface for the share to 'give away' their identities. The **ShareChange** objects have no other associations and hence no other possible clients. Shares can be confident that they have exclusive access to **ShareChange** objects. If there were other associations we would need to consider their visibilities: if there is more than one visibility arrow pointing towards the supplier, no client can be sure of exclusive access unless the associations are constrained to ensure that only one of the conflicting associations exists at a time. Shares cannot assume exclusive access to sectors because, although there is only a single association between the types, it is multiple at the client end; many shares might be simultaneously clients of a sector.

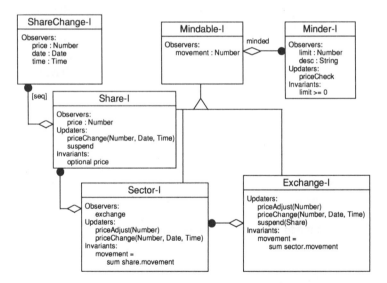

Figure 9.12 *The share minder system*

When a client has exclusive access to a supplier it is in full control; it knows that, within a particular operation, any messages it sends to the supplier will be processed in the order sent. It can also safely assume continuity between successive operations. Without exclusive access it can make no such assumptions. What, then, is the nature of the contract between a client and a non-exclusive supplier?

9.4.2 The non-exclusive contract

If the supplier places no constraints on the ordering of messages it receives there can be no problem and it makes no difference whether they are exclusive or non-exclusive. The problems arise when the supplier has definite constraints on message order.

The client could rely on detecting and handling the exceptions which will, inevitably, result from conflict between multiple clients over suppliers with message-ordering constraints. In most cases this would be unsatisfactory because the client will want to be blocked until the messages sent can be processed. Our belief is that the contract between a client and a non-exclusive supplier must allow the client to send any message defined for the supplier at any time without the supplier raising a **wrongState** exception. The supplier may still raise explicit exceptions, as defined by its statechart. Put simply, a non-exclusive supplier cannot restrict the order of receipt of its messages. We say an object that guarantees never to raise a **wrongState** exception supports the *non-exclusive contract*.

An object supporting the non-exclusive contract must be able to specify the conditions under which clients must be prevented from invoking its operations; that is, the conditions under which it must block clients. Although it is up to the supplier to protect its integrity by defining blocking rules, it is up to the clients whether or not to wait if they become blocked; different clients will want different behaviour.

9.4.3 Synchronisation constraints

To allow suppliers to specify their blocking conditions, we allow object types to be extended, more correctly *synchronised*, with the addition of *synchronisation constraints*. These comprise a list of conditions under which execution of operations is permitted. The synchronisation constraints are held in a separate type, known as a *synchronising type*. A synchronising type may contain only synchronisation constraints; it may not add properties, associations or invariants, and may not extend its parent's statechart.

In figure 9.13 we have introduced a synchronising type, called **BlockingAlarmStore**, that synchronises **AlarmStore**. It specifies a blocking condition for the **nextAlarm** message. We call **nextAlarm** a *synchronised message*. By including synchronisation constraints in the type, we have ensured that **BlockingAlarmStore** can support the non-exclusive contract. Although we have used the type extension triangle we have placed the letter **S** in it to show that this is not a sub-type but a synchronisation relationship.

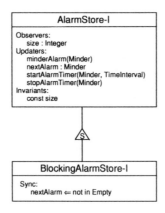

Figure 9.13 *A synchronising type*

The statement:
nextAlarm ⇐ not in Empty

means that objects of this type are permitted to begin execution of **nextAlarm** messages if, and only if, they are not in their **Empty** state. Any thread sending a **nextAlarm** message might become temporarily blocked anyway, because of the mutual exclusion restrictions, but now we are introducing a further constraint: such a thread will be unable to proceed with the desired operation until the expression to the right of the arrow becomes true. We can put a set of messages on the left-hand side if they all have the same blocking condition. Only one statement per message is allowed.

Since an object providing the non-exclusive contract must not raise **wrongState** exceptions, it follows that the set of constraints must be sufficient to ensure this. Every message which, in the non-synchronising type, might raise a **wrongState** exception must have a synchronisation constraint in the synchronising type.

Objects that conform to **BlockingAlarmStore** *do not* technically conform to **AlarmStore,** so we cannot use the objects conforming to the former in place of objects conforming to the latter. Synchronising types are not type-conformant with their non-synchronising parent types. If another client needed an alarm store with a different set of conditions we could introduce another synchronising type, but any particular alarm store object can conform only to one synchronising type or the other; we can't operate two different sets of rules on the same object.

9.4.4 Synchronisation and conformance

Conceptually, synchronising types should contain no elements other than synchronisation constraints. However, as a shorthand, we could add the synchronisation constraints directly to the **AlarmStore** type, as in figure 9.14.

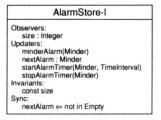

Figure 9.14 *Shorthand for a synchronising type*

This has a serious drawback: we do not allow synchronising types to have sub-types. This is because we view synchronisation as an issue orthogonal to sub-typing. Synchronising types are *not* sub-types of their non-synchronising super-types and allowing further extension of synchronising types is not helpful. It is difficult to define useful conformance semantics for synchronised sub-types, as has been shown by a number of researchers, and as is discussed in depth in [Atkin91]. As you will see later in this chapter, we have special techniques for meeting the need for polymorphic collections of synchronised objects.

So if we want to specialise the behaviour of a synchronised object we must do it by creating a sub-type of the unsynchronised type in the normal manner. We can then re-link our synchronisation constraints, as defined in the synchronising type, to the new sub-type, or define more detailed constraints.

9.4.5 Synchronisation expressions

Synchronisation expressions are most frequently related to states but may be any Boolean expression over the type's observers and states[11]. They may not refer to parameters of the message being synchronised; although the meaning of this is clear, it is very difficult to implement efficiently.

Since the truth of synchronisation expressions will change over time, we need to define exactly when they are evaluated. We define all synchronisation expressions for a type to be evaluated when an object conforming to the type is created and again each time an updater completes. When an updater completes, threads which were previously blocked because of synchronisation constraints but which could now proceed must compete against other threads blocked by the mutual exclusion constraints for access to the supplier. As with mutual exclusion, we don't specify the order in which competing threads will be chosen but we assume the competition to be fair.

---

[11] It is a restriction that the result of synchronisation expressions cannot depend on the state of any other object. That is, a synchronisation expression cannot refer to an observer that is implemented in terms of properties of another object.

We assume the results of synchronisation expression evaluation are stored, privately, so that if a synchronised message is received when no updater is in progress the results can be used to determine whether the sending thread should be blocked. The synchronisation expressions *are not* evaluated when messages are received.

9.4.6 The client's view

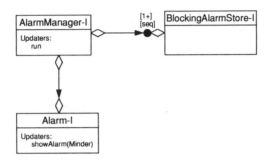

Figure 9.15 *Alarm manager*

Consider the type view shown in figure 9.15. An alarm manager manages a fixed sequence of alarm stores and passes stored alarms to the alarm itself, as shown by the statechart in figure 9.16. When the alarm manager sends a **nextAlarm** message to a store it will be blocked until the store has an alarm to forward. Other alarms in other stores will not be processed until the store currently blocking has an alarm. There is no possibility of a **wrongState** exception being raised by the blocking alarm store.

9.4.7 Post-conditions

We must also consider how the client of a supplier object providing the non-exclusive contract should interpret any post-conditions given on the supplier's statechart.

Since the supplier is not exclusive, the client can never be sure of the supplier's state. Hence, if the supplier has many possible transitions for a particular message, the client cannot know which transition will be taken. It follows, therefore, that the most the client can assume is that the post-condition of the supplier will be the logical 'or' of the post-conditions of all the possible transitions.

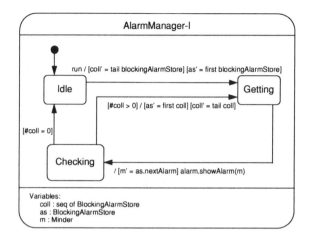

Figure 9.16 *Alarm manager statechart*

9.4.8 Timeouts

We have shown how a supplier can specify blocking conditions, and, in the example above, we have shown the effect on a client. But, as we discussed earlier, the decision as to whether or not to wait when blocked should be made by the client. The client may also wish to specify a limit to the length of time it can be blocked. These things are done using *timeouts*.

Whenever a client sends a message it can specify the length of time for which it is prepared to wait if blocked. If the specified time is exceeded, the client will receive a **timeout** exception. For example, the alarm store may decide not to wait more than 500 milliseconds if blocked when sending the **nextAlarm** message[12]:

alarmStore.nextAlarm[500ms]

If the message has parameters, the timeout is specified, inside square brackets, after the last parameter but before the closing parenthesis.

The statechart for **AlarmStore** must now be modified to take account of the **timeout** exceptions, as in figure 9.17. If the client does not want to wait at all if blocked, it

---

[12]The timeout is a value of type **TimeInterval**. In this example we are specifying the value using a literal, made up from a number and a unit post-fix. The units of timeouts are:

    ms : milliseconds
    s : seconds
    h : hours
    d : days

specifies a timeout period of 0. This means that a timeout exception will be raised immediately if the requested operation cannot be started at once.

It is important to realise that a client can be blocked in the following two ways:

- waiting for a synchronisation constraint to become true;
- waiting for another thread to leave a mutually exclusive operation.

The timeout applies to both, not just the wait on a synchronisation constraint. Therefore, it is quite proper, and sometimes useful, to specify a timeout for an unsynchronised message (i.e. one with no synchronisation constraint). This will prevent the client from being blocked indefinitely because another thread is executing a mutually exclusive operation.

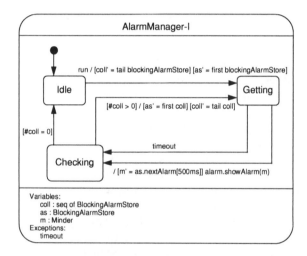

Figure 9.17 *Timeouts*

9.4.9 The synchronisation invariant

Imagine we have two kinds of alarm store, one called **BlockingAlarmStore** which, as before, blocks **nextAlarm** messages until there is an alarm available, and another, called **FullyBlockingAlarmStore**, which in addition blocks **minderAlarm** messages until there is space in the queue, rather than raising an exception. We might want our alarm manager to manage a collection containing both kinds of alarm store, as shown in figure 9.18.

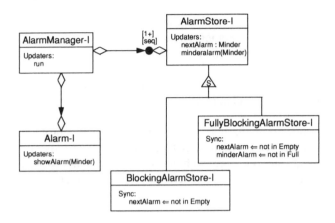

Figure 9.18 *Attempting to use synchronising types as conformant sub-types*

Unfortunately, this doesn't work because **BlockingAlarmStore** and **FullyBlockingAlarmStore** are not type-conformant with **AlarmStore** and so cannot be used polymorphically. It seems unreasonable to prohibit such designs but we need to ensure that the client's contract is maintained.

Every synchronising type guarantees, irrespective of what is in its parent's statechart, to provide the non-exclusive contract; that is, objects conforming to it guarantee never to raise the **wrongState** exception, but they may raise the **timeout** exception. To allow type-conformance between synchronising types we introduce the idea of a *synchronisation invariant*, written as **sync** in the invariants section of the type. A type with this invariant does not contain synchronisation constraints, but promises to provide the non-exclusive contract anyway. It follows that types containing the **sync** invariant must always be abstract if they do not allow all messages in every state. As with synchronising types, a type with the **sync** invariant is not a true sub-type of its super-type, and does not conform to it.

Apart from its promise to clients, a type with the **sync** invariant behaves much like a normal type. In particular, it may have sub-types, and these sub-types are conformant (and must obey the normal conformance rules). Like all other invariants, the **sync** invariant is inherited: sub-types must also provide the non-exclusive contract. A type with the **sync** invariant must have synchronising sub-types which provide the synchronisation constraints necessary to guarantee the non-exclusive contract at the leaves of its sub-type structure.

We can now produce a design with varying sub-types of **AlarmStore** by introducing a new type, called **SyncAlarmStore**, that has a **sync** invariant, as shown in figure 9.19. Notice that there is no **S** in the extension triangle between SyncAlarmStore and its sub-types: this is now true type-conformance.

To complete the story we show a revised statechart for the alarm manager in figure 9.20.

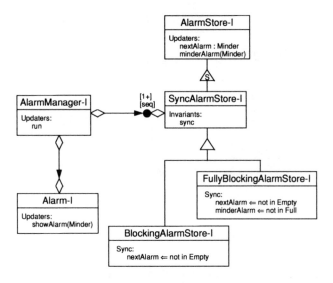

Figure 9.19 *The sync invariant*

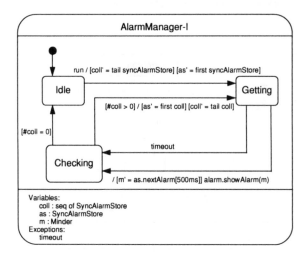

Figure 9.20 *Revised alarm manager statechart*

We can use the same technique to achieve polymorphism between objects with different behaviour, not just different blocking rules. The model shown in figure 9.21 contains a sub-type of **AlarmStore**, called **SafeAlarmStore**, which extends the behaviour of **AlarmStore** by defining a response to **nextAlarm** messages in the **Empty** state.

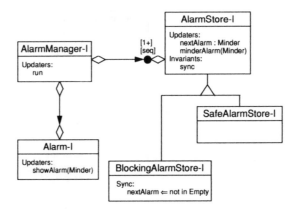

Figure 9.21 *Extending behaviour*

The extended statechart for **SafeAlarmStore** appears as figure 9.22, which you should compare with figure 9.10. When a **SafeAlarmStore** receives a **nextAlarm** message in the **Empty** state it returns a new, dummy **Minder**[13]. Notice how the existing post-conditions of **nextAlarm** have been moved from the textual part to the body of the statechart.

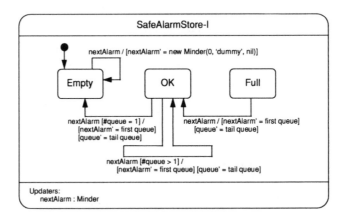

Figure 9.22 *Safe alarm store statechart*

---

[13]We have bent the rules slightly to produce this example. We have specified the third creation parameter of the dummy **Minder**, the one that represents the object to be minded, as **nil**, but earlier models indicate that this association is not optional.

Since the **SafeAlarmStore** has defined behaviour for **nextAlarm** in the **Empty** state, it can guarantee the non-exclusive contract without needing any synchronisation constraints, and hence it needs no synchronising type.

However, we must consider the impact of this on **AlarmManager** objects. Since they have a non-exclusive contract with **AlarmStores**, they cannot reason about **AlarmStore** behaviour by examining statecharts. When an **AlarmManager** sends a **nextAlarm** message the only thing it can be certain of is that it will receive a **Minder**; there is no guarantee that the **Minder** will ever have been on the queue – as we can see, **SafeAlarmStores** may return a brand new **Minder**.

9.5 Active objects

How do threads come into existence? Most frequently, their origin is buried within the run-time or operating system and our software experiences them as messages sent by the run-time or operating system. In the simplest situation we can think of the software system as a program which, when executed, is given a single thread of control that commences its execution at some defined entry point. This kind of situation is usually the first we encounter when we are learning about programming. It is also still commonplace, particularly in large-system data-processing, where the impact of concurrency on application programmers is limited to being able to run several independent, single-threaded programs at once. Single-threaded systems of this kind are becoming less common though, and are being replaced by systems integrating a variety of asynchronous information sources, such as data communication links, and featuring event-driven graphical user-interfaces. In today's software world there is much less distinction between data-processing and traditional real-time applications.

Even if our software never creates new threads of control we may need to design it to manage several. In graphical user-interfaces, each window is often associated with a thread, created by the environment when the window is created. User events cause messages to be sent to our software, executing in the window's thread. We often refer to this kind of activation as a *call-back*. If each window has its own thread, the processing of events associated with that window are inherently serialised, but our software may be dealing with events coming from several windows and these can certainly overlap. Another model used by graphical user-interfaces is to give each event its own thread – now we must deal with overlapping events from the same window. There may be constraints on the way we handle threads originating from outside the software; frequently, we are not permitted to block them or use them to call-back into the operating system. We may need to detect events and queue them for later execution. This requires the ability to create new threads of control in the software.

Sometimes we need to create new threads of control to prevent our software from stopping. If we had to manage several communication lines, each controlled by a separate object whose interface for reading was a blocking message, we would need a separate thread for each line. As soon as a thread sends a message to the line controller to read data it will be blocked until data is available. If we had only one thread, the entire software system would stop execution the first time we asked a line controller for data. The traditional solution to this problem, polling, is inelegant and inflexible.

9.5.1 Active types

An object which initiates a thread is called an *active object*; we introduced this idea earlier in the chapter. Active objects are objects that conform to one or more *active types*. The design of active types includes specification of the execution pattern of the thread, in a way that we will describe shortly. Each time an active object is created, a new thread is also created to execute the defined execution pattern.

Although the thread of an active object 'belongs' to the object it has no privileged access to the internals of the object. It may use only the defined message interface of the object, just like any other client. It is free to interact with associated objects in any way it wishes, obtaining their identities by invoking the relevant observer operations.

9.5.2 Execution patterns

The execution pattern of an active object's thread is shown by a concurrent state machine, consisting only of states with unnamed transitions, drawn at the outermost level of the statechart of the active type. This machine is distinguished as active by having a white, rather than black, circle at the tail of the initial state arrow (or arrows, if they are guarded).

Each active object can have only one thread. An active type can define only one active state machine. We make this rule because we don't want to have to define the sequence of activation of multiple threads. A collection of objects each with a single thread is always an alternative to a single object with multiple threads.

The active parts of statecharts are inherited by sub-types in the usual way, but they may not be refined. If the sub-type wishes to refine the super-type active part, or if it has more than one active super-type, it must define its own active part which completely replaces those of the super-type(s).

If you wish to specify a priority for the active thread, place it inside the circle at the tail of the initial state arrow.

In our consideration of the share minder system we have referred many times to examples where a share object receives a **priceChange** message. We will now look at an example of how these messages might be sent. We propose the existence of a message feed object which uses data from a communication line to instantiate message objects. Each message object knows the identity of the affected share and its new price. The message feed queues these incoming messages until they are read by a client, using the **nextMessage** updater. The messages are read by a price feed object, which knows how to use them to update shares. Fragments of the type view of this system are shown in figure 9.23.

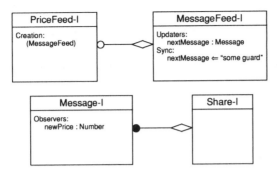

Figure 9.23 *Price feed*

We will make **PriceFeed** an active type. The thread must repeatedly read a message from the message feed and pass details of it to the share. Since the **nextMessage** updater has a blocking constraint, the thread will be blocked if no message is available. The execution pattern of the thread is a loop, as we can see clearly from the statechart in figure 9.24.

The active state machine has two 'states' but these are not the stable states of a normal state machine but unstable intermediaries between two message-sends. The stable state of this machine is when the **nextMessage** message blocks. The *initial state* arrow of the active state machine is unrelated to object creation; the post-conditions for creation shown in the textual part apply not to the initial state arrow of the active machine but to an implicit creation arrow on the omitted 'proper' machine.

The syntax of the transitions is similar to that for unnamed transitions in normal state machines. The messages on the transition are sent in the order shown. Taking a transition in the active part does not, in itself, cause the object to become secured or locked in any way, but if the transitions in the active part invoke observers or updaters on **self** the normal mutual exclusion rules (and possible blocking) apply. The active part behaves exactly like an external client.

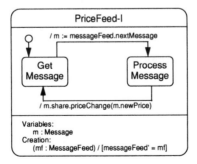

Figure 9.24 *Active objects*

It is important that we define the exact moment when the thread is created; it cannot be before the creation operation has established its post-conditions because, in the example above, the message feed association is not established until then. The thread is created after completion of the secured section of the creation operation but before commencement of its relaxed section (if it has one).

9.5.3 Thread synchronisation

We might want the thread of our price feed to wait until it is told by another object to start. We can achieve this very simply by making the thread send a synchronised message as its first action, as shown in figure 9.25. The thread will be blocked on the send of the **active** message until another object sends **start**.

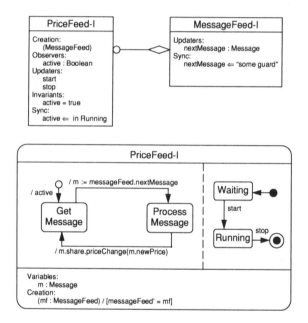

Figure 9.25 *Thread synchronisation*

9.5.4 Finalisation

Figure 9.25 also shows a finalisation state for the price feed. We have to consider what this means for active objects. When an object enters its finalisation state it is unreachable, that is, it has lost all its associations with other objects. With or without explicit finalisation, objects normally become eligible for destruction after they become unreachable; the exact moment of destruction depends on the implementation language. An active object does not become eligible for destruction until its thread stops execution, if it has not already done so. The thread stops execution when its owning object is unreachable and when it (the thread) next enters a state in the active state machine, such as **GetMessage** or **ProcessMessage** in the example above. We do not want to stop execution of the thread at any other time because it could compromise the integrity of any objects whose operations are in the thread's message-sending chain.

Applying this rule to the example above, we notice that the thread might stop execution in the **ProcessMessage** state, meaning that a message will be lost: it will have already been read from the message feed but not yet applied to the share. We could fix this by removing the **ProcessMessage** state and showing all the message sends in the same transition.

9.6 Summary

- A *concurrent* system is one where the software must begin processing a stimulus before having finished processing a previous one.
- A major issue in the design of concurrent systems is locality of *threads of control*: the extent to which threads are aligned with object boundaries.
- Concurrency causes problems when two or more threads of control simultaneously execute the same code. The main technique for dealing with this is *serialisation* using *critical sections*.
- We divide the operations of an object into *observers* and *updaters*. Observers do not change the state of the object (or any part of the system); updaters may change the state of the object.
- The serialisation of observers and updaters is based on the many readers, single writer principle. Updaters must be mutually exclusive in respect of each other and of observers. Observers need not be mutually exclusive.
- These rules are loosened in three ways. First, updaters may call local observers; second, we divide updaters into *secured* and *relaxed* sections; third, updaters may call local updaters when secured provided special restrictions are followed.
- The secured section of an updater must establish the integrity of the object and the system as a whole. The relaxed section may include code that causes the object to be re-entered *in the same thread of control*.
- Orthogonal state machines partition updaters into groups. An updater in one group may, subject to some restrictions, directly invoke an updater in another, even in its secured section.
- The contract between client and supplier objects is greatly affected by the presence of multiple clients in a concurrent system. The contract between a supplier and a single client is said to be *exclusive*; the contract between a supplier and multiple clients is said to be *non-exclusive*.

- When there is an exclusive contract the client can reason about the behaviour of the supplier by examining the supplier's statechart.
- When there is a non-exclusive contract the client cannot use statecharts to reason about the behaviour of the supplier, and so there is a risk of inadvertently causing *wrongState* exceptions. In fact, we require a supplier supporting the non-exclusive contract to guarantee never to raise *wrongState* exceptions by specifying appropriate blocking controls.
- Blocking controls are normally defined in special *synchronising types*.
- A client can use *timeouts* to decide how long to wait if blocked.
- The *sync* invariant can be used to produce conformant sub-types that support the non-exclusive contract.
- An *active object* is one that initiates a thread of control. The behaviour of the thread is defined in a special part of the type's statechart.
- Active objects cannot initiate more than one thread of control.

9.7 Bibliographic notes

The book by Atkinson [Atkin91] provides an excellent introduction to the issues involved in building concurrent object-oriented systems, and explains clearly why synchronisation and sub-typing must be kept separate.

9.8 References

[Agha86] G. Agha. *A Model of Concurrent Computation in Distributed Systems*, MIT Press, Cambridge, Massachusetts, 1986.

[Ameri87] P. America. POOL-T: A parallel object-oriented language. *Object-Oriented Concurrent Programming*, A. Yonezawa and M. Tokoro (eds.), MIT Press, Cambridge, Massachusetts, 1987.

[Atkin91] C. Atkinson. *Object-Oriented Reuse, Concurrency and Distribution*. ACM Press, New York, 1991.

[Black86] A. Black, N. Hutchinson, E. Jul and H. Levy. Object structure in the Emerald system. *OOPSLA '86 Conference Proceedings*, 78–86, ACM Press, New York, 1986.

[Booch91] G. Booch. *Object-Oriented Design With Applications*, Benjamin/Cummings, Redwood City, California, 1991.

[ESA89] *HOOD Reference Manual*, European Space Agency, Noordwijk, The Netherlands, 1989.

[Meyer93] B. Meyer. *Systematic Concurrent Object-Oriented Programming*, Technical Report TR-EI-37/SC, Interactive Software Engineering, Santa Barbara, California, 1993.

Part Four

System architecture

CHAPTER 10

Relationships between models

10.1 Why three models?

We have introduced three different ways of modelling systems, one aimed at modelling situations in the world and two aimed at modelling software. Most object-oriented development methods implicitly acknowledge only one of these modelling perspectives. Are we over-complicating things? We anticipate being accused of it, but we have found that being absolutely clear about which of these three modelling perspectives is being used invariably helps us to understand systems better, even when using notations and methods other than those introduced in this book.

It has been said many times that object-oriented methods permit the software developer to 'model the real world'. The more we have explored this idea, the more potentially misleading we have found it. Firstly, the very idea of an objective 'real world' is highly dubious on philosophical grounds. This book is not the place to discuss metaphysics and the nature of reality; suffice it to say that we do not subscribe to the kind of naïve realism implicit in the idea of 'modelling the real world'. We believe reality to be a social construction, and the activity of building software to be a social activity which necessarily alters the reality it attempts to model. This is particularly true in the case of large organisations, where the introduction of software can fundamentally alter the nature of the organisation. Of course, it is possible to model certain aspects of reality – indeed, Part 2 of this book is about doing exactly that – but it is vitally important to be clear about the purpose and limitations of such modelling.

Secondly, whatever the nature of reality, we do not find it very helpful to describe it in terms of message-passing or of operations on individual objects. Real events can be detected by many observers at once; they are not sent from point to point. Message-passing and operation invocation are appropriate constructs for describing software execution, but not normally for describing what happens in the world, because they tend to over-specify the order of the consequences of events. Some authors would claim that this means that we should introduce concurrency into our models of the world. In a sense this is exactly what we have done in the essential and specification models, by allowing broadcast events with instantaneous responses everywhere. But there is a huge difference between this potentially infinite concurrency and the techniques used in the implementation model to control the interactions between a finite number of execution threads acting at a limited speed. The essential and specification models assume infinite processing power, whereas concurrency is introduced in the implementation model precisely because we only have limited actual processing power.

Thirdly, we find it very helpful to be able to describe software in abstract terms, as in the specification model, without needing to consider implementation issues such as concurrency and message-sequencing. Most of the history of computer science has been the search for abstraction, that is, for ways of saying what is needed while omitting what is superfluous. Message-sequencing is superfluous for specifying the observable behaviour of software, and only becomes relevant when we need to describe how the software implementation is mapped onto processors.

We have spent several chapters identifying and describing the three perspectives, and giving precise techniques for building models in each perspective. This chapter considers the relationships between them in more detail.

10.2 Analysis, specification, design and programming

Terminology is a problem. In the software world we often come across the words *analysis*, *design*, *specification*, *programming*, *requirements* and a plethora of other terms whose meaning the software developer is expected to understand. Unfortunately, most of these terms have meanings vastly removed from their normal English usage, only defined by small communities, and often different from one community to another. Indeed, they frequently only acquire any real meaning within the context of a single software project. Books setting out methods often attempt to provide a definition at least for *analysis* and *design*; unfortunately they usually disagree. For some, the words are simply management tools, whereas for others they carry precise technical distinctions. In short, the terminology of software development methods is in a mess.

To help us through this predicament, we propose a set of definitions which seem to return the words to something near their dictionary meanings, as follows:

- *Analysis* is discovering and describing those aspects of a software development project about which there is *no choice*, that is, which the project is already committed to.
- *Design* is creating and describing those aspects of a software development project about which a choice exists, that is, which a project is not yet committed to.
- *Specification* is creating an abstract description of the observable behaviour of a software system.

- *Programming* is creating an executable description of the implementation of a software system.
- *Requirements* are properties which the system must possess in order to succeed. These may be divided into *functional requirements* – a statement of the desired stimulus–response behaviour – and *non-functional requirements*, such as constraints on speed, space, platform, price, human factors, etc.

Note that the distinction between analysis and design depends only on whether a choice exists. This is not a difference of notation, or of technique. Also, analysis and design are applicable to things other than software, even when the goal is software development. Software is always an element of a wider system, at least part of which must itself be designed. The distinctions suggested above can be applied regardless of whether the choices concern software structures or something else.

It sometimes takes great clarity of thought to determine where a choice actually does exist. One of the most powerful experiences for the skilled analyst is to sort out the core of a problem from the implementation-oriented terms often used to describe it by unskilled people. Most people do not have the language of abstract set theory and logic at their fingertips, and are therefore compelled to describe a situation in terms which over-commit in various ways, often bound up with the way in which a problem is currently solved.

Essential modelling can be done in order to assist with analysis, or in order to create a design, or both. So can specification, or even programming. Note also that some of these terms are not mutually exclusive. For example, analysis might consist of the discovery of a set of requirements, which may or may not constitute or include a specification. Design may be needed in order to complete the specification. Requirements may be products of analysis (*a priori* requirements) or design (requirements chosen as part of the project).

With these definitions, it does not make sense to associate specific techniques with analysis or design, nor to manage a project on the basis of techniques. We discuss project management further in chapter 13.

It would be incorrect to say that the purpose of an essential model is analysis, because it may also be used to design. Nevertheless, essential modelling is often used for analysis, especially in cases where an existing situation needs to be described as a pre-requisite to software specification. We have ourselves used essential modelling in enterprises including health care, banking and insurance to formalise what goes on in the enterprise prior to specifying any software. The usual purpose of such an analysis is to model those aspects of the enterprise which are candidates for automation, as a precursor to deciding about software system scope and boundary. When software scope and boundary have already been decided (i.e. there is no choice about them), essential modelling may be unnecessary, and analysis consists of software specification. However, in our experience the situation is often ambiguous and politically charged, with confusion about what the choices are. The use of precise, abstract notations can help greatly in charged situations, because they can help to distinguish the real choices from the imaginary ones, and indeed to determine which activities are truly analysis and which are truly design.

10.3 Seamlessness

Seamlessness is another claim of object-oriented methods, closely tied up with modelling the real world. Obviously we do not subscribe to the most elementary interpretation of seamlessness, which would imply that building software simply consists of building a model of the world and automatically generating code from it. On the other hand, we firmly believe that there can be – and indeed should be – a strong correspondence between the structure of the software and the structure of its environment. With such a correspondence, when the world changes it should be reasonably straightforward to find the part of the software which needs to be changed in response. This correspondence is what we call 'seamlessness'. The fundamental relationship we are seeking is that objects in the *concept domains* – the parts of the software that mimic the world – should have counterparts in the software's environment. Indeed, as we discuss further in chapter 11, this is how the concept domains are defined.

Assuming that in a software development project it is found necessary to build all three models – essential, specification and implementation – we find that the main correspondence between all three is in the *type views for the concept domains*. A concept domain type view for the specification model is normally a subset of that for the essential model. Software scope and boundary in a concept domain can be systematically decided by considering which aspects of an essential model are to be included in the specification model. The type view also corresponds closely between specification and implementation models. The correspondence is not exact because properties and event behaviour are implemented by updaters and observers with (possibly concurrent) message access. Nevertheless, a basic structure of object types can be found in all three modelling perspectives, and this we consider to be the basis of seamless development. It is certainly open to tool support.

This similarity of type views means that each type name can have three different interpretations during the development process. In fact, when viewpoints are introduced in chapter 12, there may be many more interpretations for each type name. In this book we have used suffixes, such as **-S** and **-I**, to distinguish between the different interpretations.

State diagrams do not, in general, correspond between essential and specification models. There may be little similarity between an essential model statechart, which describes the possible state changes to objects in a situation, and the specification model statechart for the corresponding type, which describes the responses of its software instances to events. The most obvious reason for this difference is that specification model statecharts show how events are generated by software, whereas essential model statecharts just show event sequencing. A further reason for the difference is the possibility of errors occurring in the process of communicating events between the environment and the software. The difference also partially results from our definition of sub-typing in the specification model, which allows objects of a sub-type to substitute as event receivers for objects of a super-type, because we wish to be able to assemble software from components. This is not an issue for situations, which we are rarely able to assemble from components.

There are systematic correspondences between statecharts in the specification and implementation models, but the correspondence is not direct, because of the change from event semantics to message semantics, and the need to introduce implementation domains such as persistence and distribution.

10.4 Scoping essential models

We want to discuss how to build an essential model with the correct scope, that is, one which describes everything we want to describe, and nothing that we don't want to describe. To illustrate some of the issues we will build an essential model of part of the operation of a self-service petrol station. We assume that our ultimate goal is to design some software which will control the pumps and payments. We will also assume that this station is one where dispensing of petrol occurs before payment.

We know that the main activity that occurs in petrol stations is people arriving in cars, serving themselves with petrol, paying and leaving. The people who serve themselves with petrol are *agents*, in the terminology of chapter 6; we will call them **Customers**. We start very simply, by considering the relationship between the customers and the petrol station, and the events that occur during this relationship. Figure 10.1 is our first type view, showing that every **Customer** object is associated with a **Pump** object, and every **Pump** with a **PetrolStation**. We assume that the association between **Customer** objects and **Pump** objects is created when the customer chooses the pump, and destroyed when the customer eventually leaves.

Let's create an event scenario for a typical interaction between a **Customer** object called **c**, a **PetrolStation** object, and one of its **Pump** objects called **p**.

gunRemove(p)
motorOn(p)
squeezeTrigger(p)
update(p, litres, price)
.
releaseTrigger(p)
motorOff(p)
gunReplace(p)
pay(c)
receiptRequest(c)
receiptPrint(c)
customerLeave(c)

One of the choices we have made when building this scenario is whether the parameter for events such as **squeezeTrigger** is the **Pump** or the **Customer**. Theoretically, it is an arbitrary choice, because while the **Customer** exists it is always associated with the same **Pump**. However, it seems more natural to give the **Pump** as a parameter.

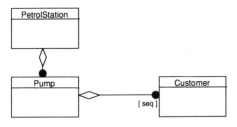

Figure 10.1 *Simple essential model type view for a petrol station*

This scenario is an example. Several other scenarios could be played out over these event types while a customer is in a petrol station. For example, the **squeezeTrigger** and **motorOn** events might be reversed.

Now let's try to create statecharts for the types **Pump** and **Customer** which generalise the various scenarios that we are interested in. Figure 10.2 is a statechart for **Pump**, defining the possible sequences of events. The left-hand statechart unit constrains the physical relationship between **gunRemove**, **gunReplace**, **squeezeTrigger** and **releaseTrigger** events; the central unit shows how **motorOn** and **motorOff** are constrained with respect to **gunRemove** and **gunReplace**; and the right-hand unit shows how **update** cannot occur until **squeezeTrigger** happens after **motorOn**.

Figure 10.3 shows a statechart for **Customer** showing dispensing and payment. Observe that this statechart does not actually show all the possible sequences of events for a person entering a petrol station; it shows the expected behaviour of a customer under normal circumstances. However, an errant 'customer' might leave without paying; pay for somebody else's petrol; pay the wrong amount; or even remove the dispensing gun, wedge the trigger so that petrol starts pumping out all over the forecourt, and drive off. The only real limitation on the possible scenarios results from the physical properties of the situation. For example, the gun cannot be replaced unless it is removed. On the other hand, the statechart for the pump does seem to describe the set of physically possible scenarios for a pump, as long as it is working correctly.

We seem to have found the following two different approaches to building this essential model:

- describing all physically possible sequences of events;
- describing typical behaviour.

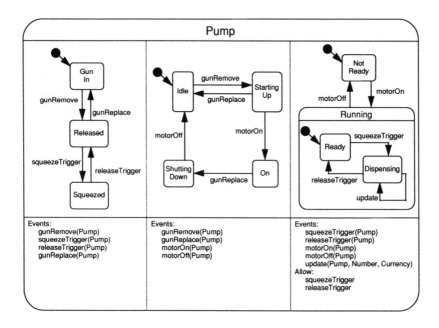

Figure 10.2 *Statechart for **Pump***

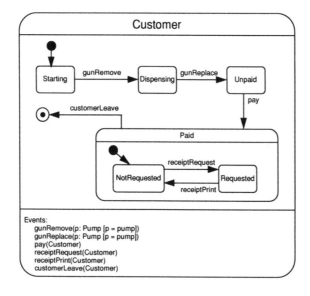

Figure 10.3 *Statechart for **Customer***

Figure 10.2 is in the first category, whereas figure 10.3 is in the second.   This inconsistency needs resolving.

Could we create a statechart for **Customer** which defines all physically possible behaviours taken from the set of events in figure 10.3? The difficulty with this is that if a person behaves sufficiently badly, they can no longer be reasonably thought of as a customer; worse, several malevolent customers could collude with corrupt petrol station attendants to subvert the system completely. We will end up with an unhelpful statechart in which almost anything is possible at any time.

We need a way to think about the problem so that we can model all possible situations without going into this kind of unnecessary detail. We have not made much headway with the customer. What might we use instead? We may note that all that is really desired from the petrol station is that it:

- dispenses petrol from pumps, and
- receives and records payments for the petrol that has been taken.

Who actually does the dispensing and paying is irrelevant. However, petrol may be taken and not paid for, or only partially paid for, and these situations should be modelled.

We invent a more abstract concept, the *transaction*, representing an obligation to pay. A **Transaction** object comes into existence the moment some petrol is dispensed, the obligation is discharged when payment is received, and the transaction is deleted at a later time when it is no longer needed for accounting and reporting purposes.

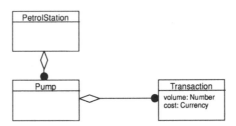

Figure 10.4 *Revised essential model type view with transactions*

Figure 10.4 is our revised type view, in which **Customer** has been replaced by **Transaction**. The proposed statechart for **Transaction** is shown in figure 10.5. Here we handle the possible misbehaviour of customers by introducing a new event: **terminate**. This is similar to the **gunReplace** event, but is initiated by the station attendant to stop delivery.   This event would occur, for example, if the attendant recognised the customer to be a known bad payer, or if petrol were pumping out over the forecourt. In any case, if the customer leaves without paying, the transaction simply remains unpaid.

We should also express the fact that only one **Transaction** object in the **Dispensing** state may be associated with a given **Pump**. This can be done by enhancing the type view, as shown in figure 10.6.

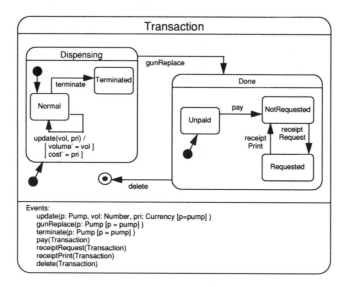

Figure 10.5 *Statechart for **Transaction***

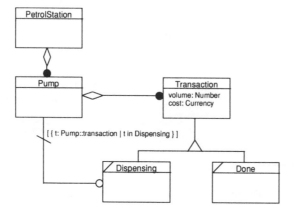

Figure 10.6 *Showing only one dispensing transaction*

We should also enhance the Pump statechart to show the **terminate** event as in figure 10.7, which also shows how new **Transaction** objects are created when the motor is switched on.

The statechart in figure 10.5 describes the delivery of petrol and payment, as long as there is no need to model the individual customers for other purposes, for example account-holding[1]. It is sufficiently abstract for the physical details of errant customer behaviour not to matter, although it does permit petrol dispensing to be terminated and transactions to remain unpaid.

The issue we have been dealing with here is scoping of essential models. Whenever we create an essential model, we have the following two competing concerns:

- We want to describe all possible behaviours, both desired and undesired, otherwise our essential model is incomplete.
- We do not want to describe irrelevant behaviour.

The choices we make about types and events are governed by balancing these concerns.

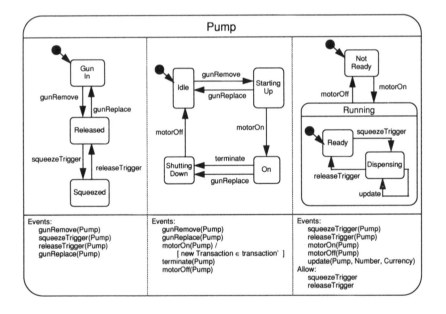

Figure 10.7 *Pump statechart with* **terminate** *event*

---

[1] If we did wish to model account-holding, we would introduce a new type of **AccountHolder**, with which **Transactions** might be associated.

10.5 The software boundary

At some point in a software development the boundary between the software system and its environment must be designed. In some cases this boundary is implicit in the situation itself; in others choosing what is to be automated is itself an act of design.

If the software boundary is implicit in the situation itself, essential modelling may not be very helpful, because the essential model would express the same behaviour as the specification model without specifying which events are software-generated. However, when the software boundary is to be designed, an essential model provides a systematic way of designing it.

Given an essential model which describes those aspects of a situation which are candidates for automation, the following questions can be asked:

1. Which types are to be included in the specification model?
   If the stimulus–response behaviour of the software depends in any way on the state of any instances of a type, then it should be included; otherwise it should be excluded.
2. Which associations are to be included?
   Normally all the associations between included types will be included. Sometimes structure in the essential model can be omitted from the specification model if the structure is not needed to support any aspect of its behaviour.
3. For each event, is it to be detected, generated or ignored by the software?
   Each event should be considered carefully. If it is to be detected or generated by the software, a way of detecting or generating it must be designed. The appropriate object identity or value must be established for each event parameter. Sometimes an event may be split into a set of differently named events depending on parameter values. Sometimes, the occurrence of an essential model event may be inferred from other events, rather than detected directly.

When designing the boundary between software and its environment, the developer must consider carefully the possibility of occurrences which 'cannot happen' from an essential modelling point of view. Events which from an essential modelling perspective 'just happen' must be input to the software, either by means of direct devices or by the intervention of an operator or user. Either way, something may go wrong, and the software must be specified to prevent, or to detect and recover from, such eventualities. Very often part of the purpose of a software system is to validate events, that is, to establish whether they are allowed to happen or not.

It is illustrative to apply these questions to the simple essential model we have developed for dispensing petrol, consisting of the type view given in figure 10.6, and the statecharts given in figures 10.5 and 10.7. The specification model will definitely need to contain the types **PetrolStation, Pump** and **Transaction** in order to manage the operation of the pumps and payments; the associations will remain as shown. What about the events mentioned in the statecharts? The following table shows how we might think about these.

gunRemove(p: Pump)	Detected, using a microswitch in the gun holster. In response, the software signals the attendant to switch the pump on
squeezeTrigger(p: Pump)	Ignored. The only thing that makes a difference is whether petrol is actually dispensed. We assume that a meter in the petrol line issues an event after each 1/100th of a litre of petrol is dispensed. This will be detected by the software. A new transaction will be created on the first such event after the pump has been enabled
motorOn(p: Pump)	Generated, in response to an action of the attendant
update(p: Pump, litres: Number, price: Currency)	Generated, in response to metering events
releaseTrigger(p: Pump)	Ignored. The software is not interested in why petrol delivery has stopped
gunReplace(p: Pump)	Detected
motorOff(p: Pump)	Generated, in response to **gunReplace** or **terminate**
terminate(p: Pump)	Detected: the attendant has hit the terminate button
pay(t: Transaction)	Detected
receiptRequest(t: Transaction)	Detected
receiptPrint(t: Transaction)	Generated, in response to **receiptRequest**
delete(t: Transaction)	We haven't yet decided how transactions are finally deleted; this depends on the details of the required reporting and accounting

As another example, figure 10.8 is the type view for an exceedingly simplified
essential model of a high-street bank. In this essential model there are, among other
things, an event **withdraw(Account, Currency)** and a statechart (left as a simple exercise
for the reader) which tells us that this event can only occur when the withdrawal does
not take the account overdrawn.

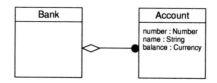

Figure 10.8 *Simple bank essential model type view*

In the specification model, we must establish a mechanism for communicating this event and its consequences between the software and its environment. One such mechanism is an Automatic Teller Machine (ATM). With an ATM, the customer inserts a card and punches a PIN in order to validate his or her identity; withdrawal of money is allowed after successful validation.

The type view for the specification model is shown in figure 10.9. Here the bank's ATMs are shown in the model, each with an optional association established after a successful PIN validation. Detected events for the specification model are as follows:

insertCard(ATM, Number)	The second parameter is the account number on the card's magnetic stripe.
validate(ATM, 4Digit)	The customer has typed the four-digit number.
requestWithdraw(ATM, Currency)	The customer has requested a withdrawal of money.

Generated events would include:

ejectCard(ATM)	The card is given back.
refuse(ATM)	The withdrawal is refused. Or else:
withdraw(Account, Currency)	The withdrawal has been authorised. This is accompanied by:
dispense(ATM, Currency)	The money is dispensed.

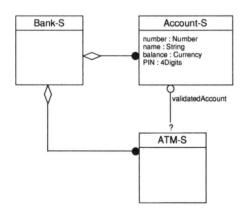

Figure 10.9 *Specification model for bank with ATM*

We can use this familiar example to underline several points as follows:

1. The essential model allows us to describe the operation of the bank account quite independently of the devices used to implement it. Holding money for

withdrawal is more 'essential' to the bank account than the particular behaviour of the ATM, or indeed any other present or future device for implementing withdrawal.

2. On the other hand we could choose to include the description of the ATM within the essential model; in fact it might be appropriate to do so.

3. The identity of the account must be communicated and validated across the software boundary. It is always necessary to do this, although schemes differ for different circumstances. Note that the identities of the ATM and bank are validated by the physical properties of the situation itself, and that bank debit cards are an attempt to apply the same principle to validating the identities of people. However, it is a lot easier to steal debit cards than working ATMs or banks (although an enterprising criminal might be able to impersonate an ATM on an electronic communications link).

4. The **withdraw** event is generated by the specification model. Frequently, an event in an essential model translates into an interaction in a specification model, started by a request of some kind and finishing either with the generation of the requested event or a refusal.

5. We would probably consider the ATM type to be in an *interaction domain*, because it is concerned with interacting with the bank account, rather than representing its essential operation. If so, the type views of the essential and specification model concept domains are almost identical.

6. We have not given any of the statecharts here. To do so, we would have to make choices about which objects are responsible for the validation process: is it a responsibility of the account itself, of the ATM, or of both? Such decisions depend on a multitude of factors, and their ultimate testing-ground is whether the software is robust and reusable in the face of changing requirements.

A further consideration is the relationship between starting configurations in essential and specification models. In some systems this is very similar, for example for the banking model above, the implicit starting configuration in both essential and specification models is a single instance of the type **Bank**. For other systems, the starting configurations in essential and specification models may differ.

10.6 Logic in essential and specification models

In both essential and specification models, the instantaneous state of the system consists of a set of related objects, each having a state and values for its properties. The state of the system can be represented by an object diagram. Every event causes a change in this state. The state change is specified using statecharts, where the new states for objects responding to each event are shown by transitions, and the new values for properties and associations are shown by post-conditions.

Invariants are statements which always hold about the structure of a model. Where there is a strong structural correspondence between essential models and specification models, similar invariants will be found in both models. For example, in the simple bank model shown above, if the **Bank** type had a property **totalBalance** with the invariant **totalBalance = sum(account.balance)**, this would apply in essential and specification models alike.

Some post-conditions can be carried across from essential to specification models; for example if the withdraw event in the **Account** type in the example above had a post-condition as follows:

withdraw(ac: Account, amount: Currency) / [balance' = balance − amount]

this would apply in both essential and specification models.

10.7 Mapping specifications to implementations

Given a specification model for a software system, how do we convert it into an implementation model? This is an important methodological question. The first thing to say about it is that the conversion process requires considerable design skill and cannot be automated straightforwardly. Issues to be considered include message-sequencing, concurrency, persistence, division of responsibilities between domains, seamlessness and traceability, design and implementation reuse, and others. In this section we discuss several of these issues. More detailed consideration of the question of domains is deferred until chapter 11, although we will assume that the general principle of domains as introduced in chapter 1 is understood.

The general idea is that the structure of the concept domain type views, including properties and invariants, are carried across into the implementation model, and each specification model event is converted to a set of message-based mechanisms. To help illustrate the process we introduce another worked example, this time of a system to manage firings in a kiln for clay pots. The specification is as follows:

This system, which runs on a personal computer with a graphical user-interface and disc drive, helps to manage an electric kiln for firing clay pots. The system may be used to pre-set a programme of future firings, and will automatically turn the kiln on and off at the correct times. There are several types of firing, each with a fixed duration and an expected temperature profile. During a firing the temperature of the kiln is automatically recorded at regular intervals and the temperature readings displayed graphically, but the system does not control the temperature of the kiln. We assume that the kiln temperature will be regulated manually by operating dampers or the like. The temperature readings associated with any earlier firing may be displayed at any time. During a firing, if the actual temperature differs from the expected temperature by more than a pre-set amount an audible alarm will be sounded to alert the operator.

The specification model type view we have designed for the single concept domain of this system is shown in figure 10.10. The starting configuration is a single **Kiln** instance associated with a fixed number of **FiringType** instances. We recommend the reader to take some time to study this specification and the associated statecharts carefully before proceeding.

Invariants on the type view establish that the times of firings cannot overlap, and that the times of readings lie between the start and end times of their associated firing. We also assert that readings are held ordered, presumably by time.

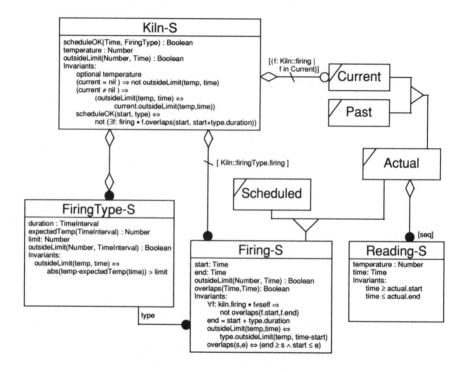

Figure 10.10 *Kiln system specification model type view*

The statechart for the **Kiln** type is shown in figure 10.11. The body of this is concerned with checking the kiln temperature against the prescribed limit. The first time the temperature exceeds the limit an alarm event will be generated. The precondition on **scheduleFiring** in the event list ensures that overlapping **Firings** cannot be created.

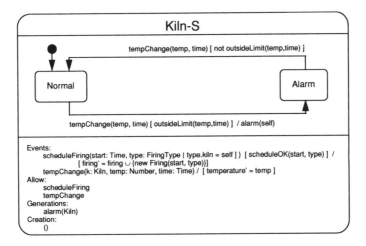

Figure 10.11 *Kiln specification model statechart*

Figure 10.12 shows the statechart for the **Firing** type. This assumes an event **readTick** occurring at regular intervals, detected by all the firing instances, which causes them to be scheduled and de-scheduled at the correct times, switching the actual kiln on and off in the process by generating the **kilnOn** and **kilnOff** events.

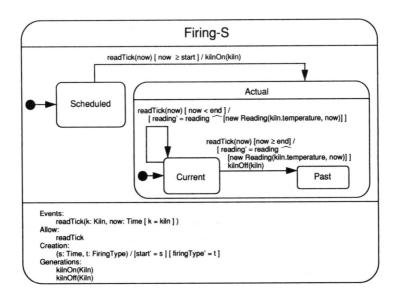

Figure 10.12 *Firing specification model statechart*

Because the readings are held in a sequence, we show the new reading being concatenated to the end of the sequence.

Figure 10.13 is the statechart for **Reading**, showing initialisation of its properties.

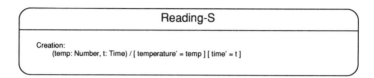

Reading-S

Creation:
    (temp: Number, t: Time) / [temperature' = temp] [time' = t]

Figure 10.13 *Reading* specification model statechart

The event table for the complete specification is as follows:

Event Name	Object Parameters	Value Parameters	Pre-conditions	Consequences	Detected/ Generated
scheduleFiring	**type: FiringType**	**start: Time**	The new **Firing** won't overlap any existing ones	A new **Firing** is created	Detected
readTick	**k: Kiln**	**now: Time**	none	If there is a current **Firing**, a new **Reading** is created	Detected
tempChange	**k: Kiln**	**now: Time** **temp: Number**	none	If the temperature goes outside limits, an alarm is generated	Detected
kilnOn	**k: Kiln**				Generated
kilnOff	**k: Kiln**				Generated
alarm	**k: Kiln**				Generated

We start to convert this specification into an implementation model by postulating that the basic structure of the type view will remain unchanged. Types and associations in the specification model will become types and associations in the implementation model, and properties will become observers. This is always a good starting-point for implementation. Carrying out this straightforward transformation gives us the type view shown in figure 10.14, which, apart from minor syntactic differences and some physical re-arrangement, is the same as figure 10.10.

In some systems it is necessary to introduce new properties, types or associations into the implementation model as a consequence of the need to manage message-sequencing, concurrency or other implementation factors. The need for these additional elements will become clear as the implementation is designed.

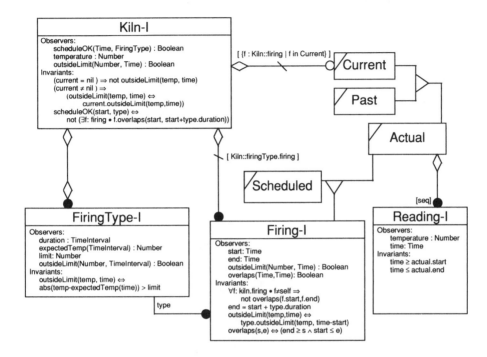

Figure 10.14 *Preliminary implementation model type view*

10.7.1 Persistence

Before making any further progress we must consider what objects will be held on persistent storage (disc) and when. The specification model assumes that the software operates continuously over time, and that there will be sufficient space to hold any number of firings and readings. In the implementation, the **Kiln** and **FiringType** objects are always instantiated in memory. We decide that the current firing (if any) and the scheduled (future) firings will be held in memory, and that all the firings will be held on disc. Past firings will only be held on disc, unless they are required to be viewed by the operator, in which case the relevant firing and all its readings will be instantiated in memory. All the readings of the current firing are held in memory and also written to disc as they are created. If the software should crash during a firing, it can be re-started and will carry on recording readings.

These decisions prompt us to change the type view. We introduce separately managed associations with each of the state sub-types of firing, and a derived association covering all instantiated firings, as shown in figure 10.15.

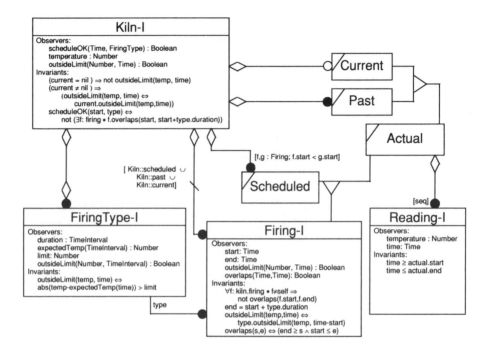

Figure 10.15 *Associating the firing states separately*

10.7.2 Other domains

So far we have only considered the concept domain. In fact, there must be other domains of the design, describing objects whose responsibility is to connect the concept domain to the system environment and to provide services to the concept domain. We don't consider the operation of other domains in detail, but we do need to document our decisions about which objects exist in those domains. We assume that the initial object configuration, established when the program is first loaded and executed, is as shown in figure 10.16. In addition to the **Kiln** and **FiringType** objects, there are objects managing the hardware interfaces with types **Alarm**, **KilnSwitch**, **TemperatureSensor** and **Clock**; a **PersistenceManager** handles the interface with the platform filing system, and a **KilnInteractor** handles the user interface. The need for these objects arises fairly directly from considering the external events in the specification model. The **scheduleFiring** event suggests a user-interface; **readTick** suggests a clock; and **tempChange** suggests a temperature sensor. The generated events **kilnOn** and **kilnOff** suggest a switch, and the **alarm** event suggests an alarm object.

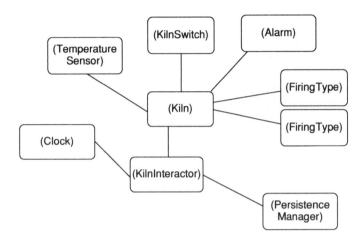

Figure 10.16 *Initial object configuration*

The type view in figure 10.17 shows the additional types introduced in the implementation model. As well as the types of the static instances shown in figure 10.16, this view defines three interaction object types corresponding to windows in the user interface: **FiringViewer**, for looking at a past firing, **FiringScheduler**, for scheduling future firings, and **KilnInteractor**, for interacting with the current firing. The annotations on the view indicate different domains.

Because instances of **Reading** and **Firing** need to persist, we make them sub-types of a type **PersistentObject**. We do not go into any further detail in this example about how the **persist** updater works; this subject is briefly revisited in chapter 11. We simply assume here that sending the message **persist** to an instance of either of these types causes a retrievable representation of it to be stored or updated on disc, and that the interface to the **PersistenceManager** provides operations to retrieve and instantiate these objects.

10.7.3 Mechanisms

The way to drive the implementation design process is by considering the key mechanisms of the software, event by event. The first event we investigate is the **readTick** event. In the specification model, all the firings are listening for these events. This is not practical in the implementation model, not least because some of the **Firing** objects may not be instantiated in memory: in any case, the **readTick** event is ignored by all the firings in the **Past** state. In the implementation model, we need to send messages only to the appropriate objects. To help with this, we introduce a new association into the type diagram, indicating which of the scheduled firings is next to be scheduled. The type view, enhanced with the new association, is shown in figure 10.18.

We make the kiln responsible for receiving **tick** messages from the clock, scheduling firings and dispatching **readTick** messages to the next and current firings. Looking at the specification model, we see that **readTick** events cause changes of state from **Scheduled** to **Current** and from **Current** to **Past**. Each time the next firing receives a tick from the kiln, it checks whether its start time has been reached. If it has, the kiln is asked to turn on. The mechanism below shows this particular tick, which also causes a new next firing to be established.

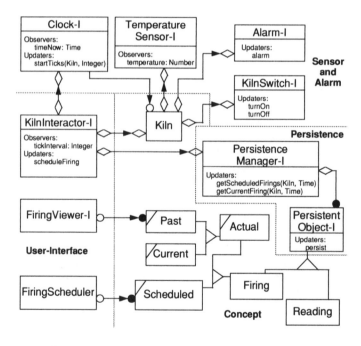

Figure 10.17 *Implementation model type view with domains*

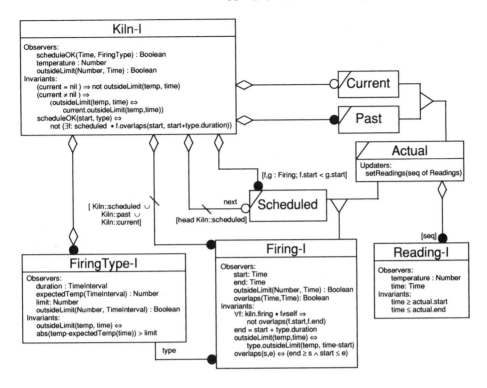

Figure 10.18 *Enhanced type view*

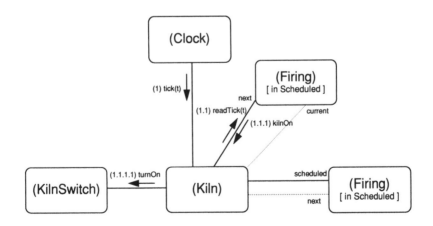

Figure 10.19 *Switching the kiln on*

In this mechanism the kiln sends the **turnOn** message to the switch in response to being asked to go on. We have decided that the kiln should act as an intermediary between the firings and the switch, rather than the firings sending the message directly to the switch. This allows the kiln to use **kilnOn** messages to rearrange its firings. We note that the **readTick** message must be sent in the relaxed section of the kiln's **tick** updater, otherwise the **kilnOn** message would cause a deadlock in the kiln.

As a result of exploring this mechanism, we have introduced some updaters: **tick** and **kilnOn** for the kiln, and **readTick** for the firing.

The next mechanism we explore, in figure 10.20, is when a tick arrives during a firing. Here we must decide how to handle temperature and time information, because in the specification model both **readTick** and **tempChange** events carry time information. We decide that the kiln first polls the temperature sensor to obtain the temperature (**temp**). It then sends **tempChange** to itself to simulate the **tempChange** event. The kiln checks that the temperature is within the limit expected at the time: in this mechanism the temperature is outside the limit for the first time so the alarm is sounded. Then the kiln interactor sends **readTick** to the current firing, which obtains the temperature from the kiln and creates a new reading. This sends itself the message **persist**, which causes it to be written to disc.

Note that there is an assumption about performance in our implementation architecture, namely that the total processing of a tick – including writing the reading to disc – can take place before the next tick.

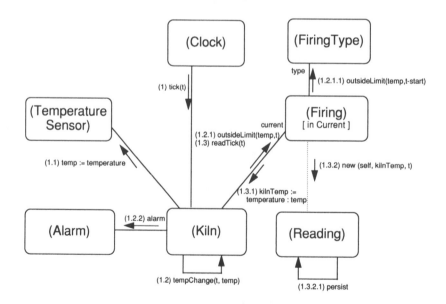

Figure 10.20 *Creating a reading*

The third tick mechanism we explore in figure 10.21 is the one when the current firing is due to finish. The firing creates a final reading and switches the kiln off by sending the **kilnOff** message. The kiln now knows that the current firing has finished and forgets about it at this point (i.e. has no instantiated association with it). We could have omitted messages 1.2.1 and 1.2.1.1 from this mechanism for simplicity if we had wanted to.

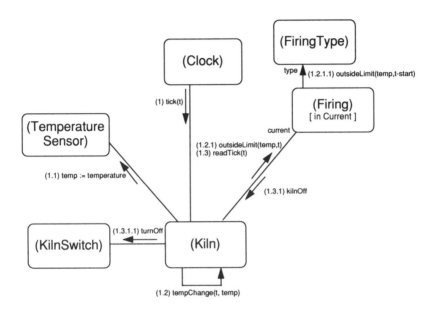

Figure 10.21 *Switching the kiln off*

In figure 10.22 we explore a mechanism which shows how a new firing is scheduled. As a result of a user interaction, the kiln interactor receives a **scheduleFiring** message. A firing scheduler is created. This asks the kiln object for all of the currently scheduled firings, and the known firing types. Then, an interaction with the user (not shown) takes place to determine the firing type and start time. The firing scheduler takes responsibility, during this interaction, for ensuring that the new firing is in the future and will not overlap with an existing scheduled firing. After this interaction a new firing is created. This sends itself the message **persist**, which causes it to be written to disc, and is then added to the kiln's scheduled set using a **scheduleFiring** updater. Because the firing scheduler has already ensured that the new firing does not overlap with any existing firings, there is no need for the kiln to check explicitly that the pre-condition for **scheduleFiring** is satisfied. In the mechanism shown, the next firing is not altered by the mechanism.

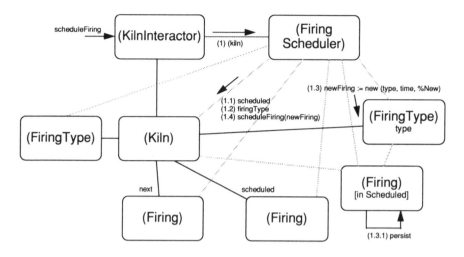

Figure 10.22 *Scheduling a new firing*

The last mechanism we investigate is the program execution itself. When there is persistent storage, it is usually necessary to start execution by instantiating objects from persistent storage to represent the current state of the system. In this case we assume that the program can be executed at any time, even in the middle of a firing (in which case we assume that the physical kiln is already switched on).

Figure 10.23 is a mechanism showing the **startUp** message sent to the kiln interactor object. This is the beginning of program execution. The kiln interactor first asks the persistence manager to instantiate the scheduled firings. The persistence manager knows which firings are scheduled from the time: any firings with starting times in the future must be scheduled. There are two of these, called **firing1** and **firing2** in the mechanism, which are instantiated with parameters telling them which kiln they belong to, which firing type they have, their starting time and which state they are in. After each is instantiated, its identity is passed to the kiln in the **scheduleFiring** message sent by the persistence manager. Then the kiln interactor asks the persistence manager to instantiate the current firing, if there is one. Again, the persistence manager can find it using the current time. The diagram shows a current firing, called **firing3**, being instantiated and having its existing readings attached by the **setReadings** message. The persistence manager then sends the kiln the **addCurrentFiring** message. Lastly, the kiln interactor asks the clock to start ticking.

We show the statecharts for **Firing** in figure 10.24 and for **Kiln** in figure 10.25. These have been designed by reasoning about the mechanisms and the specification model to produce generic descriptions of the behaviour of the implementation model types. The reader is strongly recommended to compare these statecharts with the corresponding specification model statecharts given earlier, and to examine the reasons for their similarities and differences carefully.

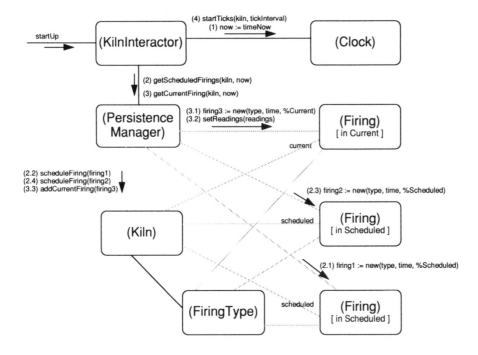

Figure 10.23 *Start up mechanism*

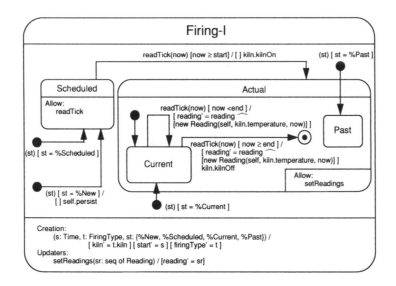

Figure 10.24 *Implementation model statechart for* **Firing**

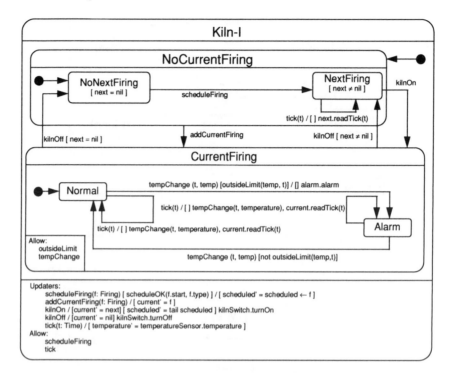

Figure 10.25 *Implementation model statechart for* **Kiln**

Finally, figure 10.26 is the implementation model type view enhanced with all of the additional information we have gleaned during this implementation model design process.

Note that the **scheduleOK** observer in the **Kiln** type does not have to be implemented because it is only referred to in a pre-condition which is not evaluated at run-time. On the other hand, it may be implemented as a service to the interaction domain which needs to validate the proposed contents of new firings.

Notice also that the invariant in **Kiln** defining the value of the **outsideLimit** property has been simplified; this is because we have introduced an *allow* statement in the state **CurrentFiring,** showing that it is invalid to call this observer except in this state.

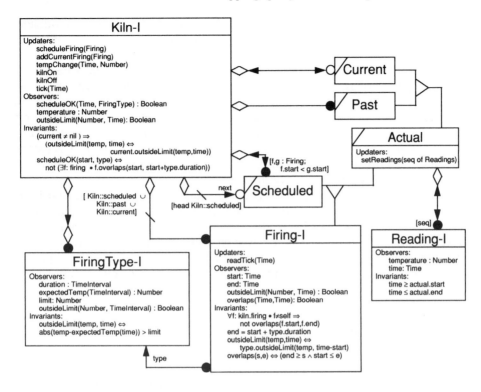

Figure 10.26 *Completed implementation model type view*

10.7.4 Conclusions

Let's attempt to draw some general conclusions about the conversion of a specification model into an implementation from our experience with this example. Firstly, our hypothesis that the type view can be carried over directly, converting properties into observers, works fairly well.

The mapping from events to messages is more involved. The generated events **alarm**, **kilnOn** and **kilnOff** map straightforwardly into messages to device-controlling objects. However, neither of the detected events is transformed straightforwardly into an updater.

Some of the complexity of the transformation results from a shift of responsibilities. In the specification model, each firing is responsible for knowing when it is due to start, and they all receive the **readTick** events. In the implementation model, to reduce the message traffic we decide to make the kiln responsible for knowing the next firing to start. As a result, the **readTick** event detected by all firings has been converted into a **readTick** message sent only to the next or current one.

Implementing the **scheduleFiring** event involves gathering the required information (firing type and start time) from the human operator, via the user-interface. When the information is gathered, the firing is created and the kiln is told about it. Again this involves a shift in responsibilities: in the specification model, the kiln is responsible for creating the firings, whereas in the implementation model, firings are created independently of the kiln (by the user-interface and persistence manager) and the kiln is notified of their existence using the **scheduleFiring** and **addCurrentFiring** updaters. On the other hand, we use a policy much more aligned with that of the specification model to create new readings. The main reason for the difference in policy is the fact that some of the firings are kept on disc, and are thus much more loosely coupled with the kiln than is implied by the specification model.

The statechart for **Firing** is reasonably similar to that in the specification models, the main differences being due to the various different ways that a firing can be instantiated in the implementation model, and the fact that firings in the past state are not kept in memory – they are only retrieved on demand. The statechart for **Kiln** bears some resemblance to that for the specification model, but is considerably complicated by the need to manage the relationships between the kiln and the different firing sub-states explicitly.

10.8 Transformation or invention?

We should emphasise that the *formal* relationship between essential, specification and implementation models is far from straightforward. Transforming from one to another is not simply a process of adding logical detail. Considered as a black box, our objective in building the implementation model is to produce something which is – as far as possible – formally equivalent, considered as a complete stimulus–response mechanism, to the specification model. This does not mean that each component of the implementation model is formally equivalent to a component of the specification model. However, there are correspondences, and our approach is based on exploiting these.

We must also emphasise that there are no right answers in the process of transforming a design from a specification to an implementation. Having designed the implementation model, we could revisit the specification model and alter it to match the implementation model much more closely. We could model persistence, for example, by introducing additional states – even in an essential model. We could model messages using events detected by only one object. We might want to move backwards and forwards between the specification and implementation models several times, until we create an overall structure in which each of the models captures our design intent best. In our minds we will also have considerations of reuse. We don't want our specification models to take on too much implementation detail because this would prevent us from reusing these specifications in systems with a different implementation architecture – a different approach to persistence, for example. On the other hand, we don't want specification models and implementation models to diverge wildly or gratuitously, because the mental effort needed to understand their relationship would be too great.

The essential point is that understanding does not come from following a recipe, it comes from working with the materials. The activity of creating all these different views of a system and struggling to understand the relationships between them and make them consistent gives insight into the problem. By dealing with all the different perspectives, the chances of leaving something out are minimised, and hence the chances of getting the result to work correctly, as well as producing design artefacts which are real assets for the developing organisation, are maximised.

10.9 Summary

- 'Modelling the real world' can be a misleading idea.
- Analysis and design are distinguished by the existence of choice, not by the use of techniques.
- The main correspondence between models is in the type view for the concept domain.
- State diagrams differ between essential and specification models, mainly because specification model statecharts show event generation.
- Essential models should be scoped to describe interesting behaviour completely.
- The software boundary can be designed by considering essential model events systematically, deciding whether each one is detected, generated or ignored by the software.
- Identities of objects in the environment must be communicated and validated across the software boundary.
- Post-conditions and invariants often correspond in essential and specification models.
- A preliminary type view for the implementation model can be created by reproducing the specification model type view replacing properties by observers.
- Persistence and performance must be considered when designing the implementation model.
- The design process proceeds by considering key mechanisms corresponding to each event, and refining the type view accordingly.
- Implementation model statecharts can be completed after mechanisms have been designed.
- The formal relationship between the three models can be complex.

10.10 Bibliographic notes

On the subject of reality, analysis and design, we recommend to the interested reader an excellent discussion of computer technology, the nature of human existence and the philosophy of language in [Winog86].

The methodological contributions of Booch [Booch91], Wirfs-Brock [Wirfs90] and several others are solely about implementation modelling. Shlaer and Mellor in [Shlae91] use a fairly precisely defined implementation-oriented technique for software specification. The work of Rumbaugh *et al.* [Rumba91] is somewhat ambiguous, in that many of their examples are obviously essential models, whereas others are clearly implementation models, but the distinction is not rigorously supported by their notation. Jacobson's work [Jacob92] introduces a number of different modelling perspectives, without distinguishing between them using formal notations. Martin and Odell in [Marti92] appear to be primarily concerned with essential modelling, but some of their examples such as 'car chases' seem to fall into the 'real-world' trap, as well as only describing 'normal' behaviour rather than being complete descriptions.

The Fusion method from Coleman *et al.* [Colem94] agrees quite closely with our specification/implementation modelling distinctions. However, they adopt global descriptions of events, especially global variables, which we think are somewhat contrary to object-oriented principles; in addition some of their formalism is not sufficiently powerful to describe some important overall behaviours, such as an arbitrary number of interleaved instances of an individual behaviour.

Building event scenarios to describe sequences of events in the world is a common feature of many systems development methods, notably [Marti92] and [Jacob92]. As we have seen, the interpretation of these sequences when humans and machinery both participate can be a subtle affair, a fact typically not acknowledged in the object-oriented literature, but discussed in some depth by Jackson [Jacks83].

10.11 References

[Booch91] G. Booch. *Object-Oriented Design with Applications*, Benjamin/Cummings, Redwood City, California, 1991.

[Colem94] D. Coleman, P. Arnold, S. Bodoff, C. Dollin, H. Gilchrist, F. Hayes and P. Jeremaes. *Object-oriented Development: The Fusion method*, Prentice-Hall, Englewood Cliffs, New Jersey, 1994.

[Jacks83] M. Jackson. *Systems Development*, Prentice-Hall, Englewood Cliffs, New Jersey, 1983.

[Jacob92] I. Jacobson, M. Christerson, P. Jonsson and G. Övergaard. *Object-Oriented Software Engineering*, ACM Press, Addison-Wesley, Wokingham 1992.

[Marti92] J. Martin and J. Odell. *Object-Oriented Analysis and Design*, Prentice-Hall, Englewood Cliffs, New Jersey, 1992.

[Rumba91] J. Rumbaugh, M. Blaha, W. Premerlani, F. Eddy and W. Lorensen. *Object-Oriented Modeling and Design*, Prentice-Hall, Englewood Cliffs, New Jersey, 1991.

[Shlae91] S. Shlaer and S.J. Mellor. *Object Lifecycles: Modelling the world in states*, Yourdon Press, Englewood Cliffs, New Jersey, 1991.

[Winog86] T. Winograd and F. Flores. *Understanding Computers and Cognition: A new foundation for design*, Ablex Corporation, Norwood, New Jersey, 1986.

[Wirfs90] R. Wirfs-Brock, B. Wilkerson and L. Wiener. *Designing Object-Oriented Software*, Prentice-Hall, Englewood Cliffs, New Jersey, 1990.

CHAPTER 11

Domains

11.1 Domains

Software developers must partition a system of any significant size into smaller parts, or sub-systems. We call these *domains*. A domain is a set of object types together constituting a coherent sub-system which can meaningfully be considered as a group. We can indicate the division of a system into domains by bubble diagrams, as shown in figure 11.1. The bubbles represent domains and the arrows represent dependencies between one domain and another.

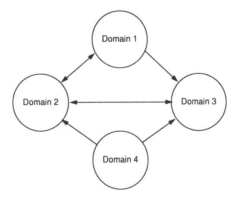

Figure 11.1 *Domains and dependencies*

Dependency between one domain and another is a consequence of relationships between types in the two domains. A dependency exists between two domains *a* and *b* if any type in *a* requires the existence of any type in *b*. Typical causes of dependency are visible associations and sub-type/super-type relationships. Dependencies may be uni-directional or bi-directional.

Normally, we insist that domains do not overlap, that is, no types exist simultaneously in more than one domain. If a particular type seems to belong simultaneously in two or more domains, it is almost certainly appropriate to divide it into parts which belong in the separate domains, and connect these parts using associations or sub-type relationships.

Note that domains are a way of dividing the system *description*, not of the system *execution*. Most software projects have some kind of overview diagram describing how the system execution is partitioned. Object diagrams are one example, and dataflow diagrams would be another. However, the main disadvantage of partitioning a system according to its execution characteristics is the loss of potential reuse of descriptions between the resulting sub-systems. Achieving this reuse within a system requires careful attention to be given to how its description is partitioned into domains.

11.1.1   Concept, interaction and infrastructure domains

Broadly speaking, domains are of three types: *concept* domains, *interaction* domains, and *infrastructure* domains. Concept domains model the phenomena in the problem being solved. Interaction domains model the software-implemented mechanisms by which the concept domain objects are kept up-to-date with the external environment and vice-versa. Infrastructure domains provide general-purpose abstractions which provide application-independent services to the other domains.

The distinction between concept and interaction domains serves two purposes. Firstly, it allows us to separate those object types which we expect to be traceable through the various model interpretations – the important concepts in the problem – from those introduced to support a particular solution.

Secondly, it supports an important architectural principle: changes to the ways in which objects modelling important problem concepts are connected to their environment should not affect the conceptual objects themselves. For example, we would like to be able to replace one user-interface by another that is completely different without having to modify the concept-domain objects with which the user-interface interacts. Ideally, our conceptual model, represented by the object types in the concept domains, should be totally independent of the means of interaction. The implication of this is that, ideally, concept domains should not be dependent on interaction domains. As we will see later in this chapter, this is not always possible. A consequence of this architectural principle is our rule that:

> *Objects of types in concept domains never interact directly with the mechanical devices that detect external stimuli or generate external responses: interaction domain objects always act as intermediaries.*

Infrastructure domains provide low-level building-blocks for the other domains to call upon. They may be used from either concept or interaction domains. In this chapter we only consider infrastructure items which are explicitly represented in our design formalisms. An implementation technology for an object-oriented design will also contain components such as collections, dictionaries, tasks and semaphores which are used to implement the fundamental concepts of our design formalisms; we can think of these components as comprising an implicit infrastructure domain.

There are many ways in which a good domain division benefits a software development. We have already discussed separating the concept model from the user-interface. In general, domains allow concerns to be separated, so that changes in requirements have the least impact on the software as a whole. Domains promote reuse: for example, parts of a concept domain which do not depend upon the details of interaction are much more likely to be usable in another context than are parts in which details of interaction are inextricably wound up with problem-domain concepts. Domains also provide the natural units for breaking down the effort on a project, as long as the domain boundaries are properly defined, and changes in the boundaries agreed, managed and understood.

11.1.2 Some examples

One example is the kiln control system introduced in chapter 10. This system automates the operation of a kiln for firing clay pots. Our implementation for this system has the following domains:

- concept domain;
- user-interface domain;
- sensor and alarm domain;
- persistence domain.

The relationships between the domains can be determined from the type view, shown in figure 11.2.

The corresponding domain diagram is shown in figure 11.3. There may be further domains unidentified here, because so far we do not have complete knowledge of the problem. For example, there might be common hardware components in the interaction domains; if so it would be appropriate to abstract out the common components into a separate hardware infrastructure domain. Above all, we want to isolate our design as far as possible from changes in the make of temperature sensor, alarm, etc.

For a rather different example, in a simple word-processor we might find the following main domains:

- logical domain, concerned with paragraphs, words, characters, fonts, styles, etc.;
- layout domain, concerned with the physical location of the words on the screen or page, interpreting position information in terms of logical structure and vice-versa;

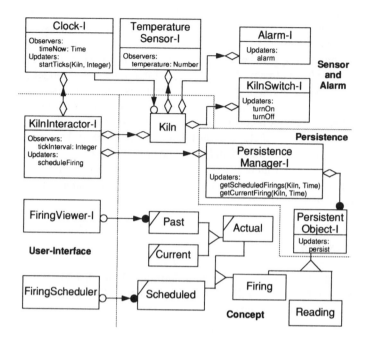

Figure 11.2 *Kiln type view showing domains*

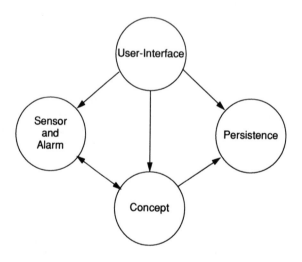

Figure 11.3 *Kiln domains*

- command domain, concerned with the interpretation of menu commands, 'undo', etc.;
- window management domain, concerned with assembling editing windows from user-interface components such as display areas, title bars, menu bars, scroll bars, etc.;
- printing domain, concerned with sending the correct commands to the printer to get documents printed.

The first three of these can be classified as concept domains, because they model the essence of the word-processing situation; the last two are interaction domains, because they act as intermediaries between the abstractions of word-processing and their concrete manifestations on the screen and printer.

A third, and rather more complex, example would be a music composition system with an interactive user-interface allowing the user to change the music's representation as conventional musical notation by direct manipulation, as well as direct input from a musical keyboard and output to electronic musical instruments using the MIDI[1] protocol. The suggested main domains are as follows:

- music domain, concerned with musical sounds and their relationships in a composition;
- notation domain, concerned with elements of musical notation and their relationships with each other and with the music domain;
- MIDI domain, concerned with translating sequences of MIDI impulses into the representations of musical sounds, and vice-versa;
- user-interface domain, concerned with creating manipulable visual displays of musical notation;
- other interaction domains concerned with interfacing to devices, operating system, persistent storage, printing, user-interface management, etc.

We would regard the first two as concept domains and the remainder as interaction domains. Figure 11.4 is a suggested domain diagram for this example. It is arguable that the notation domain is an interaction domain, because its role is to provide a way of interacting with the composition. However, in a system whose primary purpose was to edit notation, the notation domain would definitely be a concept domain. This example shows that the division into concept and interaction domains can be debatable in certain circumstances. Nevertheless, we still find the distinction extremely valuable, and even in the simplest system we always identify at least one concept and one interaction domain.

Figure 11.4 is roughly hierarchical. This is typical for multi-domain systems: normally the hierarchy has infrastructure domains at the bottom, concept domains next and interaction domains at the top, as shown in figure 11.5.

---

[1] Musical Instrument Digital Interface.

The domain hierarchy is often not strict because interaction domains often mutually depend upon each other, and exceptionally a concept domain may depend on an interaction domain. Later in this chapter we present some examples of how to manage inter-domain dependencies.

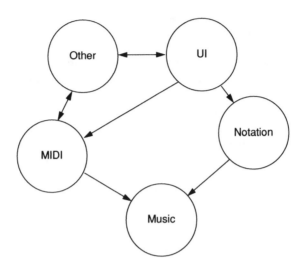

Figure 11.4 *Domains for music composition system*

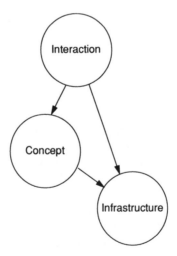

Figure 11.5 *Domain hierarchy*

11.2 Domains and model interpretations

Having introduced domains, we discuss how they are applicable in each of our modelling interpretations: the essential, specification and implementation models.

The intended purpose of an *essential* model is to describe a system whose meaning lies outside the operation of the software, so that the system being described can be formally understood. Therefore, an essential model does not normally describe interaction domains. Although it would be possible in theory to describe the structure and behaviour of the software that implements an interaction domain using the formalism and concepts of essential models, in practice there is usually little value in doing so because in this case there would be no significant difference between understanding the situation and specifying the software, and by using essential modelling concepts we would lose the distinction between detected and generated events and the discipline of behavioural type-conformance.

Domains in the essential model correspond to natural conceptual groupings or layerings in the subject-matter being described. Usually these domains are arranged hierarchically, with a single most essential domain not depending upon any others. The music domain in the example given earlier depends upon nothing else, whereas the notation domain is tightly coupled to the music domain.

A *specification* model is concerned with describing the behaviour of software and hence, in principle, contains interaction domains. Concept domains in a specification model mimic the external environment, receiving events from it and generating events back into it, and are completely independent of the actual mechanisms used to detect and generate the events. Events received by concept domains are generated by interaction domains and vice-versa.

However, we often do not build a specification model for an interaction domain because many of the design details are closely bound up with issues which are properly the concern of the implementation model, such as message-sequencing or object persistence. Also, interaction domains for interactive user-interfaces are usually constructed in practice using existing class libraries or software development tools such as Graphical User Interface (GUI) builders or User Interface Management Systems (UIMS) which have their own formalisms more closely related to the implementation model. In such cases, there may not be any great value in building a specification model. Nevertheless, for complex interaction domains, such as communication protocols or highly interactive user-interfaces (e.g. the musical notation editor suggested above), building a specification model can be extremely worthwhile.

In the *implementation* model we must deal with the practical problems of point-to-point control flow, object management, persistence and the other issues which become important when we implement an abstract specification in a finite execution environment. All domains should therefore be fully described to an adequate level of detail in the implementation model.

11.3 Domains in the implementation model

Assume that we have a specification model for a concept domain, and wish to design an implementation model. The specification model describes the structures of objects which will implement this domain, the events which will arrive as input into the domain and the events which are generated as a result. The designer of an implementation model must deal with the following questions for the implementation of the concept domain:

- When and where are objects instantiated?
- How are input events implemented as messages, which objects are they sent to, and what are the consequences?
- How are changes in the state of the concept-domain objects made visible to the interaction domains?
- How are output events implemented as messages?
- How do the interaction domains query the state of the concept domain?

In addition, the designer must of course implement the interaction domains themselves, and designing interaction domains can be at least as difficult as designing concept domains.

A real project might be implementing a large, distributed, real-time application, and a complete discussion of all the issues that would arise in such a project is outside the scope of this book. For completeness we would have to consider the overall topic of distributed object management, involving large, often complex, and indeed sometimes unanswered questions about object persistence, replication, sharing and mobility. As an example, imagine a multi-user game with shared interactions over a wide-area network where each participant's 'spaceship' can be seen on every participant's screen simultaneously, with its position updated in real time. Considered as a specification model this is relatively trivial, but as an implementation model it is rather complicated and very dependent upon the details of the implementation environment.

We reduce the discussion to a manageable scope by focusing particularly on the implementation of a concept domain and its boundary with the other domains. We also assume that the implementation being designed is for a single-user system, with objects in a single virtual address space, some of which may be stored and retrieved from backing storage using a persistency mechanism – which may be files or some kind of database management system.

11.3.1 Object instantiation

We must decide how and when an object will be instantiated in memory. There are two reasons for doing this: creating it in the first place, and retrieving it subsequently from backing storage. An object may be put in backing storage because of insufficient room in memory, because it needs to be stored between separate program executions, or to allow it to be shared (particularly with applications which are not object-oriented)[2]. The simplest option for storing objects between program executions is to retrieve all objects at the beginning of an execution, and store them all again at the end. A more flexible option is to retrieve sets of objects for well-defined user interactions, and to store any that have changed at the end of the interaction.[3]

In our kiln example, introduced in chapter 10, some objects, such as the kiln itself, are created afresh in memory each time the program is started and are not stored persistently because their state can be reconstructed. Others, such as the scheduled firings, are re-created from backing store when the program starts and held in memory during execution. The past firings are only instantiated when needed and are removed from memory when no longer required.

In chapter 10 we designed a starting configuration for the kiln system, reproduced here as figure 11.6. Of course, this configuration does not spring into life by magic; the implementor must decide how to initialise it. The initial configuration could be created either at compile time or at run-time, the exact mechanism being very dependent upon the implementation technology in use. The individual objects must be created and associated correctly; either one or more of the initial objects must have this responsibility or another object has it. We would not want this responsibility to belong to a concept domain object because this would result in excessive coupling between the concept and other domains.

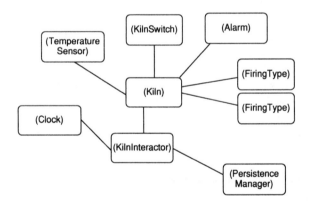

Figure 11.6 *Starting configuration for kiln system*

---

[2]We are interpreting 'memory' rather liberally here to mean 'virtual object space'. This contains all objects which may be reached directly by navigation without the intervention of explicit mechanisms to retrieve and instantiate them. This definition certainly includes virtual memory, and also some kinds of object storage system which make navigation transparent.

[3]This solution is readily generalised to a multi-user system, and various levels of protection against contention can be provided using locking mechanisms. Normally, the strategy to be adopted is largely dictated by the characteristics of the database management system chosen to support the implementation.

Other issues arise when we consider the dynamic creation of new objects. Consider the mechanism shown in figure 11.7, which illustrates the creation of a new **Firing** object.

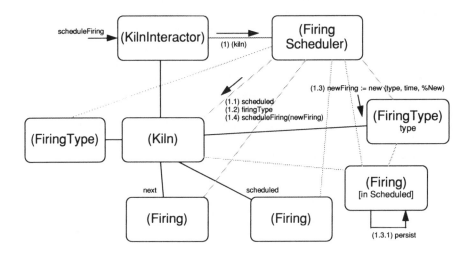

Figure 11.7 *Mechanism to create a **Firing** object*

Notice how the firing scheduler queries the kiln to obtain the identities of the currently scheduled firings (message 1.1) and the available firing types (message 1.2). It does this because it needs to have a dialogue with the user to select the correct properties for the new firing. The user will examine existing firings to decide on the required start time and select from the available firing types. We will have more to say about this in a moment. The firing scheduler creates the new object and then notifies the kiln about it. This is a design decision. An alternative would have been to ask the kiln to create it, using a message such as:

createScheduledFiring(FiringType, Time)

It is difficult to make hard-and-fast rules about whether to create concept domain objects inside the domain or outside. In this example it makes little difference, but we can make the following general observations:

- When a new concept-domain object is created as a result of user-interface action, as here, it is usual for the new object to become the subject of the user-interface: the user-interface will need to know its identity. If it is not created by the interaction domain, the identity of the new object must be returned by the concept domain.

- Whichever choice is made, it should be adhered to throughout the design. For example, if a kiln ever has to create a firing other than in response to a firing scheduler request, then it would be better for all firings to be created by the kiln.

11.3.2 Identities and keys

Object identities are a superb way of managing references to objects *within the software*, but they are meaningless outside it. A user-interface cannot ask a user to select between a number of objects on the basis of their identities; it must show the user the value of one or more of the objects' properties.

To continue with the example in figure 11.7, consider how the user is to select a firing type for a new firing. The design given in chapter 10 defines the following properties for firing types:

- duration;
- expected temperature at any time;
- limit of temperature deviation;
- a function determining whether a given temperature is outside limits;
- kiln (by virtue of association);
- firings of this type (again by association).

None of these taken alone suggest themselves as suitable ways of selecting a firing type, but we might display in the user-interface all the details of each firing type and let the user select from that information. Alternatively, we might introduce a new property to help the user with this selection, such as a number or string allocated uniquely to each firing type, analogous to a *key* in a relational database design.

In the concept domain we always prefer to distinguish objects by their identities. Although external keys may be stored in the concept domain, they are almost never used for navigation or access within that domain.

Converting between external keys and internal identities is in general a complex matter. How it is done depends upon many factors including the following:

- the number of objects involved;
- the style of the selection being carried out;
- whether the objects are currently instantiated in object space;
- the persistence scheme in use.

Conversion is normally a responsibility of interaction domains, although sometimes helper operations may be provided in the concept domain.

For an example of how *not* to use keys, consider creating a new firing by sending a message to a kiln with the following format:

createScheduledFiring(Number, Time)

where **Number** is the key of a **FiringType** object. If the user-interface already has the identity of the **FiringType** object, this would be very poor design, because it is horribly inefficient to pass the key of an object when its identity is already known.   Very frequently we see inexperienced designers passing keys rather than identities as parameters throughout the system – with catastrophic consequences for performance.

11.3.3 Input events

In interaction domains objects detect events, such as button presses, temperature changes or time passing, and translate them into messages. The actual detection is by interaction with hardware devices, either by polling or by interrupts[4]. Either way, a thread of control executing inside an interaction object will, at some point in time, know that a particular event has occurred.

In the concept-domain specification model for the kiln example there is an event **scheduleFiring**. This event causes a new firing to be created. What does it mean in the implementation model to detect that event?

We decide that the event occurs at the moment the user confirms the details of the new firing that they have already entered into the firing scheduler. Let us imagine a graphical user-interface for the firing scheduler with an on-screen button that generates this event. There might also be an option to invoke the same behaviour with a menu option. We activate these user-interface gadgets by clicking the mouse. So the lowest-level event is:

> **mouseClick(s: Screen, pos: Point)**

There are also two somewhat higher-level events, say:

> **buttonPress(f: FiringScheduler, buttonNumber: Integer)**
> **menuSelect(f: FiringScheduler, optionNumber: Integer)**

The relationship between these events is far from straightforward. A mouse click within a certain rectangle generates a button press and a mouse click within another rectangle generates a menu selection. However, one particular button and menu selection will imply scheduling a firing. Assume that we design **FiringScheduler** so that when it detects **buttonPress** with **buttonNumber=3**, or **menuSelect** with **optionNumber=6**, it generates a **scheduleFiring** event.

If we now consider how to implement this using messages, it is clear that several objects are involved. The mechanisms in figure 11.8 show what might be happening. The **FiringScheduler** object has parameterised the **Button** and **MenuOption** objects to send the appropriate number when they are clicked. The firing scheduler must itself

---

[4]At a higher level of abstraction, the interaction might be with the operating system and interrupts are replaced by call-backs. Of course, the operating system is still interacting with the hardware in some manner.

convert the abstract notions of button press and menu select into application-specific terms, and thus send the correct messages into the concept domain. This is typical, because we want the user-interface devices to be application-independent. So, interaction-domain objects must first raise events to the correct level of abstraction before they can be applied to the concept domain.[5]

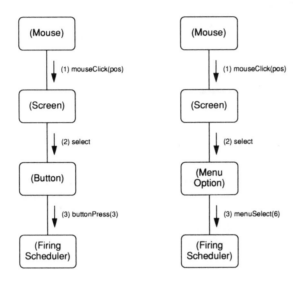

Figure 11.8 *Mechanisms to schedule a firing*

A further responsibility of the interaction domain in this example is to validate the event. Referring again to the specification model type view, the **scheduleFiring** event has a pre-condition, based on the **scheduleOK** property, to ensure that overlapping firings are not scheduled. In the specification model the behaviour is undefined if this event occurs when **scheduleOK** is false. The precise method of validating the event depends upon the details of the user-interface design; we assume the buttons and menu entries representing the action of confirming the new firing are disabled if the details entered would violate the pre-condition.

Having detected and validated an event, the interaction-domain object must apply it to the concept domain. It does this by sending one or more messages. The first act of design is to decide which messages are to be sent and which concept-domain objects must receive them. In this case, the event must cause a **scheduleFiring** message to be sent to the kiln. The event causes a single message-send, the simplest of the three alternatives depicted in figure 11.9.

---

[5]In practice user-interface libraries often provide facilities to do most of this.

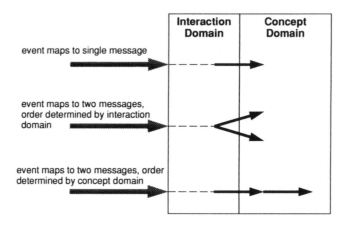

Figure 11.9 *Converting input events to messages*

We could predict that the event will correspond to a single message by examining the specification model statecharts.   Only one type of object, **Kiln**, detects **scheduleFiring** events; therefore only kilns need to be told about them. Furthermore, as only the kiln associated with the event detects it, only one object in total is interested in the event. If the event were of interest to many objects we would need to ensure that each was told about it. There are two implementation strategies for this: the first, and most common, is for the interaction object that detects the event to notify each interested object in some order it determines. The other is for the interaction object to notify one interested object and then let it notify the others, in some order it determines.   The real difference is where the order of notification is determined. Usually, the order is unimportant and can be left to the interaction object; sometimes it is important and the concept-domain objects must decide.

11.3.4 Output events

Objects in the concept domain need to generate responses whose consequences are felt in the environment, such as activating the kiln temperature alarm. In the specification model we merely show concept-domain objects generating the events, without considering how the event will be propagated to the environment. We are forced to consider this when we design the boundary interface between the concept domain and the interaction domains.

Since concept-domain objects do not generate external events themselves, we need to arrange for them to send messages requesting such generations to objects from interaction domains. To do this directly they must have associations with objects in one or more interaction domains, giving the concept domain an undesirable coupling to interaction domains. We can try to minimise this coupling. The important thing to consider is how the association between the concept-domain object and the interaction-domain object was established. We offer the following three alternatives:

1. The tightest coupling occurs if the concept-domain object obtains the identity of the interaction-domain object by creating it. This is the worst situation because the concept-domain object must know the exact type of the interaction-domain object required, and must know everything required to instantiate it.

2. Looser coupling is achieved by having objects outside the concept domain 'plug' together concept-domain objects with the required interaction-domain objects. This is done by sending the concept-domain object a message with the identity of an interaction-domain object as a parameter; the parameter is remembered for later use. By building the association in this way the concept-domain object does not need to know the exact type of the interaction-domain object, merely the type that defines the required interface and to which the interaction-domain object conforms. Different sub-types could be used without affecting the concept-domain.

3. Slightly looser coupling still can be obtained by passing the identities of all required interaction-domain objects as parameters of the message that is sent to the concept-domain object and triggers the event generation.

A further option is for the concept-domain object to adopt an indirect approach, by using the techniques in the following section to communicate its changes in state to an interaction domain, which will infer the need to generate the external event.

11.3.5 State changes

In the specification model we assume that the state of the system is visible at all times, and we do not design events whose purpose is merely to interrogate or report the state. But if, in the implementation model, we *really* want to provide a dynamic view of the state of objects in the concept domain to agents in the environment (such as people looking at user interfaces) we must design a way of propagating state changes automatically.

Consider the possible user-interface for the kiln interactor shown in figure 11.10. During a firing, the graph is updated on each temperature change. We assume some link between the kiln interactor and the alarm device. How does the kiln interactor know it should update its graph and how does it obtain the necessary information? Figure 11.11 shows two of the more obvious ways that it could be done.

Neither is very satisfactory. The left-hand mechanism requires the clock to know it must send the tick to the kiln first, making the design very dependent upon correct behaviour of the clock. The right-hand mechanism attempts to alleviate this by only requiring one tick direct to the kiln; unfortunately this requires coupling between the kiln and the kiln interactor, which is bad because now the kiln must be aware of the objects viewing it. If another kiln interactor was created for the same kiln (as often happens in graphical user-interfaces), the kiln would need to be aware of that object, too.

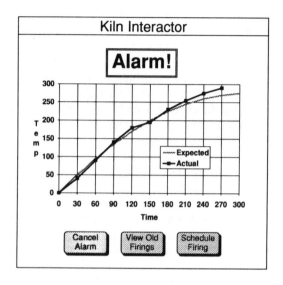

Figure 11.10 *Kiln interactor user-interface*

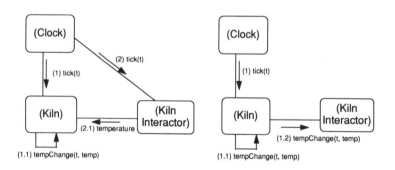

Figure 11.11 *Update mechanisms*

We can avoid this direct coupling by introducing a general mechanism for objects to notify interested parties of changes in their state using infrastructure domain types **ChangeGenerator** and **ChangeAcceptor**. The idea, outlined in figure 11.12, is often called *dependency*[6] and appears as a feature of a number of languages and class libraries.

---

[6]Not to be confused with the notion of domain dependency discussed elsewhere in this chapter.

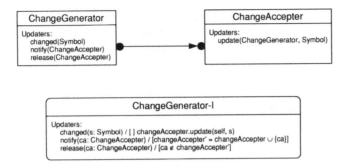

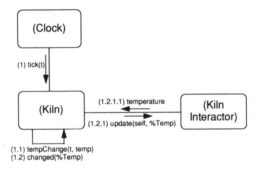

Figure 11.12 *Implementing dependency*

If we make **Kiln** a sub-type of **ChangeGenerator** and **KilnInteractor** a sub-type of **ChangeAccepter**[7], we can arrange for the kiln to notify the kiln interactor without being aware of it, provided it sends *itself* the necessary **changed** message, as shown in figure 11.13. This is a useful technique for breaking direct coupling between the concept domain and the interaction domains.

Figure 11.13 *Dependency mechanism*

11.3.6 State mirroring

There is a conflict between our desire to keep problem-domain concepts localised in the concept domain and our need to expose those concepts in friendly and powerful user-interfaces. If the user-interface is to guide the user in the appropriate choice of commands it may need to know the possible state changes of the underlying concept-domain object being viewed and changed.

---

[7]Most commonly, a sub-type extending both **ChangeGenerator** and **ChangeAccepter** is created, allowing objects both to generate *and* accept changes.

Consider the simple statechart for a business invoice shown in figure 11.14. We assume that an invoice is viewed and manipulated by an **InvoiceInteractor** object The interactor may wish to display a menu of possible next actions but, in keeping with today's standards for menus, the other, invalid, options should be shown but greyed-out. Therefore, the interactor must at all times know the current state and possible next state changes for the invoice. The strong implication is that it operates against a statechart such as that shown in figure 11.14.

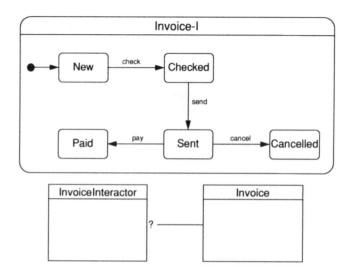

Figure 11.14 *Invoices with interactors*

It is for this reason that we often find designs where the concept-domain type's statechart is replicated in an interaction-domain type; indeed, sometimes the statechart is actually *transferred* to the interaction domain, leaving the concept-domain type as merely a data store.

This mirroring of concept-domain state in interaction domains is undesirable because it makes changes to the software more difficult and may fail to operate correctly if the underlying object (the invoice in this example) is changed via another route.

Once again, we need to devise a standard generic solution to this problem. We can devise a standard message protocol by which objects can expose their state and provide information about valid changes. A simple solution which can be used when there are no guards is to provide an observer **allUpdaters**, which returns a set of symbols naming all updaters of the recipient, and **validUpdaters**, which returns a set of symbols naming all updaters applicable in the current state. The behaviour of these observers follows directly from the statechart. Much of this detail is 'boiler-plate', and could be generated automatically from a smart tool, or by using macros, or meta-programming facilities[8]. It may be convenient simply to assume that these observers are defined as standard within a type whenever they are required.

11.3.7 Inter-domain sub-types

We frequently couple domains using sub-typing. An example of this appears in the kiln system, shown in figure 11.2. The concept-domain object types **Firing** and **Reading** are sub-types of **PersistentObject**, a type in the persistence domain. This kind of sub-typing occurs frequently because we often design domains, such as the persistence domains, as frameworks, where the entire point is to sub-type. Sub-typing in the opposite direction, with sub-types of concept-domain types in interaction domains, is very unlikely.

When we sub-type a framework type, such as **PersistentObject**, it may be necessary to override operations to support mechanisms in the framework. In this example, **Firing** and **Reading** might override the **persist** operation to specialise its behaviour. For example, we could define persist in **Firing** as follows:

> **persist / [ ] persistenceManager.persistFiring(self)**

and similarly for **Reading**[9]. In doing this we have allowed design information from one domain to 'leak' into another. Many other solutions exist, but this leakage is unavoidable[10].

We can see another need for inter-domain sub-typing in this example. If we look at the definition of the **Clock** type, as in figure 11.15, we can see that it can only tick kilns. This seems an unnecessary restriction.

Here we have a dependency between the clock domain and the concept domain. This is not a bad thing in itself, but in this case we want to make the clock more general-purpose. We break the dependency (but introduce another of a different kind) by creating a new type that is the prototype for all ticked objects. We show this design in figure 11.16. By introducing **TickedObject** we permit the design of a general-purpose clock, at the cost of having to make **Kiln** a sub-type of **TickedObject**. This is a very small cost, because **Kiln** needs to define a response to **tick** in any case; unlike the

---

[8]So far we have resisted including meta-level facilities in our formalisms, but this is one area where they would be very useful.

[9]To implement persistence, the persistence manager would need unique keys for all the persistent objects. It might be able to extract these automatically from object IDs, or they might be allocated on object instantiation.

[10]Another approach would be to provide and use meta-level facilities. If objects contained run-time information about their types, and types were themselves objects, we could implement persist generically in **PersistentObject** as follows:

> **persist / [ ] persistenceManager.persistObject(self)**

This would avoid domain leakage at the object level, at the expense of leakage at the type level: the objects representing the **Firing** and **Reading** *types* would provide operations to implement persistence for their instances.

persist updater considered earlier, this should not be thought of as 'leakage' from the clock domain (now best thought of as an infrastructure domain) into the concept domain.

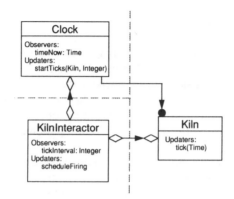

Figure 11.15 *Clocks which tick kilns*

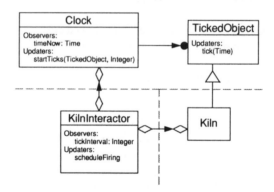

Figure 11.16 *Clocks which tick anything*

11.4 Domain dependencies revisited

The issue of domain dependencies is not really as cut-and-dried as we suggested at the beginning of this section. Domain dependencies are difficult or impossible to avoid and may be beneficial in some cases. We really need to consider the strength of the dependency rather than the fact of its existence. We can make some general observations as follows:

- The strongest type of inter-domain dependency comes when an object of a type in one domain creates an object of a type in another. We definitely wish to avoid this kind of dependency between concept domains and interaction domains.
- A visible association between two types in different domains is a fairly strong dependency and we should seek to limit the number of such associations from concept domains to interaction domains.
- Sub-type dependency is similar in strength to a visible association, but tends to have more beneficial consequences, as illustrated by the example in figure 11.16. We should expect concept domains to have this kind of dependency on domains that define frameworks.

11.5 Summary

- Domains are sub-systems which represent separate areas of concern.
- A domain is a set of object types.
- Domains don't overlap, but may depend upon each other.
- Concept domains model the phenomena in the problem being solved; interaction domains model the mechanisms by which concept-domain objects are kept up-to-date with the external environment, and vice-versa.
- Concept domains never deal directly with hardware, or system-level software that controls hardware.
- Domains promote reuse and provide a natural way of breaking down project effort.
- Domains form a rough hierarchy, with interaction domains being more dependent on concept domains than vice-versa.
- An essential model normally only describes concept domains.
- A specification model may describe interaction domains, but often doesn't.
- An implementation model describes all domains.
- In the implementation model we must decide how and when an object will be instantiated in memory.
- Objects in the concept domain may be created dynamically by interaction domains or by the concept domain.
- Object identities are not visible externally; instead, objects are referred to by combinations of properties called keys.
- Converting between keys and identities is a complex matter, and is normally a responsibility of interaction domains.
- Keys should not be used for navigation within the model.
- An interaction domain converts input events at a low level of abstraction to messages at the level of abstraction of the concept domain.
- A single event may map to several messages, whose order may be determined by an interaction domain or a concept domain.
- To generate output events directly a concept domain must have an association with an interaction domain: we try to minimise the coupling this causes.

- A scheme called *dependency* may be used to communicate concept-domain state changes to an interaction domain without creating an undesirable coupling.
- Sometimes the state of a concept-domain object is mirrored in an interaction domain. A standard set of observers may be provided for this purpose.
- Sub-typing may be used to couple domains cleanly. Interaction domains are often designed as frameworks containing types specifically intended for sub-typing.
- Domain dependencies are not cut-and-dried; there are different strengths of dependency with benefits and disadvantages.

11.6 Bibliographic notes

Many of our domain ideas originate in the Model-View-Controller concept introduced by Smalltalk [Goldb83]. Models live in concept domains and Views and Controllers in interaction domains. MVC also introduced the dependency scheme used for communicating model state changes: this has subsequently been adopted by many other class libraries.

Shlaer and Mellor have a well-developed notion of domains in their work [Shlae91]. They distinguish between application, service, architecture and implementation domains. Their ideas differ from ours in many details but the overall intent appears similar.

Jacobsen introduces entity objects, interface objects and control objects in [Jacob92]. Entity objects and control objects naturally correspond to our concept domain, while interface objects correspond to interaction domains.

11.7 References

[Goldb83] A. Goldberg and D. Robson. *Smalltalk-80: the Language and its Implementation*, Addison-Wesley, Reading, Massachusetts, 1983.

[Jacob92] I. Jacobson, M. Christerson, P. Jonsson and G. Övergaard. *Object-Oriented Software Engineering*, ACM Press, Addison-Wesley, Wokingham 1992.

[Shlae91] S. Shlaer and S.J. Mellor. *Object Lifecycles: Modelling the world in states*, Yourdon Press, Englewood Cliffs, New Jersey, 1991.

CHAPTER 12

Encapsulation and reuse

12.1 Encapsulation

Encapsulation is a fundamental concept in object-oriented systems. Encapsulation means hiding some or all of the details of the construction of part of a system from other parts. Without encapsulation, the idea of a software component has no effective meaning, because there is no way of drawing a boundary around part of the system to define a component; and without components there can be no effective strategy for reuse. When details of a system component are encapsulated, its clients are insulated from those changes which they cannot see, and hence the management of system evolution is greatly simplified. With encapsulation, the designer can defeat complexity using the divide-and-conquer strategy: large systems built by assembling completely understood small models can themselves be understood.

Encapsulation also brings advantages when reasoning about concurrent systems. As explained in chapter 9, it is crucial to be able to deduce how knowledge of a particular object is communicated around a system, in order to establish what kind of contract this object may have with its clients. Encapsulation techniques can help to reason about how this knowledge may spread.

For these reasons, a proper treatment of encapsulation is vital in any method for object-oriented analysis, design or implementation. The encapsulation techniques in this chapter can be applied to essential, specification or implementation models. Encapsulation is most important for implementation models[1], at least for the foreseeable future, because it enables libraries of re-usable executable software components to be created and disseminated. We envisage such libraries being marketed in conjunction with detailed models built using techniques such as those in this book. Such models would assist users to understand the intricacies of these libraries much more readily than they can with just the code and informal documentation.

---

[1]Despite this remark, all the examples given in this section refer to the essential or specification model for simplicity.

12.1.1 Principles

We give the name *features* to those aspects of a type (such as properties, associations and operations) to which we want to control access. We wish to specify which types have access to each individual feature of every type. Most programming languages provide facilities for controlling access to individual features in various ways; for example, C++ has a somewhat limited scheme in which class members may be marked as public (accessible from anywhere), private (accessible only within the defining class or its 'friends') or protected (accessible by the defining class, its 'friends' and its sub-classes).

In general, we think about access to features in terms of *suppliers* and their *clients*. One type is a client and another is its supplier if the client uses the features of the supplier in any way.

A supplier may have several different *kinds* of client. Each kind of client is distinguished by the set of features which the supplier makes available to it. The most remote kind of relationship between a supplier and client is where the client just knows of the existence of the supplier, but does not access any of its properties.

The most general kind of control would be to specify access to each feature individually on a type-by-type basis. Although very flexible, controlling access permissions in this way has the serious disadvantage that nominating which types have access to each feature is a lot of tedious work, which may discourage developers from making use of the facility.

To resolve this problem, we propose the concept of a *viewpoint* on a type. A viewpoint is a restricted view of a type which defines the access for a particular kind of client. A viewpoint contains a subset of the features of a type. One kind of viewpoint would be the set of features intended for use by sub-types; this would correspond to the protected+public parts of a C++ class. Another kind of viewpoint might be the set of features intended for use by *collaborating* types, that is, the types which work together with the supplier to implement the behaviour of a sub-system. In principle there could be any number of different viewpoints of a type, although typically there will be two or three.

12.1.2 Ownership and permission

A vital issue with encapsulation is the question of permission. Who is allowed to define a viewpoint, and who is allowed to access it? The answer to this question can only be properly framed in terms of human roles during the software development process. Types should have owners, such that only their owners are allowed to create viewpoints, and to nominate which other owners are allowed access to these viewpoints. There may be many owners per type, and many types per owner. A full treatment of roles in software development is well outside the scope of this discussion, but a proper consideration together with proper tool support is vital for achieving systematic reuse of software components between software systems.

12.1.3 Example

To illustrate the basic principles we re-visit the kiln example once again. We start by looking at the specification model, whose type view is reproduced in figure 12.1, and relevant statecharts in figures 12.2 and 12.3.

Consider how we might construct different viewpoints of the **Firing** type defining the availability of its features for use by other types. Looking at each of the other types, we need to include the following properties:

1. **Kiln** needs to access the **outsideLimit** and **overlaps** properties, and the creation operation.
2. **Reading** needs to access the **start** and **end** properties, because of its invariant.
3. One **Firing** object needs to access the **start** and **end** properties of others, in order to define the **overlaps** operation.
4. The state sub-types and related associations, and the association with **FiringType** need not be accessible outside the individual **Firing** object itself.

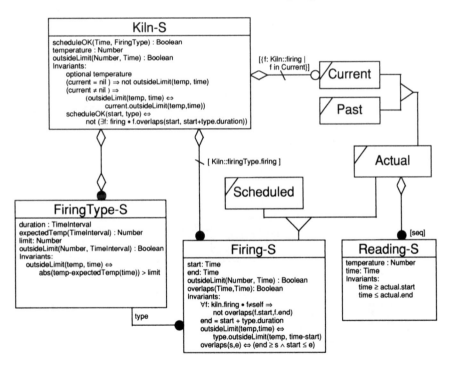

Figure 12.1 *Kiln system specification model type view*

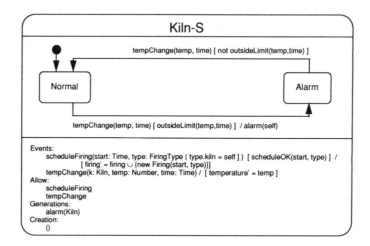

Figure 12.2 *Kiln* specification model statechart

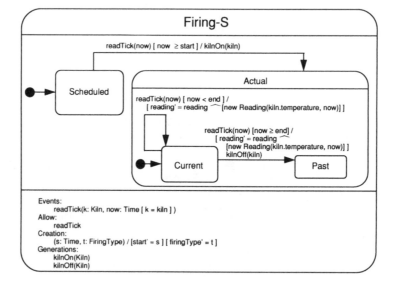

Figure 12.3 *Firing* specification model statechart

Thus there seem to be three potentially meaningful viewpoints:

1. providing access to **start** and **end**;
2. providing access to **outsideLimit, overlaps** and **creation**; and
3. providing access to all properties and associations.

The first viewpoint is needed by **Reading** and **Firing**, the second by **Kiln** and the third only by the individual **Firing** instance itself. We assume that an instance always has complete knowledge of its own type, and never define an explicit viewpoint for this purpose. Hence we only define explicit viewpoints for the first two cases. We might show these two viewpoints superimposed on the type diagram, as in figure 12.4.

To avoid clutter we have left out the internal details of **FiringType, Kiln** and **Reading**. The two viewpoints are shown as rectangles without corners. Thick arrows show that they actually belong to the **Firing** type, and thin arrows show the access granted to the viewpoints from **Firing, Kiln** and **Reading**. We've shown the creation operation on the type view for the purpose of this discussion.

The arrow from **Firing** to its own viewpoint describes the visibility one **Firing** object has of another; we return to this point later in the chapter.

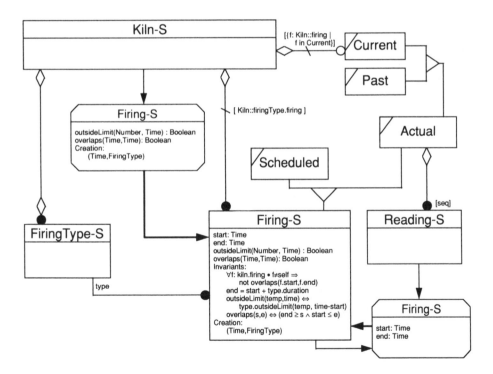

Figure 12.4 *Viewpoints*

We might produce a complete diagram of this kind by carrying out similar reasoning for all of the other types in the system; the resulting diagram would show all types, all viewpoints and the visibility relationships between all types and the viewpoints they access. However, such a diagram would be very cluttered and not particularly useful. *Viewpoint diagrams* focusing on specified sets of types and showing what they access are much more useful in practice. Because there are a large number of possible diagrams of this kind, using these diagrams to define all the access relationships in a system only makes real sense in conjunction with computerised tools. Paper versions of the diagrams may nevertheless be used for reasoning about specific aspects of the system.

12.2 Viewpoint diagrams

A viewpoint diagram focuses on a set of types (often a single type) called the *focus type(s)*, showing its access to other types in the overall system. Figure 12.5 is such a diagram, focusing on the single type **Kiln** and showing its access viewpoints on **Firing** and **FiringType**. Notice the following points:

- the **Reading** type is unknown;
- navigation of associations back from **Firing** to **Kiln** is not visible; and
- the association with the current firing, derived by a rule in the original type diagram, has been 'pushed up' into the **Firing** type itself, because the state sub-types are no longer visible.

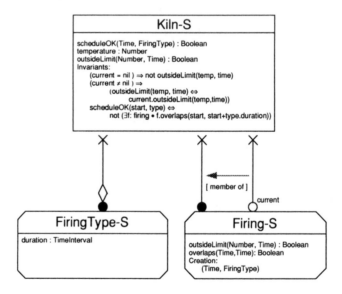

Figure 12.5 *Viewpoint diagram focusing on **Kiln***

Each viewpoint diagram must be consistent, in the sense that all names used in all expressions in the focus types must be in scope in the viewpoint diagram. Thus given that figure 12.5 is the viewpoint diagram focused on the type **Kiln**, it would not be valid for **Kiln** to mention **Reading**, or to invoke any of the properties of the other types not shown in the diagram, within its type rectangle or its statechart.

Importing a viewpoint such as **Firing** into a viewpoint diagram makes its statechart available in a limited way. The focus type needs some access to the statechart in order to reason about the way in which it makes use of the facilities of the viewpoint, but cannot have access to all of the statechart because it may include references to features of other types not visible in the viewpoint. The way we deal with this is to substitute all expressions on the statechart which refer to inaccessible features by an ellipsis consisting of dots: '...'. Thus the statechart corresponding to the **Firing** viewpoint in figure 12.5 is shown in figure 12.6.

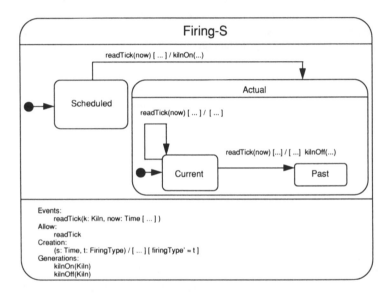

Figure 12.6 *Statechart for the **Firing** viewpoint*

If tools are available, the diagram shown in figure 12.5 may be used for editing features of the **Kiln** type. If, during development, it is decided that access to features of other types are needed which are not available in the visible viewpoints, additional viewpoints must be imported into the diagram. This naturally implies the availability of a repository of viewpoints with suitable facilities for navigation.

Note that a type can only have access to a single viewpoint of another type. Although in figure 12.5 the **outsideLimit** property of the current firing is only accessed from the kiln via the **current** association, we do not introduce a separate viewpoint for this association. In principle, we could define several viewpoints from one type to another, depending on the particular access route; in practice, this idea seems unnecessarily cumbersome and so we discard it (with one exception introduced later), although with very sophisticated automation the idea might be workable.

Sometimes a type may need access to a viewpoint of another type without having any explicit associations to it. This happens if the focus type:

- defines properties or creation operations which mention the viewpoint type as a parameter;
- defines local statechart variables of the viewpoint type; or
- in the essential or specification model, mentions the viewpoint type as an event parameter without using it elsewhere.

In such a case, the viewpoint is simply shown detached on the viewpoint diagram, with no associations. For example, figure 12.7 illustrates a **Person** type, whose instances are created by copying the name from a **Message** object, but which has no association to the **Message** type. If **Person** also had an association with a viewpoint of **Message**, then this detached viewpoint would be connected via an association line.

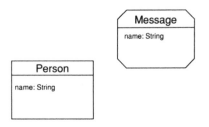

Figure 12.7 *Viewpoint with no association*

Sometimes a viewpoint may itself have visible outgoing associations to another viewpoint. For example, figure 12.8 focuses on the **Manufacturer** type, showing how it has visibility of the **Bottle** type and its association to the **Label** type. These visibilities are used to construct the derived association between **Manufacturer** and **Label**.

Given figure 12.8, we might construct a viewpoint of **Manufacturer** for use by its own clients, as shown in figure 12.9. In this diagram the fact that the association between **Manufacturer** and **Label** is derived is not visible, and not shown.

Constructing viewpoint diagrams which show long chains of associations is generally a bad idea, because such diagrams increase the coupling between types by exposing details of their relationships to clients.

A diagram may focus on several types. Returning to the earlier example, figure 12.10 shows a viewpoint diagram focusing on both **Kiln** and **Firing**. Notice that a single viewpoint of **FiringType** is shared between **Kiln** and **Firing**, even though both types do not use all of the properties exported in the viewpoint.

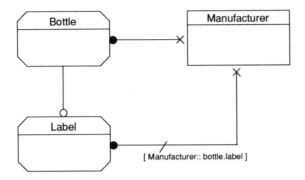

Figure 12.8 *Viewpoint with a visible association*

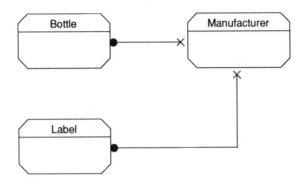

Figure 12.9 *Viewpoint of **Manufacturer***

Figure 12.10 has two different interpretations, as follows:

1. Access restrictions exist between the types **Kiln** and **Firing**, but are not shown in the diagram.
2. The diagram specifically indicates that the types **Kiln** and **Firing** have complete access to each other: each is a 'friend' of the other, in C++ terminology.

Both these interpretations are in fact useful, and both are permitted. The first is most useful to show the viewpoints at the edge of a complete sub-system, especially a domain. The second is particularly useful when no viewpoints have yet been defined between two types, and the designer is making decisions about the relationships of the types to each other.

The difference is that the first interpretation is 'read-only'. If the diagram were shown by an automated design tool, the first interpretation does not show which features of **Firing** are actually accessible to **Kiln**. Hence it gives the designer no guidance about how to refer to **Firing** when editing the implementation of **Kiln**. Hence we do not allow such editing to occur.   On the other hand, with the second interpretation, the designer knows that he or she has complete access to the features of the other type, and so editing is allowed.

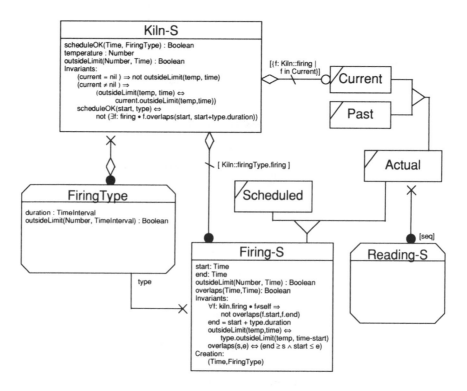

Figure 12.10 *Viewpoint diagram focusing on two types*

12.2.1 Self-access

One rather subtle question is whether a type's features are exported to itself. Perhaps it seems immediately obvious that they should be, but this is not necessarily so. There are two cases to consider: exporting features from an instance of a type to itself, and from one instance of the type to another[2]. We have already noted that all features of a type are automatically accessible from an instance to itself. However, features are only accessible from one instance to another if the feature is explicitly exported to the type

---

[2]This distinction represents an important difference between the Smalltalk and C++ views of encapsulation: in Smalltalk, instance variables are only visible within the instance in which they are stored, whereas in C++ private members are accessible to any instance of the same class.

itself, that is, a viewpoint is constructed showing which features of the type are to be made accessible between different instances – in fact we did this in figure 12.4 to show access from the **Firing** object to itself.

You have probably noticed that all the diagrams so far show associations from the focus type(s) as non-reversible; this is because navigating from an object to another object and back again is just a special case of navigating along two associations, and if possible at all, ends up with a viewpoint on the original type rather than the total access enjoyed by **self**.

Consider figure 12.11, which slightly extends an example first introduced in chapter 3. We wish to construct a diagram showing the viewpoint one **Person** object has of another, because it is possible to navigate from one to another in two ways via the recursive association. The viewpoint we need describes the access that the original object has to the features of the objects obtained by navigating.

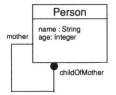

Figure 12.11 *A recursive association*

This viewpoint is shown in figure 12.12, which tells us that by navigating from a child to its mother or vice-versa gives a **Person** object of which only the **name** property is visible. The properties which are not visible for the remote object are the **age** and the ability to navigate any further. Note the mandatory use of the crosses to show that the association may not be navigated from the **Person** viewpoint back to the **Person** type.

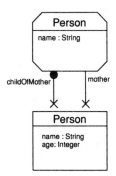

Figure 12.12 *Viewpoint showing navigation of a recursive association*

Figure 12.13 illustrates an extended situation where the viewpoint allows further navigation, but the **age** property is still private.

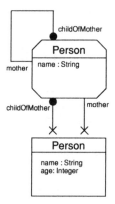

Figure 12.13 *Extended viewpoint navigating a recursive association*

We now understand how to show a reversible association starting at the focus type; it must be shown ending up at a viewpoint on the focus type, as shown in figure 12.14, in which the association to **Bottle** may be navigated back to a viewpoint of **Manufacturer**.

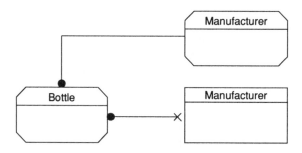

Figure 12.14 *A reversible association*

12.2.2 Sub-types and super-types

There are four main questions that need to be answered when considering a sub-type relationship, concerning the viewpoint (if any) that:

1. a client of a sub-type has of the super-type(s);

2. a client of a super-type has of the sub-type(s);
3. a sub-type has of its own super-type(s);
4. a super-type has of its own sub-type(s).

We consider each of these in turn.

Client viewpoint of super-types
Super-types are not always visible to clients. Let us consider an example.

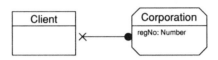

Figure 12.15 *Client's viewpoint on Corporation*

Figure 12.15 focuses on a type called **Client** (whose purpose is irrelevant to the discussion) showing its access to a viewpoint of **Corporation**. In fact **Corporation** extends **Company**, as shown in figure 12.16.

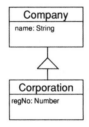

Figure 12.16 *Corporation is a sub-type*

If we wish to give **Client** access to the name property of **Company**, we may do so by creating a combined viewpoint showing **name** as though it were part of **Corporation**. If **Company** and **Corporation** both had non-trivial statecharts, they would be combined in this viewpoint.

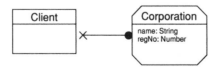

Figure 12.16 *Viewpoint showing Company properties as part of Corporation*

Alternatively we can create a viewpoint of **Corporation** in which the super-type relationship is shown explicitly, as shown in figure 12.17. We would need to do this, for example, if there were a separate association from **Client** to **Company** and we wished to take advantage of the sub-type relationship by adding **Corporation** objects to the **company** association.

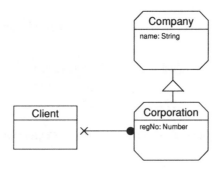

Figure 12.17 *Viewpoints showing **Company** separately*

Client viewpoint of sub-types
The existence of sub-types is only visible to clients if they acquire viewpoints of them. The existence of the type extension relationship must be explicitly included in a viewpoint; the situation illustrated in figure 12.18 is perfectly possible, where **Client** has separate access to viewpoints of **Company** and **Corporation**, but cannot treat them as related types, because the super-type relationship of **Corporation** has not been explicitly included in the viewpoint.

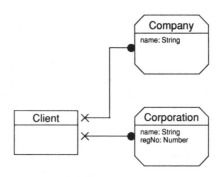

Figure 12.18 *Viewpoints omitting super-type relationship*

Sub-type viewpoint of super-types
There are two kinds of viewpoint that a sub-type can have of a super-type, distinguished for similar reasons to those discussed in the section above on self-access: an object may invoke features defined in a super-type either on *itself*, or on *another object*. We do not make all features of super-types automatically visible via self, because this would limit the ability of designers to alter the design of a super-type without affecting its sub-types. So we define an explicit viewpoint which describes this kind of access. However, this viewpoint is quite different from the viewpoint describing access to super-type features for a distinct object. In this case we break our rule that one type only has a single viewpoint of another: two viewpoints may be provided from a type to its super-type, one for self-access and one for remote access.

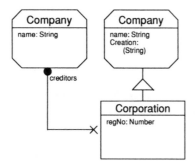

Figure 12.19 *Two viewpoints on the same super-type*

Figure 12.19 illustrates these two viewpoints for our current example. The self-viewpoint includes access to the creation operation for **Company**: to create a **Corporation** object it is necessary to be able to create its **Company** features. However, the remote viewpoint, which shows the access that a corporation has to each of its creditors, does not allow creation.

Note that the viewpoint on the super-type describes access to those features which may be *invoked* by a sub-type. To extend the super-type properly, the sub-type must have knowledge about the structure of the super-type's statechart; this is always available in full, regardless of which features are included in the viewpoint.

Super-type viewpoint of sub-types
Since super-types have no privileged access to their sub-types, a super-type's relationship with its sub-types is exactly the same as any other client's.

For example, figure 12.20 illustrates the viewpoint that a type **Message** has of two sub-types, **PriorityMessage** and **SimpleMessage**. The viewpoints show the sub-types as extensions of a viewpoint of **Message**. Note that the associations are navigable in both directions from the viewpoints.

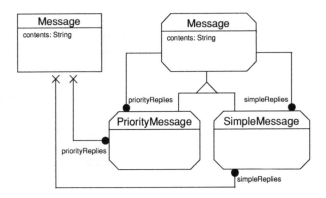

Figure 12.20 *Viewpoints on sub-types*

12.2.3 Constructing viewpoints

Viewpoints are constructed from types (or possibly from other viewpoints) by nominating features to be included. How this is done in practice is an issue for automated tools. We often talk about *exporting* a feature when including it in a viewpoint.

The most basic feature of a type is its existence (including its name). Knowledge of the existence of a type **T** gives a client the ability:

1. to construct an association to **T**;
2. to mention **T** as a parameter or result type for a property, observer or updater;
3. to mention **T** as a parameter to a creation operation;
4. to list events having **T** as a parameter in the event list (in essential and specification models only).

Simply knowing the existence of **T** does not give the client the ability to invoke any operations on **T**, or create an instance of **T**.

Each property, observer/updater, association and creation operation is a separate feature which may be exported individually. Exporting a property (in essential and specification models) or an observer/updater (in implementation models) to a client grants the ability to invoke that property in invariants, guards, post-conditions, etc. The same applies to associations (which are observers in the implementation model). Exporting a creation operation to a client grants the ability to create new instances of the exporter using that operation. A sub-type/super-type link is a separately exportable feature of the sub-type.

A type invariant appears in a viewpoint if all the elements of the expression are in scope in the viewpoint. A viewpoint may include a restricted invariant, implied by the full invariant but only mentioning elements in scope. For example, if the full invariant is **x=3** ∧ **y<z**, but **z** is not in scope in the viewpoint under consideration, the invariant **x=3** should still appear. A clever tool would automate this.

Explicitly depicted state sub-types are exported as a whole: either all of the state sub-types appear in a viewpoint, or none of them do.

12.3 The viewpoint repository

So far in this section we have introduced the concept of a viewpoint, and shown how viewpoint diagrams can be used to define the access that one type has of another. This provides a simple theoretical basis for a discipline of reusable software components. Much more important in practice is the discipline used to manage these components during a software development.

Up to now, for the purposes of explanation we have tended to imply that the purpose of viewpoints is to formalise the visibility relationships between the types in a pre-existing complete model. At this point we should loosen this assumption: we envisage viewpoints on pre-existing types as providing the building blocks from which complete models are constructed. The overall process of model development consists of defining types and their viewpoints, placing them in a repository and subsequently selecting elements from the repository for defining new types and viewpoints. Viewpoints should be designed to minimise the dependencies between one type and another; nevertheless these dependencies still exist, and the repository must help to manage the effects of changing the definition of any type. A complete model is defined simply by nominating an initial type, in which case the complete model consists of all the types which have viewpoints reachable directly or indirectly by navigation from the initial type.

A vital issue is how viewpoints should be named and catalogued. We envisage that every viewpoint has a descriptive name which indicates its intended purpose and which appears in the catalogue. A decent repository should support many strategies for finding viewpoints, apart from simply searching by name; a discussion of these is outside the scope of this book.

12.3.1 Re-naming

Whenever a viewpoint is imported from a repository into a viewpoint diagram, selected names may be substituted in order to make it more useful to the importing context; either because the existing names conflict with names already in scope in the importing context or simply because different names are desired.

Consider figure 12.21, which shows a viewpoint on a specification model type called **Customer**, with a property called **name** and an association with another viewpoint called **BankAccount**. Imagine that we wish to import the **Customer** viewpoint into another diagram, but wish to change the name of the type to

BankCustomer because there is already a **Customer** type in the target diagram. We may rename the type locally for the importing diagram with an expression, thus:

BankCustomer ← **Customer.**

Any name in a viewpoint may be substituted, as long as the overall result is legal. A re-naming expression is evaluated at the point where the viewpoint is imported into a new context. The practicalities of this must be managed by automated tools; there is no realistic way that this kind of re-naming can be managed on paper.

Once a viewpoint appears re-named in a diagram, it would be an error to import another viewpoint on the same type into the same diagram with a different re-naming.

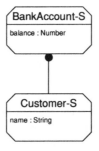

Figure 12.21 *Viewpoints on **BankAccount** and **Customer***

12.4 Parameterised types

Any type can be parameterised on a value type. Figure 12.22 shows three types which together define a tree structure, parameterised on the type of the **contents** property.

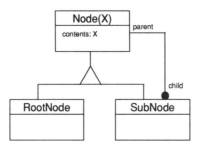

Figure 12.22 *Defining a parameterised type*

A parameterised type may be (but does not have to be) instantiated when a viewpoint is created of it. For example, we might instantiate figure 12.22 to create the diagram in figure 12.23, in which the parameter **X** has been substituted by the type **Integer**. As with re-naming, the pragmatics of substitution are managed by the repository. The viewpoints in figure 12.23 may be manipulated further according to the normal principles.

Any number of different instantiations of the same parameterised type may appear in the same diagram.

A parameterised type may restrict the types which may be used to instantiate it, by including on its defining diagram a viewpoint of the parameter type itself. Any instantiation must be a type for which this viewpoint is valid. For example, figure 12.24 extends the example with a viewpoint which requires the type **X** to provide an infix $\leq$ operation, which has the normal axioms for a total ordering. The types **Integer** or **Number** would be valid instantiations for **X**.

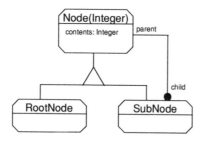

Figure 12.23 *Instantiating a parameterised type in a viewpoint*

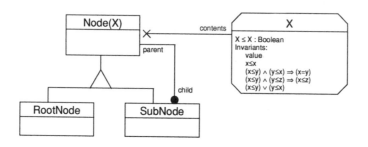

Figure 12.24 *Restricting a type parameter*

Note that this is the only case in which we allow the definition of a viewpoint on a currently unknown type[3].

---

[3]To allow this for object types in general would require a logic for testing conformance between arbitrary statecharts. This might be desirable in the long term.

12.5 Summary

- Encapsulation is a fundamental concept in object-oriented systems which promotes reuse, simplifies system evolution, and assists reasoning about concurrent systems.
- Our unit of encapsulation is the *viewpoint*, which defines the set of features of one type which are accessible from another.
- Including a feature in a viewpoint is called *exporting* it.
- A viewpoint diagram focuses on one or more types and shows their access to other types via viewpoints.
- A type can normally only access one viewpoint of another type.
- A viewpoint may define the access one instance of a type has of different instances of the same type.
- A viewpoint on a sub-type may show features of the super-type as though they belong to the sub-type.
- The sub-type/super-type relationship between two types is a separate feature which may be omitted or included between viewpoints on those types.
- A sub-type can have two viewpoints on a super-type, defining access on the same instance and different instances.
- Elements on the statechart are never exported.
- State sub-types are exported as a whole.
- Viewpoint diagrams need computerised tools to manipulate.
- Viewpoints and the types they are derived from live in a repository, which provides the foundation for reuse of software components.
- Names in viewpoints may be substituted when they are imported into diagrams as long as no two viewpoints on the same type appear in the same diagram with different re-namings.
- Types may be parameterised on value types. The parameterisation may be restricted by defining a viewpoint of the parameter type.

12.6 Bibliographic notes

Some of our ideas on encapsulation and parameterised types have been influenced by the Eiffel programming language [Meyer92].

12.7 References

[Meyer92] B. Meyer. *Eiffel: The language*, Prentice-Hall, New York, 1992.

Part Five

The development process

CHAPTER 13

The development process

13.1 The process of software construction

A criticism frequently levelled at books on object-oriented method, and we fully expect similar criticism for this work, is that they spend most of their pages discussing techniques and notations and few describing how those techniques and notations are used to manage software development projects. Without wishing to speak for other authors, we offer an explanation for this apparent failing: the implicit message is that techniques and notations need not be used as the basis for software project management and control.

For all that has been written about the vision of software development as a considered, deducible, ordered and, above all, repeatable process, we don't see it that way – at least, not yet. The key activities of designing software systems are creative and chaotic, relying in the main on the skill, intuition and experience of individual designers. A software system is, above all, a work of art; not fine art, since it is the product of craftsmen rather than artists.

The introduction of new techniques, new ways of organising software and new working practices is likely to change matters in the future. Although we are not convinced that component-based software reuse will bring significant benefits as quickly as many people claim, it is clearly a factor which, if carefully managed, could make some aspects of software construction more routine. As important will be the impact of standardised software architectures, giving designers a head-start by providing proven frameworks for particular kinds of systems.

For the moment, though, we feel it necessary to separate clearly the design process from the management process. The design process is the process by which the designer's skills are harnessed and directed. As befits a creative process, it cannot be rigid and constraining. By contrast, the management process must be rigid and disciplined because it is the basis for important commercial decisions, the kind of decisions influenced entirely by logic not beauty, and underwritten by the root of commerce: *money*.

We suggest that the design process uses the techniques described in the rest of this book to develop an understanding of the problem and a suitable solution. It is a targeted but not always predictable process, where the design grows over time. By contrast, we suggest that the management process be based on cyclic, evolutionary development and delivery, with a formal monitoring and reporting structure.

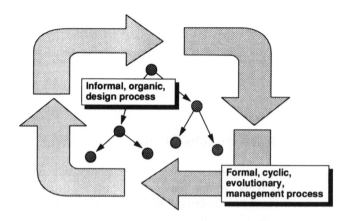

Figure 13.1 *Management and design processes*

13.2 Management process

13.2.1 Systematic development

We call any software project managed with a clear and logical process a *systematic development*. A systematic development must be planned, measured and controlled. There have been many software management processes promoted in the past which could justly claim to be systematic, and we do not take issue with that. Here we try to show how a management process can still be systematic, even when divorced from design techniques.

Conventional wisdom has it that progress in software development can and should be measured in terms of the application of particular design techniques. For example, many projects have milestones such as '50% of entity-relationship diagrams completed', or '75% of data-flow diagrams completed', thereby coupling closely the design techniques to the management of the project. Managing projects in this way constrains the creativity of designers by forcing techniques, valuable in themselves, to be used in a particular order.

Not all software projects have the same starting conditions. In some cases, the specification for the software is completely given, often through existing standards. This is common where the primary clients of the system are other machines. Many telecommunication switching systems are like this.   In other cases it is extremely unclear what the software needs to do, and part of the problem is establishing the needs.   Systems where the primary clients are people fall into this category: people rarely know what they want.   On the whole, software projects tend to be far less well defined than most people admit.

We believe that software must be built incrementally, and that milestones should measure completion of demonstrable software, not designs. The main reason for this is that no other kind of milestone is really worth having.   Designs can't crash, so there is no sure-fire way of knowing whether they are any good[1].   More importantly, in many cases the only people who know whether a design will meet the needs will not be computer-literate, and so won't understand the design.   Customers of software care little or nothing for good design in itself, although they might care about the spin-offs of good design, such as reduced life-time costs and better quality.   Customers of software care about the software itself, and they perceive only what they see by their interaction with it.   They care about when they get it, how much it costs, and how well it fulfils the organisational need.   These qualities are difficult to perceive by studying a design specification, even for experts.

13.2.2 Software development organisation

The software factory
The development of software is not, as some authors have claimed, analogous to large-scale industrial manufacturing, because software development is primarily an activity of design, as opposed to replication.   We might more usefully compare software development with individual feats of design, such as the Apollo spacecraft or the Channel Tunnel.   These were possible only because they were underpinned by engineering principles identified and systematised through many years of theoretical research and empirical study.   By analogy, software development must be underpinned by software engineering, a discipline still in its infancy, whose impact on current developments is extremely limited.   Software development today relies almost entirely on the skills of craftsmen, not engineers; craftsmen who have learnt their trade through years of application and experimentation, typically through apprenticeship with other craftsman.

This situation is slowly changing as we move towards standardised architectures for different kinds of systems.   The skills of the craftsman, focused on building from scratch, are being replaced by those of the technician, skilled in assembly.   For this change to have much impact we must examine the way software development is organised.

---

[1]But design models can be animated, particularly if they are well defined, like those described in this book. Proper animation of design models might solve this problem: we would obtain a true assessment of the quality of a design by executing it directly.

Software development is currently organised, and funded, around *projects*, which bring together a team of people for a limited period so that a particular software system can be constructed; indeed, much of this chapter makes the assumption that software development will be organised like this. But we should challenge this assumption because of the following:

- A software system is typically enhanced and modified throughout a long lifetime; there is no clear end point of development.
- The trend towards software component assembly implies a major shift in funding towards the development of components, as opposed to systems.
- Rapid response to changing requirements is seen by many organisations as more important than provision of rich functionality.

The ultimate goal of a software development organisation should be to establish an environment where new requirements can be assimilated into the existing body of software with as little effort as possible.

Team organisation

The traditional approach to software development, as taught in universities and colleges in recent years, doesn't seem to scale. By this we mean that the effort required to complete a big software project is far in excess of twice the effort required for a project half its size: effort increases faster than size. This is a direct consequence of the non-linear increase in human communication channels that results from the informal design process obligated by today's level of knowledge.   As our understanding of software development grows, and the design techniques used improve, we will be able to tackle larger projects with more confidence. We see the improved powers of abstraction provided by software objects as an important part of this change.

As Brooks [Brook75] noted many years ago, we cannot hope to deal with the problems inherent in big projects merely by allocating to them a large number of development staff. We must recognise that big projects, just like small ones, depend for their success on the presence of a few highly skilled and experienced designers. Therefore, we recommend that the critical design tasks of every project, irrespective of size, be undertaken by a very small team.

We suggest that every development project be organised with a *core team* which assumes primary responsibility for the project, and one or more development teams which work as instructed by the core team. For smaller projects, the core team is also the development team.

The core is made up as follows:

- **Project Manager** – Responsible for development planning, reporting and co-ordination. One of the main jobs for the Project Manager is to ensure that the Chief Designer and his/her colleagues are given full opportunity to do their work and are not forced to spend hours 'playing politics'.

- **Chief Designer** – Ultimately responsible for making the thing work. Must understand every aspect of the system and be comfortable with all the related technology. Responsible for devising and keeping a vision of how the whole thing will work. The Chief Designer will probably be the person who makes the key design presentations to others.
- **Designers** (probably not more than two, possibly none) – Aides to the Chief Designer.
- **Project Administrator** – Ensures project procedures are followed, gathers metrics, collates and indexes documents.

It goes without saying that members of the core team must be exceptionally skilled and motivated, since the success of the development rests entirely on their shoulders. The core team designers are not just pen-pushers; they must be prepared to get their hands dirty by building prototypes and working closely with development teams. In theory, any one of the designers is sufficiently skilled that they could build, or learn how to build, the entire system, given enough time. They are capable of grasping the design as a whole, and reasoning about the global consequences of design decisions. Although the same does not necessarily apply to the Project Manager, he/she must be capable of reading and understanding program code.

The responsibilities of the core team are as follows:

- Take crucial design decisions.
- Establish system architecture.
- Set out global policies on things such as error handling.
- Verify system feasibility.
- Specify tools and techniques.
- Develop a plan for testing and integrating the development.
- Devise development team cycle plans.
- Co-ordinate integration of development team tasks.

In the early stages of the development the core team might be supplemented in two ways: by technical specialists and by requirements researchers. During their early investigations, where the aim is to establish feasibility and overall architecture, the core team assigns specific tasks to the technical specialists. The requirements researchers investigate the exact end-user requirements and feed these into the system specifications.

The technical specialists are expert in some particular field, such as data communications, hardware interfacing or databases. They might later join or lead development teams to seed them with project-related experience.

Each development team must have an assigned leader, who is responsible for ensuring that the team delivers as required. On larger projects, each development team might have a part-time project manager, responsible for cycle planning and reporting.

Factors affecting risk

An important part of a project manager's job is assessing and controlling risk. The risk of a project is proportional to the levels of inexperience in a variety of areas:

- **The people** – Using a team that is inexperienced in software development increases risk. To make matters more complicated, there is also a very large difference in productivity between developers.
- **The problem domain** – If the members of the project team are not experienced in the kind of problem being tackled the risk increases.
- **The technology** – Introducing new technology, such as object technology, increases risk.
- **The size** – Large projects carry a greatly increased risk.

The effect of project size on risk is so marked that every effort should be made to split large developments into several smaller ones. People often argue this can't be done with their development, for some reason or another, but this is rarely true.

Establishing system requirements

Broadly speaking, there are two kinds of system requirements: *functional needs* and *operational constraints*. A functional need is a feature or facility that the system needs to provide. An operational constraint is something that limits freedom of choice in deciding how to provide the functional needs. A typical functional need might be the need to produce a particular report. An operational constraint might limit how long the report can take to produce or define a range of printers on which it must be producible.

Historically, the software industry has been much better at establishing functional needs than operational constraints. Unfortunately, the operational constraints often include many of the critical success factors.

Our contention is that, in the vast majority of cases, the full system requirements will not become known until the software is provided to the users. We use this contention to justify our recommendation of evolutionary development, as described below.

System requirements should always be stated in a form that makes it easy to determine whether they have been met. A requirement that the system should be 'reliable' is useless. We recommend you to the work of Tom Gilb in this area [Gilb88].

Estimation

It shouldn't come as any surprise that estimating the effort required for a software development project is difficult. Consider the facts:

- Rarely, if ever, do we build the same system twice. The only organisations known to the authors who produce reliable estimates are those which build similar systems time and time again.

- As an industry we regularly undertake development projects wildly different from anything we or, in extreme cases, anyone has done before. Such adventures into the unknown (frequently *misadventures*) are impossible to plan accurately.
- We often use different tools for each project. Experience and knowledge of the tools to be used is vital for correct estimation.

Use of an evolutionary process allows costs to be managed even when estimation is difficult or impossible. It allows the project manager to keep track of what has been spent and what has been produced.

13.2.3 Recommended management process

Phases
The job of the designer is to produce a workable design but to do that he or she must learn about the problem, the constraints, the tools, the people, and so on. Design is very much a learning experience. You can never say, with any certainty 'This part of the design is finished; I don't need to consider it any longer.' We don't think the *design* process can be phased.

Therefore, we do not support the division of projects into analysis, design, coding, integration, testing, etc. Instead, we identify three major development activities: *project preparation*, *construction* and *approval*.

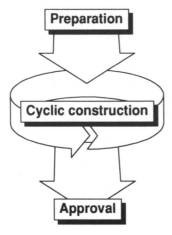

Figure 13.2 *Development activities*

The overall order of work in a development project should be:

1. Preparation, involving (in no particular order):
    - establishing the general scope of the project;
    - agreeing the time and money constraints;
    - identifying the personnel involved, including:
        project sponsor: the person or organisation which controls the funding of the project,
        development staff,
        user representatives, who may actually be users,
        specialist support staff, including external consultants;
    - establishing the critical success factors;
    - checking project feasibility (possibly with prototypes);
    - assessing risk;
    - deciding on the development environment and tools;
    - obtaining organisational commitment to the project;
    - deciding on the documentation scheme to be used;
    - opening the necessary channels of communication between all parties;
    - production of preliminary design models;
    - identification of sub-systems;
    - design of overall system architecture (to some level);
    - construction of prototypes;
    - preparation of design documents;
    - cycle planning.
2. Construction cycles, involving (in no particular order):
    - constructing and refining design models;
    - constructing prototypes;
    - writing and testing code;
    - document creation and update, including user documentation;
    - integrating code;
    - testing of integrated code;
    - reviews.
3. Approval. Subsequent to the final cycle (or in parallel with other cycles for phased approval) there must be a process of project approval. This involves (in no particular order):
    - formal acceptance of the system (including documentation) by the users;
    - installation;
    - training of users;
    - post-development review by developers (including the production of a report).

Although the project preparation activity is largely the responsibility of the core team, we must take account of any overriding learning objectives. With an inexperienced development team, or a team with widely varying experience, we may wish to involve many more people in the project preparation tasks.   This will inevitably *reduce* productivity rather than improve it, and thus lengthen the project preparation stage, but, depending on circumstances, we may accept that penalty in return for the learning benefits.

Evolution and cycles

Our development philosophy is one of *cyclic development*.   For any project of significant size, we consider it impractical to determine at the outset exactly what order development should take and exactly what the focus of attention at any point in the development should be.   With cyclic development we set out to build a regular succession of working functional subsets of the system. This approach allows progress towards delivered functionality to be assessed, rather than progress against a theoretical plan.   It allows the development team to respond rapidly to problems and opportunities that arise during the development process.

The system evolves through cycles. Cyclic development requires feedback from the appropriate parties at the end of each cycle. This feedback may necessitate rework to ensure the system best meets the needs of its users. There must be user representatives as part of the project team who can approve, from time to time, the direction being taken. User representatives should review progress at least at the end of each cycle.

The development of a software system is rarely 'finished'.   Instead, development stops when a system good enough for the purpose has been created. This will be at the end of some cycle. The project is planned to last for a certain length of time, translated into a number of cycles. Development may stop before the end of this time because the sponsor doesn't wish to spend more money, but it should certainly stop *at that time*. If, as a result of incorrect estimation or the extra effort required for rework, there is insufficient time to deliver all desired functions, some will have to be omitted. This should become clear well before the end of the planned duration. In nearly every case the system is still useful without some of its features and an additional project can, if required, be defined to add those features that are still desired.

In cyclic development, the project is divided into cycles of work, where each cycle advances the development activity. Each cycle has specified objectives and a *fixed length*. During the cycle, developers build software, using the results of the preceding cycle as their base. At the end of the cycle the cycle products are integrated with the results of the previous cycle to produce a new system. During the cycle review this new system is approved as the base for the next cycle. Any work not completed at the end of a cycle must be re-scheduled for a later cycle. The cycle products integrated into the new system need to be production quality; that is, they must meet standards, have the right documentation and have been tested to the prescribed level. They do not have to be 'perfect'.   The cycle review may identify errors in specification or construction that must be fixed during later cycles but need not prevent the software becoming an integrated part of the system. If the cycle products are clearly unsuitable, either because their reliability is so poor that they would impede progress in the next cycle, or because they fail to address the requirements adequately, there must be no hesitation in discarding them.

The overall scheme for cyclic development is shown in figure 13.3.

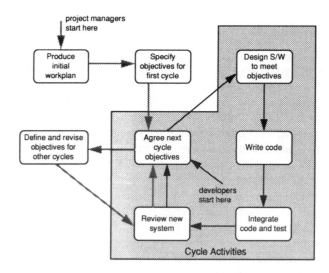

Figure 13.3 *Cyclic development*

The formality with which the cycle process is applied will depend on the size of the project, the experience of the developers and the organisation's culture.

Cycle length
Ideal cycle length depends on the tools being used and the stage of development of the project. Every cycle has fixed overheads: the time taken to agree objectives and to review results. If the cycles are too short, these overheads become too large a proportion of the available development time and productivity suffers. If the cycles are too long, so much development may be done during a cycle that there is a reluctance to discard cycle products when they prove not to meet requirements and, if they are discarded, developer morale suffers. Projects using powerful development tools can have shorter cycles because more real development will be finished in a shorter time. It may be wise to increase cycle length as the project proceeds. In the early cycles there will be many unknowns and the risk of producing unsuitable cycle products is higher.

Our experience suggests that the minimum cycle length for any project involving more than two developers is two weeks. When there are only two developers the process is invariably less formal and cycles may be of only a few days. For large projects the cycle length, particularly towards the end of a project, may be many months. A typical project plan for a nine-month project might be as shown in figure 13.4.

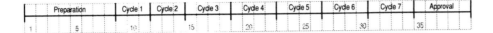

Preparation		Cycle 1	Cycle 2	Cycle 3	Cycle 4	Cycle 5	Cycle 6	Cycle 7	Approval
1	5	10		15	20	25	30	35	

Figure 13.4 *A typical project plan*

Cycle objectives and priorities

Every cycle must have clear objectives and a work plan, both captured in a cycle plan document. It must be easy to discern whether the cycle objectives have been met. This implies careful cycle planning and specification. Experience suggests that cycle planning and specification require considerable resources.

It is impossible to make hard-and-fast rules about how work should be allocated to cycles, but we have found by experience that an objective of an early cycle should be to prove the viability of the project by constructing a version of the system which covers the full breadth (but not depth) of activity: it should show that stimuli can be detected and responses generated.

The nature of cyclic development requires that the priorities assigned by the user to various features be well understood by the developers. The project manager must take these priorities into account when planning cycles and when dealing with problems that occur during a cycle.

13.3 Design process

13.3.1 Systematic design

Our aim in devising a management process is to provide systematic development. A similar goal for design is to perform *systematic design*. In this section we examine the issues affecting the design process and show that systematic design is not always a reasonable objective.

Since the management process described above calls for the production of new executable code every few weeks or months you might well ask 'What's the point of building abstract design models; I might as well just write the code. I'll soon find out if I got it wrong.' As time-served programmers, we have done just that ourselves at times in the past, and can readily understand this view: but long experience tells us that, although superficially attractive, this way of working almost inevitably leads to poorly structured and unmaintainable code.

Even so, it is true that experienced designers, good at manipulating abstract concepts and working alone, can often construct very complex design models in their heads, and transform them directly into code. The design techniques described in this book embody some important design principles, and their purpose is to facilitate the application of those principles. Experienced designers who have a sound grasp of those principles can, and frequently do, bypass the actual techniques and associated notations while still remaining loyal to the principles themselves. We claim that an understanding of the techniques, and thus of the underlying principles, will improve your ability as a designer *whether or not* you use the techniques rigorously.

Having said that, we must strongly defend the use of design techniques to capture design intent explicitly. Implementation languages such as Smalltalk and C++ do not allow design intentions to be fully expressed. Important design concepts, particularly associations and invariants, must be diluted for implementation in these languages, and no amount of systematic 'reverse engineering' will ever recover the full design intent without intervention from a designer. The techniques described in this book allow the design intent to be captured and reasoned about by a single designer or a whole team. Very rarely is it acceptable for the design intent to be lost, as it inevitably must be if it is never captured.

Also, systematic design implies the use of design techniques which allow consideration of the design at various levels of abstraction. Systematic design requires conscious and deliberate design; it requires that the executable software be a consequence of the design models and their evolution, and not the other way around. With systematic design, the primary representation of the software is the design models, not, for example, a collection of C++ source-code files[2]. Systematic design requires the designers to take account of all the issues and address them up front. Waterfall-style development, where a 'complete' design is produced before coding begins, is compatible with our notion of systematic design but incompatible with our management philosophy. A design does not have to be done all at once to be systematic; the designers must merely understand what they are doing and recognise (and record) what is being left out. To be systematic, each piece of executable software must be the result of design.

Producing design models that address all the issues, as required for systematic design, will take time, and designers will be forced to commit to design decisions, to make choices. There must be some way to validate these choices: either the design team has that freedom itself or it must validate them with others who have it, such as the users' representative. In every project it will be impossible to validate all these choices without constructing executable code and running it.

We have observed the following reasons for this:

(a) A genuine lack of understanding about the 'right' solution to a problem – the problem represents a new or different challenge where it is impossible to validate alternatives before 'seeing them in action'.

(b) A lack of creative ability in the designers – the designers do not know how to formulate the right questions or decide on possible answers.

(c) A lack of intellectual skills in the designers – the designers are unable to manipulate or reason about abstract concepts.

(d) A lack of organisational commitment to design – the organisation has a belief that time spent not writing code is time wasted.

---

[2]This implies a need for very sophisticated design support tools.

(e) A lack of commitment to the project by the potential users or the organisation as a whole – the project is not motivated by a real organisational need and so the people who could validate decisions will react only to demonstrable software and will not, or cannot, make the extra effort required to examine a design model.

If (e) prevails it is probably unwise to continue the project because, unless the situation changes, it cannot be successful. For the remainder of the above list, the immediate way out of the predicament is to build some software using a series of informed guesses. With some running software available to focus minds, decisions are frequently much easier. The least sophisticated of users (or designers) can usually look at a piece of running software and say 'that's what I want' or 'it would be better if...'.

The real dilemma, and the key issue in systematic design, is how to use the information gained by writing the software. There are two possibilities, as follows:

1. Treat the software as a baseline and enhance it, using the principle of evolutionary development, into second and subsequent versions, and, ultimately, into the final system. This approach has become very popular recently, under names such as *incremental prototyping*.

2. Treat the software as a disposable prototype and add the information gained to a knowledge-base that captures design policy decisions. The prototype might still be enhanced to answer further questions but it never becomes the basis for the 'real' system. The 'real' system will be an implementation of the knowledge-base, ideally built using the principle of evolutionary development, probably in parallel with ongoing prototyping. We will call this approach *dual-track design*.

Both can be made to work but you need to decide which option you are following before building the initial software. With incremental prototyping, the initial software must be production quality because it will become part of the final system. We can therefore assume that it will take longer to build than in the second approach, where, as a prototype, it need not be production quality.

Both approaches have risks. Incremental prototyping poses the major risk that successive evolutions will undermine or distort the design basis, leading to a poor quality solution even if the initial design was sound. Another risk with this approach is that inadequate design documentation will be produced, making it even more difficult to rectify emergent failings in the original design. The major risk with dual-track design is that the 'real' system will never be built, and the undocumented and insupportable prototype will become, as a result of organisational pressure, the *de facto* 'real' system.

If the degree of uncertainty about design choices is small, and thus the prototypes are also small and built infrequently, dual-track design is by far the best. Small prototypes, each covering only a small part of the system, are unlikely to be forced to become the final system. But dual-track design is viable only if the reason prototypes are being constructed is (a) in the list above (a lack of understanding about the right solution); the designers must have the necessary creative and intellectual abilities and there must be organisational support for design.

When the degree of uncertainty is large, and thus it is necessary to prototype most parts of the system, incremental prototyping wins out, not because it is conceptually better but because it is viable; in such cases it takes a very disciplined organisation to follow the dual-track approach[3]. Incremental prototyping is also the only viable option when designers lack the necessary skills or the organisation is not committed to design.

We seem to be suggesting that incremental prototyping is incompatible with systematic design. It need not be so. The design for each evolution of the prototype can be carefully integrated into a consistent design model, and the code then brought into line with this new model. But all too often the ultimate reference point for the project is the software not the design model; the software drives the design model and not the other way around[4]. Then incremental prototyping is not systematic design. Conversely, following the dual-track approach does not necessarily guarantee systematic design, although it is much more likely.

Systematic design is demanding. It requires a high level of maturity and intellectual ability in the designers, and a strongly supportive organisational culture. It is time-consuming and painstaking. The pay-back comes in the long-term, with reduced costs over the life-time of the software.

The simple fact is that for many, perhaps most, projects the ability or desire to be systematic does not exist, and no amount of hand-wringing will change this. Such projects will be designed in a piecemeal, *ad hoc*, fashion and are unlikely to want to utilise the full depth and formality of the techniques presented in this book. We recognise and accept this. Software built without systematic design in a reasonable time is either the work of exceptionally gifted designers, who need no help from design techniques anyway, or is, by implication, uncomplicated. Uncomplicated software is increasingly built using high-level tools by relatively unskilled practitioners. We offer the depth and formality of our techniques to satisfy the needs of systematic designers building complex software.

The choice of approach affects the way in which design techniques are used on the project. For projects following systematic design, the full range and depth of design techniques are applicable and appropriate. For projects unable to be designed systematically, the extent to which design techniques can be used for forward planning is limited, but, depending on organisational culture, they might be used to record what was done, after the event. In these circumstances we may choose to restrict the choice of techniques and limit their complexity by, for example, omitting the use of mathematical constraints and specifications.

---

[3]Although we might reflect on Brooks' remark: 'Plan to build one and throw it away – you will anyway'.

[4]This argument disappears if the software and the design model *are the same*, as they would be if, for example, the design models were directly executable.

13.3.2 Techniques

A designer needs three things: a set of techniques to help tackle issues in the design; a set of notations to capture the design and communicate it to others; and guidance on what to do next when stuck. The notations used in this book serve the second of these, although we must consider the extent of their use. The other two areas we will try to deal with here.

Lots of techniques have already been described in this book, such as structural and state modelling. These techniques are there to be used as and when the designer wishes. They are the set of intellectual tools in his or her box, to be pulled out and applied at the right moment. All the techniques will not always be used during a single development project; it is a matter of selecting the right ones for the job.

Techniques satisfy needs; we can formulate some questions that might arise during a software project and see which techniques might help in each case (see table 13.1). The techniques mentioned in the table are not separate or necessarily at the same level of abstraction. For example, building an implementation model implies using the type view, state view and mechanism techniques, to some extent at least.

Fitting techniques to the problem

In this book we have set out three different modelling perspectives: essential, specification and implementation. We do not intend to imply that all three are vital to every software development project, nor that the order of their construction, if used, must be in the order presented in this book. Indeed, it is our strong opinion that all three models can, to some degree, be built and enhanced together, as a set. The utilisation of the different models depends on the situation faced by the designer. Here we consider four possible situations and suggest how to tackle them.

> *We are a bank and we have a complex business process for dealing with mortgage payment arrears. This process involves many people and departments, many forms, many decisions and many different stimuli and responses. We want to computerise all or part of the process to reduce our staff level and to deal with arrears more effectively.*

The first thing to note here is that the problem to be solved has already been defined. The business goals are to reduce staff level and to deal with arrears more effectively – presumably this means faster or with better consultation with the borrower. Our techniques can help by providing behavioural descriptions of situations but they say nothing about how to determine the business goals. Much can, and has, been said by others about this; for instance by [Wilso84]. With this proviso, it seems clear the first thing to do in this situation is to produce an essential model, which will capture the current or desired behaviour for arrears processing and provide a vocabulary and structure within which decisions about computerisation can be made.

How can I understand the problem better?	Build an essential model
How can I explore the problem without pre-judging the boundary between the software and the other parts of the system?	Build an essential model
How can I specify the required behaviour of the software without having to consider implementation details?	Build a specification model
How can I specify fully, but abstractly, the boundary between the software and its environment?	Build a specification model
How can I deal with implementation issues, such as concurrency, in an abstract, language-independent, way?	Build an implementation model
How can I find likely kinds of objects given a textual description of a problem?	Perform a textual analysis
How can I find likely kinds of objects given only the events that occur in the situation?	Look for the event parameters
How can I explore the design of a solution informally, in a group?	Run a CRC workshop (see appendix C)
How can I find out if the proposed user-interface is acceptable?	Build a prototype
How can I ensure my computation algorithms are fast enough?	Build a prototype
How can I check my understanding of the hardware?	Build a prototype
How can I ensure my design will work?	You can't, so implement part of it and check
How can I determine the required interfaces of my objects?	Construct mechanisms
How can I explore the structure of my design?	Draw type views
How can I explore the dynamics of my system in a formal manner?	Draw state views
How can I explain the structure of my design?	Draw object diagrams
How can I formalise the inputs and outputs of my system?	Construct an event table
How can I explore the external event–response behaviour of my software?	Construct event scenarios
How can I partition my design?	Consider domains and responsibilities

Table 13.1 *Matching techniques to needs*

Once these decisions have been made, and again we offer no techniques for making these decisions, the boundary between the software and its environment can be formalised in a specification model. It may then be necessary to revise the essential model to reflect the needs of the software[5]. An implementation model based on the specification model can be developed, probably in parallel with the specification model.

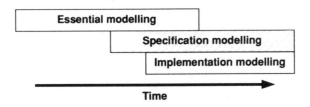

Figure 13.5 *Activities in the bank example*

This represents the archetypal design process, as illustrated in figure 13.5. Our experience in practice is that these situations occur less frequently than you might imagine, and, when they do, the needs and desires of the potential users of the software are so poorly understood that there is no realistic alternative but to rely heavily on prototyping.

We are a telecommunications company and we want to build a network switch and network monitor in accordance with CCITT standards.

Here there is little doubt about the boundary between the software and its environment: it is mostly given by the standards. The major task is to specify the behaviour of the software when it receives stimuli. Therefore, the first activity is to begin an specification model and to use that model to drive the production of an implementation model, as shown in figure 13.6.

In the absence of powerful support tools, the designers might decide to move straight from the specification model to the code. This would mean having to deal with all the implementation issues, such as concurrency, at the level of the code, without the help provided by the abstraction of the implementation model. Alternatively, the designers might omit the specification model, and go straight to the implementation model. We think this is less satisfactory because the abstraction provided by the specification model is very useful.

---

[5]In this analysis we have taken no account of possible pre-existing design patterns or frameworks. In many cases it may be better to revise needs to fit the existing designs, rather than invent new ones. Such revisions will increase the likelihood of needing to alter the essential model.

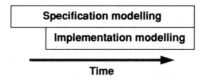

Figure 13.6 *Activities in the telecommunications example*

> *We are a development software products company and we want to develop a user-interface class library to support the development of complex GUI applications, using a variety of operating systems and hardware.*

A major problem for this company is going to be explaining to their customers how to use the class library. Design models can help. A specification model will provide an abstract explanation of structure and behaviour, showing the software's response to events. An implementation model will show how the library is arranged and illustrate patterns of usage. Ideally, the company should supply machine-readable design models with their library[6].

> *We are an insurance company and we want to understand better the activities we perform in dealing with insurance claims.*

The important question here is 'why?'. It would be possible to construct an essential model as a behavioural description of the business process but this will not directly help to answer questions about the business goals. Although essential models can clearly be used to support business process modelling, without any intention to produce software subsequently, we don't promote them for that purpose. We consider them an aid to the process of software development and not an end in themselves. If our techniques are to be used in this situation, then we can only assume the construction of an essential model, as in figure 13.7.

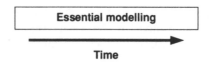

Figure 13.7 *Activities in the insurance example*

---

[6]This trend has already begun.

The relationship between techniques and project stages

There is no fixed relationship between the design techniques and the project stages. Typically, we might expect preliminary essential and specification models to be produced during the preparation stage. These models would then be refined during construction cycles, along with the implementation model.

Mechanisms versus statecharts

Mechanisms in the implementation model show sequences of messages in particular scenarios. The set of statecharts for the types involved in a mechanism can capture exactly the same information, in its generic form. What should we conclude about the order in which these techniques are used?

All our experience of object-oriented design points to mechanisms as the single most powerful technique for deciding exactly how a system will work. There is nothing to equal mechanisms to understand the end-to-end flow of control when a stimulus occurs. Producing a mechanism can ensure that an appropriate interface is defined for every affected part of the system; in particular, they allow domain boundary interfaces to be established and checked. Mechanisms make an excellent base for a debate between separate teams over the correct interfaces between their sub-systems.

So we suggest that mechanisms be used by designers to drive the design forward, to force the formalisation of object interfaces. They are also invaluable for explaining how the system works. Statecharts capture a family of mechanisms because, if used fully, they can explain the message sequence in every possible state. That gives them a completeness which mechanisms can never attain but it makes them less useful as a technique for focusing on one particular sequence. To understand an end-to-end flow we need to consider and inter-relate a set of statecharts – not a trivial undertaking.

Mechanisms and statecharts should be used together, capitalising on the strengths of each. Good tools should allow information captured using one technique to appear in views of the other.

We should also note that mechanisms are natural test cases; the logic for choosing which mechanisms are important is exactly the same as the logic for selecting test cases. This points to a possible use for mechanisms in the definition of test plans.

13.4 Tools

The availability of tools is a limiting factor in following the principles of systematic design because tools are needed to synchronise the executable software with the design models. Ideally, they are one and the same.

All three model interpretations described in this book could be executed, or at least, simulated. A simulation of the essential model would keep the state of the simulation in line with a stream of events fed to it and would detect and reject invalid event sequences. A specification model could be executed in a similar way, with a stream of input events producing a stream of output events. An implementation model could be the lowest level of abstraction required, its direct execution being the final result of a development project. We have specifically defined the implementation model so that this might be possible in the future[7].

Assuming that design models will not be executed directly, tools to support design must be closely integrated with the development environment for the chosen implementation language; if they are not it will be very difficult to keep the design models in step with the code. Integration with development environments also enables designs to be explored interactively by setting up simple experiments that exercise the code associated with the design. Tools which provide animated visualisations of designs will play an important role in the future.

The precision inherent in the notations presented in this book provides the potential for tools with very considerable checking capabilities. These tools can go much further than cross-checking names; the inclusion of logical inferencing will allow sophisticated checking of semantic integrity.

But tools don't have to be that clever (and expensive) to be useful. Informal tools that support the various views and provide simple syntactic checks, perhaps also with hyper-text-like links between arbitrary design elements to support traceability, can go a long way towards managing and assisting comprehension of a complex design.

Tools, like methods, should be aids not masters. They should give the designers flexibility and not constrain them. They should enforce syntax but not prevent invalid or incomplete diagrams from being drawn; they should, unobtrusively or when asked, point out inconsistencies and omissions.

We need to consider carefully whether tools being built to support object design methods are themselves true to the spirit of object technology. All too often design support tools are monolithic and try to expropriate to themselves the entire process of software development. Tools should be built as flexible components which can be assembled into an environment suitable for a given project. The components must inter-operate with other elements of the developer's computer system; for example, it should be possible to embed representations of design models into documents. It should be perfectly possible to treat your word-processor as the top-level support tool, with links to specialised design tool components.

The range of tool components required is vast. Amongst others, we need tools to support development standards, testing, shared reuse repositories and configuration management of all design elements (not just the code).

13.5 Completeness versus usefulness

In this book we have tried to position design as the central activity in software development. We have tried to show that it is possible to construct precise design models at various levels of abstraction, including models that come close to being – and perhaps are – complete descriptions of implementation behaviour. The time has

---

[7]But note our comments in the next section on completeness.

come to consider whether it is appropriate and useful to build models that even approach the level of completeness we have suggested.

Producing a complete implementation model, with full statecharts showing all inter-object message sending, takes a considerable time. In the absence of tools to execute such models directly, we must decide whether it is worth spending that time when it is inevitable that another model at roughly the same level of abstraction will be produced in some other language, such as C++ or Smalltalk. These languages are complex in their own right and, when coupled with the complexity of operating system interfaces and so on, the result must be a significant proportion of the developer's time spent on realising an implementation.

Given the tools available at the time of writing in 1994, it is our contention that completeness is not often a reasonable goal in software design. For any system of moderate complexity, a complete design specification (complete in the sense that it leaves nothing unsaid) would take too long to create and be of limited use since it cannot be executed. At heart, software development is actually about building executable systems, systems that work and are useful. We believe, and the evidence supports this view, that as soon as the system being built exceeds the trivial, any time spent on analysis and design activities is repaid during coding and subsequent system extension. But this does not imply that analysis and design must be exhaustive.

It is, of course, a trade-off. If we were to plot the total effort expended on a development project against the percentage of that time spent on analysis and design, we predict that the graph would be like the one shown in figure 13.8 (not to scale).

Although the shape of the curve will vary, according to such factors as the expected life-time of the software and the organisational culture, we think the principle is sound: there comes a point where spending extra time on analysis and design just cannot be justified. It is probably impossible to say where that point is without detailed consideration of the project in hand. From our own experience we know that this point is frequently exceeded.

Completeness and usefulness are not related. A few, scruffy diagrams showing the basis of operation of a system are frequently life-savers. The best guideline we can give is this: if you reach a point where you believe, on the basis of some real experience, that, given the current state of knowledge, the software can be completed in a satisfactory way, and that the amalgamation of the software with the analysis and design documents produced so far is sufficient to allow the system to be repaired and enhanced, don't spend any more time on your design models.

Hopefully, in time the software industry will develop tools that allow efficient execution of specifications. But even in 1994, we believe that a deep understanding of the design principles described in this book will empower designers to produce more elegant systems, and that the rigorous notations will provide a mode of communication between designers.

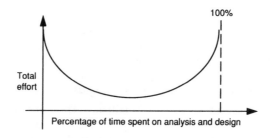

Figure 13.8 *The effort/design trade-off*

13.6 Summary

- At present, software design is a creative and chaotic process performed by skilled and experienced craftsmen.
- It is necessary to separate clearly the software management process from the software design process, so that designers are not constrained by the formality needed by managers.
- The management process must be rigid and disciplined but not based on measurement of the use of design techniques.
- The management process should establish milestones that correspond to the delivery of functioning code and achieve them in a series of evolutionary cycles.
- The ultimate goal of a software development organisation must be to establish an environment that reacts to changes in need by accommodating the need within the existing software framework, rather than meeting each set of needs with a separate project.
- Every development should have a small *core team* consisting of a project manager, a chief designer, assistant designers and a project administrator. The core team takes full technical responsibility for the development.
- There are three major development activities: *project preparation, construction* and *approval*.
- The design process has as its aim *systematic design*, a condition where the code is at all times a consequence of the design models, and not the other way around.
- It is inevitable that some design decisions can be made only by experimentation with implementations. The issue is how these experiments, or *prototypes*, are incorporated into the development process.
- We discuss two approaches: *incremental prototyping*, where each experiment is part of the system being developed, and *dual-track design*, where the results of the experiments are input to the design of the final system.
- Neither approach guarantees systematic design, although dual-track design is more likely to provide it.

- For many projects, the aim of systematic design is not achievable. These projects are unlikely to want to take full advantage of complex design techniques.
- Different kinds of development require different application of techniques; not all techniques will be used on a single project.
- Systematic design requires powerful tools.
- Completeness of design models is not always a reasonable or useful goal.

13.7 Bibliographic notes

Much has been written on cyclic and iterative development processes; of particular relevance is the work of Boehm [Boehm88].

Given our views on the tension between creativity and rigorous method, we refer the reader to the paper by Parnas and Clements on faking a rational process [Parna86].

13.8 References

[Boehm88] B.W. Boehm. A spiral model of software development and enhancement. *IEEE Computer*, May 1988.

[Brook75] F.P. Brooks. *The Mythical Man-month: Essays on software engineering*, Addison-Wesley, Reading, Massachusetts, 1975.

[Gilb88] T. Gilb. *Principles of Software Engineering Management*, Addison-Wesley, Wokingham, England, 1988.

[Parna86] D.L. Parnas and P.C. Clements. A rational design process: How and why to fake it, *IEEE Transactions on Software Engineering* 12/2, February 1986.

[Wilso84] B. Wilson. *Systems: Concepts, methodologies, and applications*, John Wiley & Sons, Chichester, 1984.

Summary of notation

A.1 Type views

A.1.1 Basic notation

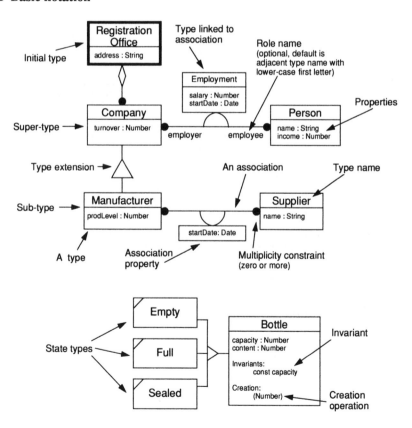

A.1.2 Associations

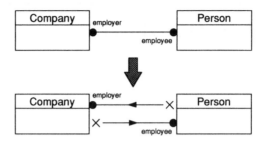

An association can be thought of as a pair of unidirectional associations, each with a source and a destination type.

Table of association multiplicity adornments:

Symbol	Name	Placement	Meaning	Restrictions
<none>	Single	Destination	Constrains multiplicity of the destination to be exactly one. Navigating the association yields an object of the destination type	Exclusive with Multiple and Optional
●	Multiple	Destination	Constrains multiplicity of the destination to be zero or more. Navigating the association yields a collection of objects of the destination type	Exclusive with Single and Optional
○	Optional	Destination	Constrains multiplicity of the destination to be zero or one. Navigating the association yields an object of the destination type or nil	Exclusive with Single and Multiple
[m..n]	Range	Destination	Constrains multiplicity of the destination to be in range m to n	Used only with Multiple
[m]	Range	Destination	Constrains multiplicity of the destination to equal m	Used only with Multiple
[m+]	Range	Destination	Constrains multiplicity of the destination to be in range m to infinity	Used only with Multiple

Table of ordering adornments:

Symbol	Name	Placement	Meaning	Restrictions
\<none\>	Set	Destination	Defines the destination collection to be unordered, with no duplicates	Used only with Multiple
[bag]	Bag	Destination	Defines the destination collection to be unordered, but with duplicates allowed	Used only with Multiple
[seq]	Sequence	Destination	Defines the destination collection to be ordered	Used only with Multiple
[...]	Sorted	Destination	Defines the destination collection to be sorted according to some predicate. A rigorous predicate has the form: [a, b: Type; expression] where a comes before b if the expression is true	Used only with Multiple

Table of other adornments:

Symbol	Name	Placement	Meaning	Restrictions
q(T)	Qualifier	Source	Defines a function, q, that selects from a multiple association using a parameter of type T. The destination can still be multiple, indicating that the parameter selects more than one object	Normally replaces a multiple. If the function is not total over T, the destination should be optional
◇	Aggregation	Source	Fixes source membership of an association for the life-time of the destination. The life-time of the destination is contained within the life-time of the source. If the source is destroyed, the destination is destroyed	
/	Derived	Anywhere on line, going across it	This association is logically derivable from others. Normally accompanied by a derivation expression	
→	Visible	Destination, with arrowhead on line	The association is definitely navigable from the source to the destination	Implementation model only

Symbol	Name	Placement	Meaning	Restrictions
?	Undefined	Destination	The association from source to destination is not fully defined	No other adornments allowed for this direction
X	Blocked	Destination	The association is not navigable from source to destination	No other adornments allowed for this direction

A.1.3 Special invariants

The table below gives details of the special invariants that can appear in type boxes:

Invariant	Meaning
abstract	There can be no objects that conform to this type without also conforming to a sub-type of this type
const *property*	The value of this property is fixed throughout the life-time of each object conforming to this type
optional *property*	This property can take the value nil.
sync	This type provides the non-exclusive contract with clients, and so guarantees not to raise wrongState exceptions, but may block callers. (Implementation model only)
unique *property*	The value of this property will be different for every object in the model conforming to this type
value	This type is a value type, and so can have no navigable associations coming from it

A.1.4 Constraints between associations

Constraints between associations are shown by drawing a dashed or faint arrow.

Constraint	Meaning
[subset of]	The membership of the destination association at the tail of the arrow is a subset of the membership of the destination association at the head of the arrow. The linked associations must have a common source
[member of]	Equivalent to subset of but used when the association at the tail of the arrow identifies a single object
[redefines]	The association at the tail of the arrow is redefining the inherited association at the head

A.1.5 Specification models

In specification models, the type names shown in type boxes in type views have a **-S** suffix.

A.1.6 Implementation models

In implementation models, the type names shown in type boxes in type views have a **-I** suffix.

Implementation model type views do not show properties in type boxes. Instead, type boxes may have two headings, **Observers:** and **Updaters:**, under which operations provided by the type are listed.

Synchronising types have another heading, **Sync:**, where expressions controlling the availability of operations are listed. A synchronising expression has the general form:

> **message ⇐ logical expression.**

A.2 Object diagrams and mechanisms

Object diagrams and mechanisms share the same basic notation, consisting of objects and links.

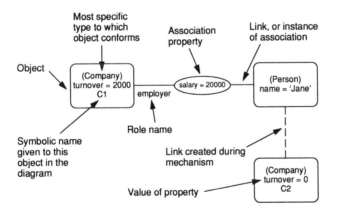

In mechanisms, links are annotated with separate arrows and legends to show which messages are sent and the order of sending.

Message-sequence
number

Message name

Expression indicating how
the result is determined,
using names from the name-
space of the receiver

$$(2.1.4)\ r := dolt(p, q) : s$$

Assignment of
message result to a
name in the name-
space of the sender

Parameters, taken
from the name-
space of the sender

A message
being sent in
this direction

A.3 Statecharts

A.3.1 Basic notation

State with
nested states

Type name

State

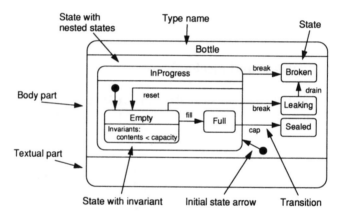

Body part

Textual part

State with invariant   Initial state arrow   Transition

Orthogonal state machines

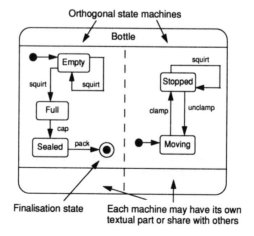

Finalisation state   Each machine may have its own
textual part or share with others

A.3.2 Essential models

Table showing the permitted section headings in the textual parts of states:

Textual part headings	Placement	Use
Events:	Outermost state only	List of events of interest to objects of this type
Creation:	Outermost state only	List of creation operations
Variables:	Any state	List of statechart variables
Allow:	Any state	List of events allowed in this state and any enclosed states
Invariants:	Any state except outermost state	List of predicates that are true in this state

Syntax for transitions (note that the '/' is optional if there are no post-conditions):

event	**(formal param names)**	**[guards]**	/	**[post-conds]**
mandatory	only those mentioned in rest of transition	optional		optional

Syntax for entries in the event list:

event	**(formal param names & types)**	**[filters])**	**[pre-conds]**	/	**[post-conds]**
mandatory	mandatory	optional	optional		optional

A.3.3 Specification models

Type names appearing as titles in specification model statecharts are given a **-S** suffix.

Table showing the permitted section headings in the textual parts of states:

Textual part headings	Placement	Use
Events:	Outermost state only	List of events of interest to objects of this type
Generations:	Outermost state only	List of events (together with their signatures) generated by objects of this type
Entry:	Any state except outermost state	List of events to be generated on entry to this state
Exit:	Any state except outermost state	List of events to be generated on exit from this state
Creation:	Outermost state only	List of creation operations
Variables:	Any state	List of statechart variables
Allow:	Any state	List of events allowed in this state and any enclosed states
Invariants:	Any state except outermost state	List of predicates that are true in this state

Syntax for transitions:

event	**(formal param names)**	**[guards]**	/	**[post-conds]**	**gens**
mandatory	only those mentioned in rest of transition	optional		optional	optional

Syntax for entries in the event list:

event	**(formal param names & types)**	**[filters])**	**[pre-conds]**	/	**[post-conds]**	**gens**
mandatory	mandatory	optional	optional		optional	optional

For guards, filters and pre-conditions:

$$[\,a\,]\,[\,b\,] \equiv [a \vee b].$$

For post-conditions:

$$[\,a\,]\,[\,b\,] \equiv [a \wedge b].$$

A.3.4 Implementation models

Type names appearing as titles in implementation model statecharts are given a **-I** suffix.

Table showing the permitted section headings in the textual parts of states:

Textual part headings	Placement	Use
Updaters:	Outermost state only	List of updater messages for which extra information (such as post-conditions) is specified in the list
Entry:	Any state except outermost state	List of messages to be sent on entry to this state
Exit:	Any state except outermost state	List of messages to be sent on exit from this state
Creation:	Outermost state only	List of creation operations
Variables:	Any state	List of statechart variables
Exceptions:	Outermost state only	List of exceptions raised or handled by objects of this type
Allow:	Any state	List of messages allowed in this state and any enclosed states
Invariants:	Any state except outermost state	List of predicates that are true in this state

Syntax for transitions:

message	(formal param names)	[guards]	/	secured msgs	[post-conds]	relaxed msgs
mandatory	only those mentioned in rest of transition	optional		optional	optional	optional

Syntax for entries in the **Updaters:** list (note that messages are not shown in the updaters list unless extra information is being provided):

message	(param names & types)	[pre-conds]	/	secured msgs	[post-conds]	relaxed msgs
mandatory	mandatory	optional		optional	optional	optional

A.4 Viewpoints

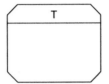

A viewpoint of type **T**.

A.5 Logic, sets and other mathematics

The mathematical notation used in this book follows closely that given in [Hayes87]. We suggest you consult that book for further details, particularly concerning the derivation of operators from first principles.

Let x and y be identifiers, let S and T be sets, let t be a term, and let P, Q and R be logical predicates (i.e. expressions yielding true or false).

A.5.1 Definitions and declarations

	Meaning
LHS ≡ RHS	Definition of LHS as syntactically equivalent to RHS.
x : T	Declaration of identifier x to stand for a member of the set T (which may be a type name or any expression yielding a set).
x, y : T	≡ x : T, y : T
( )	Groups terms in expressions

A.5.2 Logic

	Meaning
true, false	Logical constants
not P	Negation: 'not P'.
$P \wedge Q$	Conjunction: 'P and Q'
$P \vee Q$	Disjunction: 'P or Q'
$P \Rightarrow Q$	Implication: 'P implies Q' or 'if P then Q'
$P \Leftrightarrow Q$	Equivalence: 'P is logically equivalent to Q' or 'P if and only if Q'
$P \rightarrow Q, R$	Conditional: 'if P then Q else R'.
	$(P \rightarrow Q, R) \Leftrightarrow ((P \Rightarrow Q) \wedge (\text{not } P \Rightarrow R))$
$\forall x : S \bullet P$	Universal quantification: 'for all x in set S, P holds'.
$\exists x : S \bullet P$	Existential quantification: 'there exists an x in S such that P holds'.
$\exists! x : S \bullet P$	Unique existence: 'there exists a unique x in S such that P holds'.
$t_1 = t_2$	Equality between terms.
$t_1 \neq t_2$	$\equiv \text{not } (t_1 = t_2)$

A.5.3 Sets

	Meaning
$t \in S$	Set membership: 't is a member of S'.
$t \notin S$	$\equiv \text{not } (t \in S)$
$S \subseteq T$	Set inclusion: 'every member of S is also in T'.
$\{\}$	The empty set.
$\{t_1, t_2 \ldots, t_n\}$	The set containing the terms t_1 through t_n
$\#S$	Size of the set S
set of S	Powerset: set of all subsets of S.
$\{x : S \mid P\}$	The set containing exactly those x in S for which P holds.
$\{D \mid P \bullet t\}$	Given declarations D, the set of t's for which P holds.
$\{D \bullet t\}$	Given declarations D, the set of t's.
	$\equiv \{D \mid true \bullet t\}$
$(t_1, t_2 \ldots, t_n)$	Ordered tuple of $t_1, t_2 \ldots,$ and t_n
$S \cup T$	Set union.
$S - T$	Set difference.
$S \cap T$	Set intersection.
$\cup SS$	Distributed set union. Given SS is a set of sets with members taken from S, 'the union of all the members of all the sets'
	$\equiv \{x : S \mid (\exists s : SS \bullet x \in s) \}$
$S \times T$	Cartesian product: The set of all 2-tuples such that the first component is a member of S and the second a member of T

sum S	The numerical sum all of the elements of the set S.
	sum { } = 0.
	sum ({t} $\cup$ S) = t + sum S.
	Also defined over sequences and bags.
min S	Minimum of a set (or sequence or bag).
max S	Maximum of a set (or sequence or bag).

A.5.4 Functions

	Meaning
S $\rightarrow$ T	The set of total functions from S to T

A.5.5 Bags

Mathematically, a bag is treated as a function mapping elements of the bag to positive integers, representing the number of times the element appears in the bag.

	Meaning
bag of T	The set of bags whose elements are drawn from set T.
#X	The number of elements in bag X
[]	The empty bag
$[x_1, x_2...,x_n]$	The bag containing x_1, x_2...,x_n with the frequency in which they occur in the list.
members X	The set formed from the elements of bag X.

A.5.6 Sequences

Mathematically, a sequence is treated as a function mapping positive integers, representing position in the sequence, to elements of the sequence.

	Meaning
seq of T	The set of sequences whose elements are drawn from set T.
#A	The length of sequence A
[]	The empty sequence
$[a_1, a_2...,a_n]$	The sequence containing a_1, a_2..., and a_n
A $\frown$ B	The sequence formed by concatenating the sequence A with the sequence B.
A(n)	The nth element of sequence A.
members A	The set formed from the elements of A.
items A	The bag of items contained in the sequence A.
head A	The first element of a sequence or nil if the sequence is empty.
	A $\neq$ [] $\rightarrow$ A(1), nil

last A	The last element of a sequence or nil if the sequence is empty.
	$A \neq [\ ] \rightarrow A(\#A)$, nil
tail A	All but the head of a sequence.
front A	All but the last of a sequence.

A.5.7 Sorted sequences

	Meaning
$S \leftarrow e$	The sorted sequence formed by inserting element e into the sorted sequence S, following the sort rule for S.

A.5.8 Objects

	Meaning
a in Q	True if the object a is in state Q, false otherwise.

A.6 References

[Hayes87] *Specification Case Studies*, I. Hayes (ed.), Prentice-Hall, Hemel Hempstead, Hertfordshire, 1987.

Value types

B.1 Built-in types vs. user-defined types

We distinguish between built-in value types, that is, types provided by the formalism which it is unnecessary for the user to specify any further, and user-defined types. In this book we have used a number of value types in the examples, which we pragmatically divide into the following categories:

- *Built-in types:* **Boolean, Number, Integer, String, Character, Symbol**; sub-ranges of **Integer**.
- *User-defined types:* **Date, Time, TimeInterval, Point, Rectangle, Line, Currency,** and **4Digits**.

In principle we could give complete, formal, axiomatic descriptions of every one of these; however this would be a long-winded exercise of limited value. In practice we try to provide enough formal apparatus to do a reasonable amount of semantic checking. For example, if a set of elements is to be sorted, it should have a total ordering defined on it.

In this appendix we describe our formal apparatus for specifying value types, and give a specification for all the built-in types listed above, and some of the user-defined types. We intend this to be sufficient for designers to be able to construct similar specifications for their own value types.

B.2 Anatomy of a value type

A complete description of a value type has the following elements:

1. a set of *values*;
2. either a set of *literals* which denote the values, or some other way of referring to them;

3. a set of *operations,* each of which takes some values as parameters and returns a value as its result;
4. a *signature* for each operation, specifying the types of its parameters and result;
5. some *rules* which specify the operations.

Note that the parameter and result types of operations do not have to be the same; for example the < operation on the type **Integer** gives a **Boolean** value as its result: more formally, **Integer<Integer : Boolean**.

The distinction between essential, specification and implementation models does not apply to value types, which are the same in all three models. Unlike object types, value types have no **self**, and all parameters to operations are specified explicitly. And, of course, value types have no statecharts.

We specify a value type by specifying its literals, and by drawing a type rectangle defining its operations and rules. We do this below for all the built-in types used in the book, and some of the user-defined ones. First we discuss literals and syntax.

B.3 Literals

Built-in types usually come equipped with a set of literal names which denote constant values of the type. User-defined types may also have literals.

We provide no formal mechanism for specifying literals. Some are so ubiquitous as to need no definition, such as the Boolean literals **true** and **false,** and the integers **0,1,2,....** Others such as strings, symbols and dates are specified by example: **'STRING'**, **%symbol, 26th January 1994.** User-defined types can have their own special-purpose literals; alternatively, structured values can be denoted by stating their type and enumerating their components, for example **Point(x=0,y=0).**

B.4 Syntax

Built-in types also often come equipped with their own syntax for applying operations. For example, numbers can have infix binary operators such as +, –, etc., and prefix unary operators such as – and $\sqrt{}$; Booleans have infix binary operators $\land$, $\lor$, etc., and the prefix unary operator **not.** Each of these sets of operators has its own natural precedence for bracketing.

Our scheme for operator syntax allows operator signatures to be defined as prefix, infix or postfix using a positional notation. For example:

- the prefix *unary minus* for **Integer** has the signature **–Integer : Integer;**
- the prefix *not* for **Boolean** has **not Boolean : Boolean;**
- the infix *less-than* has **Integer<Integer : Boolean;**
- the postfix *squared* uses postfix dot notation as in **Integer.squared : Integer.**

Only operators defined using the postfix dot notation may take additional parameters, as in **Rectangle.contains(Point) : Boolean**. This notation is the same as that used for object navigation expressions and message-sending.

The following operator precedence rules apply, from highest to lowest, to all expressions (including those involving objects):

- non-alphabetic unary prefix;
- non-alphabetic unary postfix;
- alphabetic unary prefix;
- alphabetic unary postfix (dot notation with no parameters);
- infix binary multiplicative (*,/,∧);
- infix binary additive (+,−,∨,⌢);
- other infix binary (=, <, ⇒, ⇔, etc.);
- dot notation with parameters;
- other non-alphabetic infix (e.g. (), '→ ,').

Parentheses ( ) may be used to override these rules, in the normal way. When operators of the same precedence appear unbracketed together, the left-most takes precedence.

B.5 Boolean

B.5.1 Literals

{true, false}

B.5.2 Type specification

Boolean
not Boolean : Boolean Boolean ∧ Boolean : Boolean Boolean ∨ Boolean : Boolean Boolean ⇒ Boolean : Boolean Boolean ⇔ Boolean : Boolean Boolean → Boolean , Boolean : Boolean
Invariants: value $(true \to p , q) = p$ $(false \to p , q) = q$ $not\ p = (p \to false , true)$ $p \wedge q = (p \to q , false)$ $p \vee q = (p \to true , q)$ $(p \Rightarrow q) = (p \to q , true)$ $(p \Leftrightarrow q) = (p \to q , not\ q)$

We do not expect a type rectangle specifying **Boolean** to appear in type diagrams; nevertheless it is useful for illustrative purposes because the type is finite and simple.

There are two parts to the specification: the list of *operations*, with their signatures, and the list of *invariants*.

The statements in the **Invariants:** section give the rules which govern the meanings of the operations, using the logic defined in appendix A[1]. In this case we have defined all the operations in terms of the '→ ,' (*if-then-else*) operation. Note that an invariant such as **(true → p,q) = p** should, strictly speaking, be written as ∀**p,q: Boolean •** (**(true → p,q) = p**). We normally omit the universal quantification over unbound variables whenever the types of these variables can be inferred from the context, as in this case. It would be perfectly correct to include the quantification for clarity, or to disambiguate ambiguous cases.

B.6 Number

B.6.1 Literals

{1.0, 1.1, 123456789.987654321, etc.**}**, that is, arbitrary-precision rational numbers specified using decimal notation.

Note that **{0, 1, 2,** etc.**}** are **Integer** literals, see below: **Integer** is a sub-type of **Number,** so these literals also denote **Number** values.

Note that **Number** values can also be denoted by dividing two **Integer** values, for example **22/7.**

B.6.2 Type specification

Number
- Number : Number Number + Number : Number Number − Number : Number Number * Number : Number Number / Number : Number Number < Number : Boolean Number > Number : Boolean Number ≤ Number : Boolean Number ≥ Number : Boolean Number = Number : Boolean abs Number : Number Number.min(Number) : Number Number.max(Number) : Number

Invariants:

value	a≤a
a+b = b+a	(a≤b) ∧ (b≤a) ⇒ (a=b)
a+(b+c) = (a+b)+c	(a≤b) ∧ (b≤c) ⇒ (a≤c)
a-b+b = a	(a≤b) ∨ (b≤a)
a+(-a) = a-a	(a≤b) ⇔ not (b<a)
a*b = b*a	(a≤b) ⇔ (b≥a)
a*(b*c) = (a*b)*c	(a<b) ⇔ (b>a)
(a/b)*b = a	(a≤b) ⇔ (a.min(b) = a)
a*(b+c) = a*b+a*c	(a≤b) ⇔ (a.max(b) = b)
abs n = (n<0) → -n, n	(a≥b) ⇔ (a.min(b) = b)
	(a≥b) ⇔ (a.max(b) = a)

[1]It may seem like circular reasoning to use logic to define the meaning of Boolean. Nevertheless, we have to start somewhere, and as this is not a book about logic, this is where we start.

These invariants are sufficient to do quite a lot of reasoning about **Number** values.

B.7 Integer

B.7.1 Literals

{0,1,2,3, etc.} : the normal integer numerals.

B.7.2 Type specification

Integer is a sub-type of **Number**. This means that an **Integer** value can be used wherever a **Number** value is expected. This has the following implications:

- The set of **Integer** values is a subset of the **Number** values.
- The **Number** operations are inherited or overridden by **Integer**.
- Any operation overridden by **Integer** agrees, in the sense that the result obtained by applying it to **Integer** values is the same result as obtained by applying the overridden version to **Number** values.

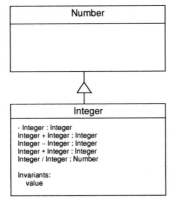

B.8 Integer sub-ranges

The syntax of sub-ranges of **Integer** is **lower..upper**, **lower** being the lower bound and **upper** the upper (e.g. **1..10**).

Declaring a property **x** having a sub-range type **lower..upper** is equivalent to declaring **x** to be an **Integer** and including an invariant **(lower ≤ x) ∧ (x ≤ upper)** in the declaring type.

B.9 String

B.9.1 Literals

{'**hello world**', ... } : strings are contained in single quotes. The empty string is denoted by ''.

B.9.2 Type specification

```
┌─────────────────────────────────────────────────────────┐
│                         String                          │
├─────────────────────────────────────────────────────────┤
│  String = String : Boolean                              │
│  # String : Integer                                     │
│  String ⌢ String : String                              │
│  String (Integer) : Character                           │
│  head String : Character                                │
│  tail String : String                                   │
│  String.prefix(Character) : String                      │
│                                                         │
│  Invariants:                                            │
│    value                                                │
│    '' = ''                                              │
│    (s = t) ⇔ (head s = head t) ∧ (tail s = tail t)     │
│    #'' = 0                                              │
│    not (s='') ⇒ (#s = #(tail s) +1)                    │
│    (tail s).prefix(head s) = s                          │
│    s(1) = head s                                        │
│    (n ≤ #s) ⇒ (s(n) = (tail s) (n-1))                  │
│    '' ⌢ t = t                                           │
│    not (s='') ⇒ (s ⌢ t = (tail s ⌢ t).prefix(head s)) │
└─────────────────────────────────────────────────────────┘
```

B.10 Character

B.10.1 Literals

{ **@a, @b, @c, ..., @A, @B, @C**, etc.}: characters are prefixed by @ signs.

B.10.2 Type specification

The only operation defined on characters is equality: **@a=@a**, etc.

B.11 Symbol

B.11.1 Literals

{ **%symbol**, ... }: symbols are prefixed by percent signs.

B.11.2 Type specification

The only operation defined on symbols is equality: **%abc=%abc**, etc.

B.12 User-defined types

Here we reproduce the geometric types **Point, Line** and **Rectangle** defined and used in chapter 8.

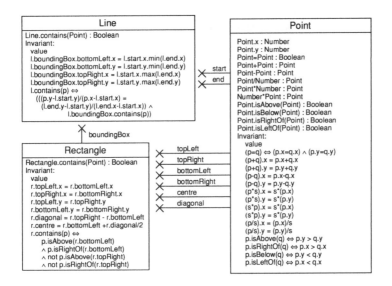

B.13 Other value type schemes

The above specifications are those that we have used in this book. The designer should feel at liberty to define his or her own schemes. The fact is that in any given project the designer has to understand the set of value types available in the given implementation technology, and design the system accordingly. For example, a given programming language may restrict the precision of integers, fixed-point and floating-point numbers, or the maximum length of alphanumeric strings; a library may provide **String, Date** and **Time** types, or geometrical types **Rectangle, Point, Line, Curve** and others. The designer must decide whether to allow the set of available value types to 'filter up' and become the built-in types of the design formalism, or to implement the types used in the design formalism in terms of the available types in the implementation. We would usually prefer the latter, but a compromise with the former may be more practical in given circumstances.

Either way, the elements available in the implementation technology are rarely already equipped with formal specifications. Many designers will not create these for themselves; however, the techniques described here will enable them to do so if they wish. Schemes for value types which may be useful in particular projects include the following:

- the OMG's CORBA (Common Object Request Broker Architecture) value types **{ float, double, long, short, unsigned long, unsigned short, char, boolean, octet, string }**;
- value types defined by COBOL, for example **PIC999V99**, for a COBOL or Object COBOL development;
- value types defined by classes in Smalltalk, or a class library for C++ or Eiffel.

Finding the objects

For many designers, both experienced and inexperienced, a common stumbling-block is identifying those kinds of objects required to build a model of the problem situation. Here we describe some techniques to help with this.

C.1 Textual analysis

The identification of object types comes from an analysis of the vocabulary of the problem situation, as expressed in specifications, process manuals and by problem domain experts.

A useful way of establishing this vocabulary is by a textual analysis of written problem descriptions. This technique originated with the work by Russell Abbott [Abbot83], who described a way of identifying program elements, including data types and operations, from English descriptions. The essence of the technique is that nouns and noun phrases imply objects, while verbs and verb phrases imply operations. By drawing up a list of the nouns and noun phrases found in the textual description we can produce a list of potential, or *candidate*, object types. This list must then be considered and refined to identify the appropriate and relevant object types. In fact, within a given situation, expressed for a given purpose, problems in doing this seldom arise; it is usually quite clear which kinds of object play an interesting and important part in the situation.

This method of coming up with a list of candidate object types has been called 'the sucker's method' because of its simplistic assumption that noun = object. In fact, this assumption holds in many cases but there are exceptions. It is important to include in the model all those things considered to be separate and interchangeable in the situation; this sometimes includes operations, such as complex parameterised algorithms, as well as more familiar entities. In such cases the operations should become object types. This follows from an important principle of object-orientation: use objects to encapsulate those things which are most likely to change.

C.2 What is a 'good' object?

When refining a list of candidate object types, there are some things to watch out for:

1. Be careful that you don't have two or more candidates that really describe the same thing (synonyms). Watch out in particular for adjectives which add little or no meaning.
2. Reject any candidates that describe types which are outside the bounds of the situation being modelled. Ask 'if the state of this thing changes, is the state of the situation affected?'
3. Some candidates might really be the names of properties of objects (e.g. the *size* of the bottle). These should be rejected and the type having the property should be annotated appropriately.
4. Some candidates might describe single objects, using their proper names or keys (e.g. Steve Cook). In this case, decide the type to which the object is conforming, and choose a name for that type: Steve Cook is an object conforming to the type Person.
5. Some noun phrases describe features that objects have only by virtue of their association with other objects (e.g. the *maker* of the bottle). Sometimes, this is a pointer to another object type as yet undiscovered (Manufacturer).
6. Some candidates describe operations on objects, rather than objects themselves. Usually this means that the candidate is not an object type, although if the operation has important properties of its own it might be. Otherwise, consider how to represent the operation as an event.
7. Watch out for mass nouns and units of measure. Use the 'how much / how many' test suggested by Abbott. He suggests putting the words 'how much' in front of the candidate – if it makes sense it is probably not a suitable object type. On the other hand, if putting the words 'how many' in front of the candidate makes sense, it might be a suitable object type. For example: 'how much water', 'how many waters'. Water is likely to be a suitable candidate only if the purpose of the model is to compare different samples of water.
8. When building essential models we are not concerned with software or any computer system implementation detail, so discard any candidates which relate to implementation.

C.3 CRC

The Class-Responsibility-Collaborators (CRC) technique for object-oriented design was first described by Kent Beck and Ward Cunningham in a paper presented at the OOPSLA conference in 1989 [Beck89]. It is a very useful technique for getting started, particularly for a team inexperienced in object-oriented design. It is positioned somewhere between our specification and implementation models. It deals with software, not the world; it places great importance on partitioning responsibilities between software components; it describes object collaborations using a client–server model. The usefulness of the CRC technique comes in large part from its incorporation of mechanism-like features.

The CRC technique is based on the following principles:

- A *class* describes the behaviour of a set of objects of the same kind.
- Each class of objects takes responsibility for particular parts of the overall system behaviour.
- Responsibilities take two forms: responsibilities for *knowing* something and responsibilities for *doing* something.
- Objects discharge their responsibilities by collaborating with other objects[1].

As you can see, the CRC technique goes beyond just finding the objects; indeed, it says nothing about how objects are found. It is useful for validating the choice of object types by considering the part they play in the software. The elements of the technique are as follows:

- The designer(s) use skill and experience to identify the classes of objects required. (Textual analysis, as described above, is useful here.)
- Details of each class are recorded on a card (see below).
- Each of the system functions are considered in turn. The responsibilities implied by the function are broken down and allocated to the relevant classes.
- Using a role-playing approach, the designer(s) decide how the responsibilities can be discharged by considering the sending of messages between objects. This, in turn, identifies other responsibilities.
- By role-playing, the classes are refined; new classes are identified; existing classes are discarded.
- The tangible nature of the cards aids role-playing. Designers frequently hold the cards and use gestures to describe interactions.
- The cards can also be arranged to show various design patterns and structures, including encapsulation and inheritance.

The CRC technique is useful for introducing the ideas of objects to beginners. Its informality, while great for breaking the ice, limits its usefulness for experienced designers. It is best used by small groups, not individuals.

---

[1]We generally assume that objects collaborate by sending messages.

Class details are recorded on cards, usually 6"x4" index cards, whose fronts have the following layout:

Class Name	
Responsibilities:	**Collaborators:**
Details of responsibilities	Details of classes which objects of this class will use to fulfil their responsibilities

It use a good idea to write a short description of the class on the back of the card, giving the role and purpose in the design of these objects.

The CRC technique does not fit precisely with the other techniques described in this book: it straddles several, including specification models and implementation models in general, and type views and mechanisms in particular. Nevertheless, we have had great success with this technique as a way of teaching about objects and for brainstorming designs.

C.4 Events

So far, we seem to have given the impression that the design process always begins with the identification of object types. This is not so. Sometimes, all the available information about the situation to be modelled is expressed in terms of events, and so it makes sense to start by producing an event table. Once we have a list of events, we must establish the parameters to each. What information must the event carry in order to identify its purpose or effect? Answering this question leads directly to the identification of the important object types in the situation.

C.5 References

[Abbot83] R. Abbott. Program design by informal English descriptions. *Communications of the ACM*, 26(11):882–894, November 1983.

[Beck89] K. Beck and W. Cunningham. A laboratory for object-oriented thinking. *OOPSLA '89 Conference Proceedings*, 1–6, ACM Press, New York, 1989.

Index